Ruby Cohn assumes realism to be the dominant mode in English theatre since 1956, the year of John Osborne's *Look Back in Anger*. She argues, however, that the most provocative plays of the last few decades have departed from realism, and she traces certain patterns of departure which are familiar in the long tradition of English drama.

The patterns, which form the chapters of the book, include the theme of England as dramatic metaphor, modernizations or adaptations of Shakespeare, stage verse, theatre within theatre, explorations of madness, dreams, ghosts, and the re-viewing of history through a contemporary lens.

Among the playwrights who avail themselves of these devices are John Arden, Edward Bond, Howard Brenton, Caryl Churchill, David Edgar, Pam Gems, Christopher Hampton, David Hare, Peter Nichols, Tom Stoppard, David Storey, Heathcote Williams, and Charles Wood.

*Retreats from realism in recent
English drama*

Retreats from realism in recent English drama

RUBY COHN

Professor of Comparative Drama,
University of California at Davis

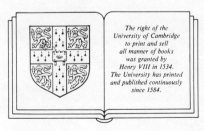

The right of the
University of Cambridge
to print and sell
all manner of books
was granted by
Henry VIII in 1534.
The University has printed
and published continuously
since 1584.

CAMBRIDGE UNIVERSITY PRESS

Cambridge

New York   Port Chester   Melbourne   Sydney

Published by the Press Syndicate of the University of Cambridge
The Pitt Building, Trumpington Street, Cambridge CB2 1RP
40 West 20th Street, New York, NY 10011–4211, USA
10 Stamford Road, Oakleigh, Melbourne 3166, Australia

First published 1991

Printed in Great Britain at the University Press, Cambridge

A catalogue record for this book is available from the British Library

Library of Congress cataloging in publication data
Cohn, Ruby
   Retreats from realism in recent English drama / Ruby Cohn.
      p.   cm.
   Includes bibliographical references (p.   ) and index.
   ISBN 0 521 40363 4 hardback
   1. English drama – 20th century – History and criticism.   I. Title.
PR736.C55   1992
822'.91409–dc20   90–25707 CIP

ISBN 0 521 40363 4 hardback

This book grew from my great debts to:

London theatres, especially the Royal Court and the Young Vic.

The British Theatre Association's invaluable library, with its indefatigable staff, especially Enid Foster.

My theatre companions through the decades, especially Renata and
Martin Esslin, Adele and Ted Shank, Enoch Brater, Dolora Cunn-
ingham, Jim Vinson, Hersh Zeifman, especially in dissension.

The lively seminar members of summer, 1978, funded by the National
Endowment for the Humanities, hosted by the Royal National
Theatre in London.

Editors who have become friends – Sarah Mahaffy and Sarah Stanton.

Contents

Earlier versions of Chapters 3 and 5 appeared in *Theatre Journal* and *Modern Drama* respectively, by whose permission I reprint my own material.

Illustrations

1

Introduction

We all had our own style, our own songs, and we were all English. What's more, we spoke English.   (Billy Rice in John Osborne's *The Entertainer*)

Recent English theatre, in brief

I propose to examine a few patterns in some hundred English plays that were first performed between 1956 and 1990. My title – *Retreats from Realism in Recent English Drama* – implies my belief that the main tradition of recent English drama is that of realism, but it does not imply that a retreat is an act of cowardice. Quite the contrary. The kind of retreat that interests me is aware of itself, at once playful and exploratory, perhaps better spelled as re-treat.

I understand realism as the mimetic representation of contemporary middle-class reality. Until the mid-twentieth century, the English proscenium usually framed a drawing-room, whose very name abbreviated withdrawing-room, with its acceptance of sexism and class privilege. Although Noel Coward, D. H. Lawrence, and George Bernard Shaw in their very different ways tried to freshen the air in the room on stage, the whole edifice trembled only after 1956. With increasing frequency, playwrights deviated from realism by relying on older English dramatic traditions. I hope to show how these traditional devices become instruments of exploration in some contemporary plays.

My examination is schizophrenic, first of all, because drama supposes and yet opposes theatre. That is to say, these dramas were written for performance, and yet the texts are printed, available to readers. Although inventive and/or rebellious young men (and a very few women) wrote these recent plays for performance, and although I have attended most of the performances, I comment mainly on published texts. A tension between text and performance is endemic

1

to all investigations of drama, and the new concern with a so-called "performance text" exacerbates the problem. The tension is, however, different in a recent play and in a familiar classic. The latter yields the pleasure of nuance, but a new play should offer entrance into a new world, which is a lesser adventure on the page than on the stage. Reading new plays can nevertheless be savored if one has a taste for language or a vision of performance in the mind's eye. But the schizophrenia persists.

Other symptoms of my schizophrenia are more personal: an American casts her foreign eye on recent English drama; a woman responds to theatre conceived mainly by men; a middle-aged and middle-class person applauds new and sometimes radical plays; a liberal humanist steers a frail craft away from the shoals of critical theory; the life of performance congeals into type; too much of my prose delivers plot summary that imposes linearity on deliberately disjointed works. I am that middle-aged, middle-class, female American linear humanist, with its attendant limitations, but I am involved in a durable if moody love affair with London theatre. My first trip to London dates from 1950, and I have been commuting to its theatre ever since, riding its waves – verse drama, kitchen-sink sets, a spurt of the absurd, epic sweep, a raw-edged Court, the birth of the National and Royal Shakespeare Companies, alternative theatre shoots and offshoots.

The hardy perennial in this panoply is the English language. In an increasingly visual and performative culture, most English drama remains unrepentantly verbal; its wit and variety (if not its depth) in the second half of the twentieth century rival those of the Elizabethan period. Despite discourses adumbrated by theorists, despite forays into non-traditional venues, most recent English drama continues to thrive on characters colored by the charismatic presence of the actors who impersonate them and give them voice, the whole illuminated against designedly telling environments.

A century ago theatre realism loudly proclaimed its proximity to the real. The heir of melodrama and the well-made play, realism soon domesticated drama, muting its climaxes. The surface familiarity of realism was intended to convey contemporary reality, and since both words – reality and realism – are today under investigation (when not under Derridean erasure), I abide by Katharine Worth's broad embrace: "I am using [realism] in its widest possible sense, to take in at one end the meticulously 'accurate' slice of life play and at the other the play which only just keeps within the bounds of ordinary . . . probability" (*Revolutions*, pp. vii–viii).

Mimetic at both ends, the realistic play is embedded in the contemporary scene. The heir of the well-made play, it too is well made in linking cause and effect within a plot. The characters behave with sociological and psychological credibility; members of the broadening middle class, they display the effects of its education and conventions. Often rooted in the stock types of melodrama – innocent ingenue, beleaguered hero, benign older man, eccentric older woman, and (modified) nefarious villain – the character can wind away from its roots, but will nevertheless remain psychologically coherent from first to last: Hedda Gabler will not settle down to hearth and home, Three Sisters will not go to Moscow, Major Barbara will not call down a plague on both her men. Even when the character's change is at the heart of the drama – Nora's declaration of independence – it is traced with credible gradualism that is expressed in a discursive dialogue.

In the many discussions of stage realism (or naturalism which sometimes serves as its synonym), dialogue has received only glancing attention – perhaps because the familiar living-room muffles the particular phrases, perhaps because most of us hear or read the masterpieces of realism in translation. Yet the coherence of realistic dialogue parallels that of plot and character. Ibsen's people speak grammatically in complete sentences. O'Casey's tenement dwellers connect one sentence logically to another; they answer pointed questions, and they swear meaningful oaths. Despite a French Theatre of Silence, English stage dialogue waited for Pinter and Beckett (who is not English; in his words, "Au contraire") to admit hesitation, disjunction, repetition, and great gaps (Kane, *The Language of Silence, passim*). Beckett's drama defies all the tenets of realism, but Pinter usually adheres to its strictures in everything but language.

Today, stage realism may be recognized as a code of conventions – picture-frame proscenium bounding a room furnished with three-dimensional objects and peopled with characters who behave predictably according to their heredity and environment, and who speak in clear sentences and concepts. Today, the realistic frame may be more flexible; the setting has moved out of the middle-class home; indeed the English stage garden has virtually displaced the drawing-room. Token objects may suffice to convey the milieu, and atmospheric lighting colors the mood. On the one hand, criticism sports adjectives for such realism – poetic, heightened, symbolic – and on the other hand, some critics confuse the words "realism" and "reality," and some – including Zola – do not discriminate between "realism" and "naturalism." Although I do not wish to quibble about terminology, I

3

think it is useful to recognize in realism, however heightened or however witty, the series of conventions that I have summarized: sociological, psychological, and linguistic fidelity to the surface of contemporary middle-class reality. For the sake of simplicity but not, I hope, oversimplification, I shall assume that naturalism also follows these conventions, but since the characters are born into lower ranks of the social hierarchy, fate constricts them inexorably, depriving them of scope. At their best, realistic plays offer audiences the very texture of experience; at their most habitual, realistic plays offer entertainment. The weekly program of London theatres makes no distinction between realism and non-realism, but it does distinguish between "comedy" and "play;" far more often than not, both groupings are faithful to familiar surfaces.

Yet some modern English playwrights have chafed against such fidelity, resorting to specific non-realistic devices to probe dramatically into what they view as reality, and the subject of this book is drama embracing these devices, which were available in the long tradition of English drama. The devices are staging the nation, Shakespeare adaptation, verse dialogue, theatre in the theatre, mental fragmentation, and costume drama (sometimes with a Brechtian infusion). A few plays blend several of these techniques, in a determined assault on realism. With some hundred examples of non-realistic dramas, I may seem to contradict my claim that realism remains the *dominant* theatre mode, but many of these plays are exceptional in the corpus of the playwright's work, and, more significantly, the most impressive playwrights tend to be non-realistic. About the others I say nothing.

The following introductory pages are not to be construed as a thumbnail history of modern English theatre. Rather, they glance at playwrights who, departing from realism in one or more of the patterns I have enumerated, will figure in later chapters. By now it is traditional to date the new English theatre from May 8, 1956, the premiere of *Look Back in Anger* by John Osborne (b. 1929) at the Royal Court Theatre on Sloane Square, several tube stops west of the so-called West End of London, and, with less than 500 seats, somewhat smaller than West End theatres. The theatre critic in David Mercer's *After Haggerty* (1970) sums it up neatly: "The crucial development in our theatre in 1956 was, as has been repeated and analysed ad nauseam: Osborne's LOOK BACK IN ANGER. (*Refers to notes card in his hand*.) At the Royal Court Theatre in London an entire generation seemed to have found its own vehement, articulate expression in the character of Jimmy Porter."

Referring to my own note cards, I see that the impact of that realistic *Anger* was less like an explosion than an avalanche that only gradually acquired momentum. George Devine, the first artistic director of the newly-founded English Stage Company, had leased the venerable Royal Court Theatre in order to lure writers to the stage. The company's opening production was a play by the novelist Angus Wilson, *The Mulberry Bush*. The second production was an American import – Arthur Miller's *The Crucible*, three years after its lukewarm New York premiere. The third production – and the first in which Devine had a voice in the choice – was John Osborne's *Look Back in Anger*, which took pride of place over hundreds of other scripts that were mailed to the Court after an advertisement in *Stage*.

Attractive to the Court's directors, *Anger* garnered mixed reviews. The playwright David Edgar selectively summarizes them: "liked by the *Sunday Times*, loved by the *Observer*, and rubbished by Milton Shulman in the *Standard*" (*Second Time as Farce*, p. 137). Even when the dynamic prose of the *Observer*'s critic, Kenneth Tynan, converted *Anger* into a cause and theatre into a banner, the Court was only half full. When a scene of Osborne's play was shown on television, however, the avalanche gathered force. The drama appealed to a generation of English graduates of red-brick universities who looked in mounting anger at their heritage, their present, their prospects. Or, as the radical dramatist John McGrath notes acerbically: "What Osborne and his clever director Tony Richardson had achieved was a method of translating some areas of non-middle-class life in Britain into a form of entertainment that could be sold to the middle classes" (McGrath, *A Good Night Out*, pp. 9–10). Perhaps *Anger*'s familiar realistic form is one of its selling-points.

John Osborne, who described his *Anger* as a "formal, rather old-fashioned" play, later sought several kinds of escape from its old-fashioned form of realism.[1] He experimented with the music-hall turns of *The Entertainer* (Royal Court, 1957), the epic sprawl of *Luther* (Nottingham, 1961), the delirious distortions of *Under Plain Cover* (Royal Court, 1962) and *Inadmissible Evidence* (Royal Court, 1964), a play about a play in *A Sense of Detachment* (Royal Court, 1972), and an adaptation of Shakespeare's *Coriolanus* into *A Place Calling Itself Rome* (no known production, 1973). What these and Osborne's more

---

1 Robert Egan argues persuasively for the histrionic quality of Jimmy Porter, but I do not agree that the whole play is therefore "presentational."

realistic plays share is a protagonist of startling articulacy who rails against his world. The *Times* critic Irving Wardle realized: "Osborne may have brought the tirade back into theatrical currency, but it was the content of the tirades that mattered" (*Theatres of George Devine*, p. 181). Jimmy Porter's content brimmed with scorn for genteel old England. David Edgar, who admits his debt to Osborne, pithily summarizes his teaching: "the proper function of playwrights [is] to 'piss in the audience's eyeballs' (the phrase is Howard Brenton's), and that exercise has defined the higher calling of the craft ever since John Osborne first opened his fly at the Royal Court Theatre on 8 May 1956" (*Second Time as Farce*, p. 141).

John Arden (b. 1930), another Royal Court playwright, engages in such micturation in his essays rather than his plays, which revel in the artifice of theatre. Dedicated to a strong (not always clear) story line, rebellious protagonists, inventive staging, and colorful language, Arden grounds many of his non-realistic dramas in British history. Although he occasionally collaborated with his wife Margaretta D'Arcy before 1972, joint authorship should be credited to most of his post-Court plays. (Only four actually opened at the Court.) Progressively disenchanted with English theatre and English politics, the Ardens in the 1970s moved to Western Ireland, spurning the blandishments of London theatre, where his early works are occasionally revived but where his new plays are not presented. From *The Waters of Babylon* (1957) to the epic radio series *Whose is the Kingdom?* (1988), Arden has blended history, humor, verse and song, and a partisan stance into his own distinctively vigorous voice, almost never muffled into the three walls of stage realism.

In the early years of the Royal Court, Edward Bond (b. 1934) was the warrior-playwright during that theatre's battle with the censoring Lord Chamberlain. His shocking realistic play *Saved* (1965) fell prey to the censor's scissors, but when his *Early Morning* (Royal Court, 1968, for two performances) was banned in entirety, a dormant Theatres Bill was revived in the House of Commons, and theatre censorship officially ended in Britain. *Early Morning* is a pseudo-historical, deadly serious farce, with cannibalistic scenes in an afterlife. After this fantasy, Bond continued to spurn realism through his own versions of Shakespearean and Greek tragedies in *Lear* (Royal Court, 1972) and *The Woman* (National, Olivier, 1978). Although he dislikes baroque devices, Bond has injected a brief play within his play *The Sea* (Royal Court, 1973). Like his colleagues Christopher Hampton and Tom Stoppard, Bond stages writers in plays more or less based on their biographies – Shakespeare in *Bingo* (Exeter, 1973), John Clare in *The*

6

Fool (Royal Court, 1975), Basho in *Narrow Road to the Deep North* (Coventry, 1968) and *The Bundle* (RSC Warehouse, 1978). Bond immerses his writers in the spiritual desert of their respective social environments. Like Brecht, Bond dramatizes social and spiritual poverty through parables based on legend or history, and he returns only rarely to the realism that first gained him attention at the Court.

Sometimes grouped with Osborne, Arden, and Bond, Arnold Wesker (b. 1932) was first produced at the Belgrade Theatre in Coventry, but it is at the Royal Court that he became known in London. Of the first Court wave, he has adhered most faithfully to realism, but his sets displace the traditional drawing-room with humbler shelters. Wesker's plays were dismissed as kitchen-sink drama, and several of his plays are indeed set in the kitchen, the literal living-room of working-class people. In *Roots* (Coventry, 1959), perhaps his most searching play, the Norfolk kitchen lacks the luxury of a sink with running water, but *The Kitchen* of that same year is set in the well-equipped kitchen of a restaurant. Other Wesker plays take place in the bunk-room of a class-corroded army, and in the offices of a modern newspaper. In mercilessly realistic environments Wesker's characters are often seen *at work* – an unusual activity on the modern English stage. In this book about non-realistic plays Wesker appears by virtue of a rebuttal of Shakespeare's *Merchant of Venice*.

Harold Pinter (b. 1930) was early paired with Wesker as a kitchen-sink dramatist, but the artifice of his dialogue soon distinguished his plays as deviants from realism. Pinter himself has said (somewhat reluctantly): "I'm convinced that what happens in my plays could happen anywhere, at any time, in any place, although the events may seem unfamiliar at first glance. If you press me for a definition, I'd say that what goes on in my plays is realistic, but what I'm doing is not realism" (*Complete Works*, II, p. 11). Perhaps that is why his drama found no home at the Court, where Osborne's *Anger* had set the ambience of social specificity, rather than "anywhere, at any time, in any place." Ignored by reviewers and audiences, Pinter might have continued his acting career while his drama languished stillborn, were it not for the admiration of Harold Hobson of the *Sunday Times*, who, however, did not grasp that Pinter's characters jockey with an infra-language lying below the telling rhythms that we hear. At first mistakenly admired for a tape-recorder ear, Pinter is now recognized as a master stylist, whose stripped dialogue has seeded the contemporary English comedy of manners, a genre that adheres to realistic tenets. With few exceptions, Pinter's plays present a realistic surface, for all the mystery at their core. His non-realism does not, however, fall into any of the patterns I examine, so he does not enter this study.

In the same generation of mid-century playwrights, Robert Bolt (b. 1924) and Peter Shaffer (b. 1926) are even further than Pinter from the Court. Fortunate enough to leap from children's plays on radio to a vehicle for Ralph Richardson – *Flowering Cherry* (Oxford Playhouse, 1957; with Richardson at the Haymarket), Robert Bolt has zigzagged between stage and screen (after overcoming aphasia). Best known for his *A Man for All Seasons* (Globe, 1960), he has acknowledged the influence upon his work of Brecht, and yet that influence is one of surface alone. Similarly, Peter Shaffer has combed the surface of Artaud – after arriving on the West End's Shaftesbury Avenue in 1958, with a well-made drawing-room play, *Five-Finger Exercise*. Shaffer turned away from realism with *The Royal Hunt of the Sun* (Chichester, 1964), the first new play to be produced by the new National Theatre. Not unlike Osborne in centering his dramas on a tormented and articulate hero, Shaffer surrounds his quasi-historical Pizarro with spectacular visual effects, which adorn his obsessive theme of reason versus passion.

Shaffer's contemporary, James Saunders (b. 1925), has had a contrasting career. Beginning with absurdist rather than realistic plays, he has always paid close attention to the nuances of language, eschewing the visual lavishness of Shaffer as well as the seductions of the irrational. Although Saunders has had several small West End productions, he has not been wooed by the subsidized companies. Nevertheless, he has survived for three decades by varying his media – radio and television, as well as the stage – and by limiting himself to small casts and inexpensive sets. Two little theatres have been especially hospitable to his work: the Questors in Ealing and the Orange Tree in Richmond. Deft with dialogue, he sometimes sets his plays in the theatre – *Next Time I'll Sing to You* (Questors, 1962), *Games*, and *After Liverpool* (both Questors, 1971).

Another highly verbal playwright of that generation was never produced at the Court – David Mercer (1926–80). Like some Court writers, Mercer was an auto-didact from a working class family, and his first plays – produced on television – reflect "where the difference begins" (the title of his first play) between an older generation and the children they educated through self-sacrifice. "A whole generation of working-class parents pushed their sons and daughters across what turned out to be a chasm that would stand between them for the rest of their lives" (Don Taylor, *Days of Vision*, p. 50). When Mercer's first play was rejected by several theatres, the television director Don Taylor helped him rewrite it for that medium, to which Mercer subsequently contributed twenty-five scripts, but between 1965 and 1980 he also wrote nine stage plays, and in both media he often exploded the frame of realism. Not only did Mercer reach out from his native Yorkshire to all of Europe, but in both media he made free with time and space; he fragmented the narrative line while honing and concentrating verbal repartee. In Don Taylor's summary: "The . . . dramatic tension between art and life informs a good many of [Mercer's] best plays. They are all to some degree autobiographical. They are none of them autobiographies" (p. 110).

A contemporary of the first wave of new English playwrights, Pam Gems (b. 1925) did not begin to write till the 1970s, when she and her family moved to London. A mother of four, she started with children's sketches but soon shifted to women-centered plays in various fringe venues. Her *Queen Christina*, written in 1974, was rejected by the Royal Court as "too sprawly, too expensive . . . and appeal[ing] more to women" (Wandor, *Carry On Understudies*, p. 161). It became the first play by a woman to be produced at the RSC's Other Place in Stratford in 1977. Her most successful play *Piaf* (1978) also opened there, but moved on to praise in London and New York. Although Gems has done several adaptations of older plays, most of her work adheres to the conventions of realism, with emphasis on women's problems.

As suggested by Gems' career, the 1970s saw the Royal Shakespeare Company and the National Theatre competing with the Royal Court for new writers. Although the Court from its inception announced itself as a writers' theatre, some writers were more welcome than others. "1969 was the year when a quite coherent generation of playwrights began appearing, including David Hare, Howard Brenton, and Snoo Wilson, and they were being staunchly resisted by the establishment of the Royal Court" (Doty and Harbin, *Inside the Royal Court Theatre*, p. 100). In 1969 the Artistic Director of the Court, William Gaskill, opened the Theatre Upstairs for more experimental work, the first alternative stage in a major English theatre. Whether in the West End, the subsidized theatres, or the still upstart Court, the new drama was grounded in humanism. Overtly or covertly, the plays appealed to audience sympathy, but this changed in the 1970s, when audiences rushed to the London theatre to be assaulted.

Their forerunner was Joe Orton (1933–67), who inaugurated the shocking comedy of manners at the Court. In the three years between his first production *Entertaining Mr. Sloane* and his brutal death in

1967, Orton's acid pen etched caricatures of blackmailers, murderers, and rapists of insatiable sexuality, to the delight of presumably respectable audiences. Something of a culture hero in the amoral 1980s, Orton has been the subject of a film *Prick Up Your Ears* (Orton's title). Orton has sharpened traditional forms of English comedy through the disparity between formal prose and heinous deed, but he rarely strays from the surface of realism in the form of the well-made farce. *The Erpingham Camp* (1966 for television, but adapted for the stage) is an exception, modeled as it is on *The Bacchae*.

Far less flamboyant than Orton, David Storey (b. 1933) may have more staying power. Son of a Yorkshire miner, Storey attended art school, played professional rugby, and taught school before committing himself to writing. Fiction was his first genre, but he turned in discouragement to drama: "I think *Sporting Life* was about the eighth novel I'd written and I got so tired of trying to get them published that after *Sporting Life* had been turned down about eight times, I thought 'Well I've got nothing left here, perhaps I'm really a dramatist'" (Hayman, *Playback*, p. 8). Nine productions at the Royal Court render the "perhaps" less nebulous. Storey's own categorization of his plays is often quoted: (1) the poetic naturalism of *The Contractor* (1969) and *The Changing Room* (1971); (2) the traditional literary drama of *In Celebration* (1969) and *The Farm* (1973); and (3) the overt stylization of *Home* (1970) and *Cromwell* (1973). In the lineage of J. B. Priestley and D. H. Lawrence are Storey's realistic studies of alienation in the spiritual poverty of the north of England. *The Contractor* sidesteps a dramatic plot, however, to dramatize the raising and lowering of a gigantic tent that usurps the stage space and hints at extra-spatial symbolism. Most subsequent Storey plays devalue the plot in order to stage metaphors for the decline of contemporary England – irreligious, crazily familial, but untethered to an ethic. What Storey said of *Mother's Day* (Royal Court, 1976) applies to most of his plays: "They are a family who intrinsically invert every decent value. But I think they're genuinely a microcosm of English life with their delusions, illusions and fantasies, and their inveterate capacity to live in the past" (Kerensky, *New British Drama*, pp. 16–17).

If the Royal Court Theatre of George Devine had done no more than house that first generation of playwrights, its place in theatre history would be assured. John McGrath, who spent a brief period at the Court, writes sourly: "Many another young writer has followed Osborne into the Royal Court or the Aldwych or the National Theatre. They have been served by an array of ex-working-class directors and actors whose ranks are ever growing . . . More important, this particular *kind* of theatre has become equally respectable, conventional and pernicious" (*A Good Night Out*, pp. 8–9). Perhaps. But because the Court has continued to welcome new playwrights, it is usually in dire financial straits, periodically closing the bold Theatre Upstairs for lack of funds.

Some members of the second wave of English playwrights – the phrase of John Russell Taylor – graduated from their respective universities directly or indirectly to various fringe theatres. John McGrath (b. 1935) went from Oxford to a brief stint at the Court (1958–61), later reacting against both. He wrote for and directed on BBC television, and also worked with the Everyman Theatre of Liverpool. In 1971 he founded the 7:84 Company, named for a statistic: 7 per cent of the people of Britain own 84 per cent of the wealth, and the theatre company is dedicated to plays that expose this anomaly. Opposed to naturalistic thesis plays, McGrath favors song-laden productions that delight while they teach alternative views of history. Working largely in Scotland, McGrath lies beyond my province geographically, but also structurally, since his non-realistic devices are not accommodated by the patterns I analyze.

Other university-to-fringe playwrights include Howard Brenton (b. 1942), who moved from Cambridge to the Brighton Combination, and who also worked with the Portable Theatre and Foco Novo. In all these venues he indulges in shock effects to open audience eyes to the deplorable state of their country. For that purpose non-realistic devices are included in his arsenal, but he reverts to realism for his collaborations with David Hare in *Brassneck* (Nottingham, 1973) and *Pravda* (National, 1985).

After graduating from Cambridge David Hare (b. 1947) joined Tony Bicat (b. 1948) and Snoo Wilson (b. 1948) to found the Portable Theatre in 1968. Hare, along with the directors William Gaskill and Max Stafford-Clark, in 1974 founded the collective Joint Stock Company, so often composed of Court actors that Edward Bond named them the "Royal Court in exile" (Doty and Harbin, *Inside the Royal Court Theatre*, p. 148). Hare has received too little credit for his initiatory abilities, even while directing and playwriting. He admires theatre that exposes lies, and many of his plays – both realistic and non-realistic – are dedicated to that enterprise, from *Slag* (Hampstead Theatre Club, 1970) to *Racing Demon* (National, 1990).

David Edgar (b. 1948) graduated from Manchester University into political activism, writing skits for fringe companies – 7:84, the General Will, and Monstrous Regiment – before attaining fame at the Royal Shakespeare Company with his 1980 adaptation of *Nicholas*

Nickleby. Consistent in all his work is an awareness of the seductions of evil. Technically, Edgar excels in adaptation – not only the world-famous *Nicholas Nickleby*, but also the diary of the South African activist Albie Sachs, the case history of the schizophrenic Mary Barnes, and the documentation of the rise of English fascism in *Destiny* (1976). Partial to realism, Edgar has strayed into Shakespeare and verse, mainly for parody.

These university-to-fringe playwrights have later worked within formal theatres, whether the small spaces of the subsidized companies, their main houses, or even the West End. Howard Brenton and David Hare, later to collaborate on three plays, met at the Court during the 1969 production of Brenton's *Revenge*. In 1972 David Hare lampooned the typical first-wave Court play in *The Great Exhibition*: the exhibition is at once a flashing of genitals and an exposure of emotion à la Jimmy Porter of *Look Back in Anger*. Brenton, Hare, and Edgar have adapted easily to the "aggro" effect first introduced by Bond at the Court. Whereas Brecht's estrangement seduced audiences to use their reason, the Court aggro was intended to punch the complacency out of their audiences.

A more recent university-to-Court graduate is Caryl Churchill (b. 1938), who arrived via radio. In sympathy with feminism, she collaborated in the enterprises of Joint Stock and Monstrous Regiment. Not attracted to realism, she has attained fame with the imaginative leaps of *Cloud 9* (Dartington College, 1979), *Top Girls* (1982), *Fen* (University of Essex Theatre, 1983), *A Mouthful of Birds* (Birmingham Repertory, 1986), and *Serious Money* (1987), all playing in London at the Royal Court, sometimes after research with the Joint Stock group. Although Joint Stock no longer exists, her allegiance to joint actor–writer exploration continues, as she recasts her stage language for the needs of the specific project. At the suggestion of the director Mark Wing-Davey, she has even ventured (with students of the Central School of Drama) into another language – the Romanian of *Mad Forest*, in which she blends documents with an angel, a dog, and a vampire. Caryl Churchill is the most profound and theatrical writer of her generation.

Alan Bennett (b. 1934) is the only *playwright* member of the university quartet who tickled the funny-bone in the 1960s as far beyond the fringe as Shaftesbury Avenue and Broadway. Bennett has also played at the Court with *Kafka's Dick* (1986). For the most part, however, Bennett's wit is appreciated on the larger stages of the West End. His irrepressible humor ranges from television skits to scenes centered on English spies. His plays are rarely concerned with reality, but they often succumb to realism, though his first and most ambitious play *Forty Years On* (Manchester, 1968) stages England through an intricate lacing of plays within the play.

Like Bennett, Michael Frayn (b. 1934) began his theatre career in a university musical, but then graduated to journalism, fiction, and dramatic scripts for several media. In the theatre he is best known as a translator of Chekhov, and like that master he usually confines himself to realism, but occasionally he breaks out of the box set, notably in his manic farce *Noises Off* (Lyric, Hammersmith, 1982), a hilarious play within a hilarious play.

About the same age as Bennett and Frayn, Simon Gray (b. 1936) left academe for the West End. For the most part, his plays are witty renditions of sexual peccadilloes, the contemporary avatar of the comedy of manners. Blessed with superb directors (often Harold Pinter) and actors (often Alan Bates), he provides pleasurable evenings in the theatre without disturbing the audience. From *Wise Child* (Wyndham's, 1967) to *Hidden Laughter* (Vaudeville, 1990) Gray offers audiences protagonists who can convert their pain to aphorisms. Only occasionally does Gray stray from realism – notably in the biblical *Yonadab* (National, 1985) and *Melon* (Haymarket, 1987), whose mental distortions were, however, expunged in revision.

Certain refugees from realism have zigzagged between the subsidized companies and the West End, or, in the case of Alan Ayckbourn (b. 1939), between regional theatre (Scarborough), the National, and the West End. By far the most commercially successful of recent English playwrights, Ayckbourn has also been accorded critical esteem, most notably by Michael Billington of *The Guardian*. Ayckbourn composes rueful comedies about the minutiae of suburbia. Specializing in frustrated women protagonists, Ayckbourn has been hailed as a feminist by a few male critics. Apolitical in a political climate, genial in an acerbic climate, Ayckbourn has tinkered with stage space and realistic conventions, but never boldly enough to disturb. In *Intimate Exchanges* (Ambassadors, 1984), for example, two characters play many roles in some thirty scenes that follow inexorably from a character's decision as to whether or not to smoke a cigarette. Ayckbourn's *Woman in Mind* (Scarborough, 1985), stages the fantasies of the titular protagonist.

One might view Tom Stoppard (b. 1937) as the intellectual's Ayckbourn, or the upper-class Joe Orton, whose love of the burnished artefact he shares. Unlike Orton, however, Stoppard celebrates the bumbling humanitarian rather than the charming monster, and he plunges his characters into scenes of obstreperous theatricality, far from realism in his most famous plays *Rosencrantz and Guildenstern Are Dead* (Edinburgh Fringe, 1966), *Jumpers* (RSC, Aldwych, 1972), and *Travesties* (RSC, Aldwych, 1974). Indulging in recondite allusion, Stoppard has spurred more academic criticism than any English playwright but Pinter. He has also won applause from unacademic West End audiences.

Peter Nichols (b. 1927), who trained as an actor, evades realism by his relish for modes of popular theatre. Like Joe Orton, Nichols is able to evoke laughter from painful areas of experience – a spastic child in *A Day in the Death of Joe Egg* (Glasgow Citizens', 1967) or a hospital ward in *The National Health* (National, 1969). Nichols has been presented in such varied venues as the Glasgow Citizens' Theatre, the Royal Shakespeare Company, and the Half Moon, but mainly in the West End.

Since English theatre, film, television, and radio are all centered in London, writers sometimes skip from one medium to another. Most of the playwrights I have mentioned have received their main dramatic training in the theatre, but from the first David Hare was attracted to film. A committed socialist, Trevor Griffiths (b. 1935) has preferred television to other genres, since he frankly desires the widest possible exposure. Television's small screen and petty detail are well suited to realism, and Griffiths' few stage plays tend to follow that convention, but his best-known play *Comedians* (Nottingham, 1975), is an exception.

David Rudkin (b. 1936) exploits the potential of radio, rather than conform to the conventions of the realist stage. From *Afore Night Come* (RSC, Arts Theatre, 1960) to *The Saxon Shore* (Almeida, 1986) he probes a mystical union with a primitive earth, expressed in highly sophisticated stage imagery. Charles Wood (b. 1932) has penned several successful and wildly different screen scenarios, but his few plays offer a non-realistic and harrowing picture of army life (*Dingo* [Bristol Arts Centre, 1967]), or satire of theatre (*Fill the Stage with Happy Hours* [Nottingham, 1966]), or a farce about film (*Veterans* [National, 1972]).

Still another individualist, Christopher Hampton (b. 1946) is an atypical Court alumnus. Recruited when he was still at Oxford, Hampton did not share the Court preoccupation with the decline of England, or the Court commitment to regional voices. Rather, Hampton in his witty and elegant prose has dramatized his concern with what it means to be a writer, as in *Total Eclipse* (Royal Court, 1968), and *Tales from Hollywood* (National, Olivier, 1982). In addition to six original plays that subvert or extend realism in different ways,

Hampton has written movie scenarios that have not been produced, and many commissioned translations – Molière, Horvath, and modern classics such as Ibsen's *Hedda Gabler*. Ironically, Hampton has gained most acclaim for his translation/adaptation of an eighteenth-century French novel, *Les Liaisons dangereuses* (1985), whose title aptly sums up one of his own constant themes.

In sharp contrast to Hampton's polished prose, the stage dialogue of Steven Berkoff (b. 1937) is raucous and obscene. A native Londoner, Berkoff turned playwright after provincial experience as an actor and director. A self-proclaimed disciple of Artaud, Berkoff spurns the proscenium and its familiar three walls, to perform on a virtually bare stage, with actors playing props as well as characters. Beginning with *East* (1975), Berkoff attempts to enfold contemporary obscenities into Elizabethan pastiche – an effort that is non-realist by nature.

More adroit than Berkoff linguistically and dramatically, Peter Barnes (b. 1931) has adapted Elizabethan plays for the radio and the modern stage. Addicted to comedy from *The Ruling Class* (Nottingham, 1968) to *Red Noses* (RSC, Barbican, 1985), Barnes nevertheless condemns comedy as a narcotic that inures us to the horrors of our time. His several plays boldly blend the comic and the horrific; he is perhaps the one consistent English dramatist of the grotesque.

Playwrights born in the 1940s have been diversely asserting their own individuality, none more strikingly than Heathcote Williams (b. 1941). A unique personality who is not dedicated to theatre, he has written a Pinteresque struggle for dominance in *The Local Stigmatic* (Edinburgh Festival, 1966). *AC/DC* (Royal Court Upstairs, 1969) is a major work that has never been appreciated. His documentary novel *The Speakers* was the basis of the first Joint Stock project (jointly directed by William Gaskill and Max Stafford-Clark), initiating the audience displacement that is now called promenade style. In the mid-1980s Williams abandoned the theatre for ecological epics.

Howard Barker (b. 1946) exposes the contradictions in both history and myth, and he does so in rhythmically varied, lexically rich language demanding all the considerable resources of an actor like Ian McDiarmid. A poet as well as a playwright (perhaps a poet rather than a playwright), Barker has a cult following, crystallized in a theatre company, The Wrestling School, that performs only his work. Nevertheless, the sheer density of his dialogue increasingly discourages audiences, who perhaps have to absorb him gradually over the years.

Stephen Lowe (b. 1947) shares the left-wing bias of Barker, but his

language is spare and localized. Moreover, he eschews erudite references in favor of the specific details of working-class life. At first an
actor under Alan Ayckbourn's direction in Scarborough, Lowe soon
turned to playwriting and was produced in London at the Riverside,
before he was taken up by the Court-allied Joint Stock Company,
which developed his best-known play *The Ragged Trousered Philanthro-
pists*) (a 1978 adaptation of Robert Tressell's book). In *Touched* (Nottingham, 1977) he reaches beyond realism.

Nigel Williams (b. 1948) is equally at home in drama, fiction, and
television. Extremely versatile, he can convey a teenage milieu in
Class Enemy (1978), a working-class ethos in *Line 'Em* (Cottesloe,
1980), or English history in *Country Dancing* (RSC, The Other Place,
1986). More ambivalent than the Court writers in his political affiliation, Williams travels slowly beyond realism.

A few years younger, Stephen Poliakoff (b. 1952) has been prolific
in dramatizing the spiritual poverty of contemporary British youth.
Conventionally realistic in depicting slices of their life, he evokes a
milieu swiftly and economically through energetic dialogue. Two
recent plays work on larger canvases: *Breaking the Silence* (RSC, Mer-
maid, 1984) dramatizes a literal silence-breaker, one who invents
sound for motion pictures; *Coming in to Land* (National, Lyttleton,
1986) also literalizes a metaphor, when media manipulation becomes
a matter of survival.

Finally, more recent Court playwrights contrast markedly with the
first generation in the lineage of Osborne. Timberlake Wertenbaker
entered theatre through her translations from the French, but she
started her Court career with an unsentimental play about disability,
Able's Sister (1981); feminism and class privilege are her themes in *The
Grace of Mary Traverse* (Court Upstairs, 1986), and the power of theatre
in *Our Country's Good* (Royal Court, 1988). As a commission for the
Royal Shakespeare Company, she "feminized" the Philomel myth in
The Love of the Nightingale (The Other Place, 1987). Stealthily, optimism peeps below the surface of her plays.

Louise Page (b. 1955) studied playwriting with David Edgar, who
occasionally teaches at Birmingham University. After working on
radio and television, she became Resident Dramatist at the Court,
where her play *Salonlika* (1982) won the George Devine award. Unlike
that play, which admits a ghost, most of Page's work encompasses
realistic depictions of women's experience, but she has also shaded
the decidedly unrealistic fairy tale *Beauty and the Beast* (1985) with a
new feminist color.

The plays of Sarah Daniels (b. 1957) were first seen outside of

London or in the Upstairs Studio of the Royal Court. Dedicated to the theme of female bonding in a patriarchal society, Sarah Daniels explores such bonding in different communities from seventeenth-century *Byrthrite* (a pun on ritual and right) to her contemporary, mainly realistic plays. Almost all her work features a loving lesbian relationship as opposed to unsatisfactory heterosexual unions. In spite of the monolithic morality, Daniels' plays avoid sentimentality, and they economically render the particular society she dramatizes.

Jim Cartwright (b. 1958) is two years younger than the English Stage Company, which managed to survive through three shaky decades. Cartwright's first play *Road* (1986) begins on the far side of despair but ends with a few shards to shore against the ruin of contemporary England. Spurning realism for audience movement along a road, Cartwright blends his native northern dialect into verbal symmetries reminiscent of Beckett. His second play *Bed* (Cottesloe, 1989), commissioned by the National Theatre, is remarkable for its bed that usurps the whole Cottesloe stage. That mammoth bed is inhabited by seven characters in their seventies, who seesaw between fact and fantasy.

My swift sketch surveys some dramatists who survived into London performance and publication, but new English playwrights find it increasingly difficult to attain production, especially if they are inclined to a full stage. Once produced, however, their plays are discussed, dissected, and classified by critics who are safe from the firing-line (and who are usually relegated to Notes to Introductions such as this). The first wave of criticism (as opposed to reviews) was preoccupied with names and dates; who writes for the theatre, and what does he (or occasionally she) write? Michael Anderson, John Russell Brown, Ronald Hayman, Arnold Hinchliffe, Oleg Kerensky, Laurence Kitchin, John Russell Taylor, Simon Trussler, and Katharine Worth have provided essential information and cogent analysis of the first wave of playwrights. The second wave of critics (sometimes distinct from reviewers) leans to the left – John Bull, Colin Chambers, Sandy Craig, Catherine Itzin, Micheline Wandor, Trevor Griffiths, and Carole Woddis, although Richard Allen Cave pivots on his own eclectic taste. In the main these critics favor realistic plays that support their social goals. Individually, these critics fight against conservative condemnation, as epitomized by Paul Johnson: "I suppose we have to reconcile ourselves to the fact that our subsidised theatres, especially the Royal Shakespeare and the National, exist mainly to give second-rate playwrights expensive opportunities to peddle left-wing propaganda – one good reason for starving such places of money" (*Spectator*, May 11, 1985).

As a liberal (with a lower case "l"), I abhor Johnson's sweeping and inaccurate edict, but I also part company with many second wave critics. I do not believe theatre revolutions can be waged in an old structure, and realism seems to me the dominant old structure, cramping inchoate reality within its rigid walls. In the staging of battles, the choice of weapons reveals a good deal about the historical context of a play; similarly, in dramaturgy, the choice of techniques reveals a good deal about the imaginative context. Although I would not use the word "masterpiece" for any English drama of the late twentieth century (since Beckett is Irish), I think plays that venture outside of dusty living-rooms and dustier lives infuse vigor into contemporary culture. Paradoxically perhaps, these non-realistic patterns were first explored in earlier periods of drama, but the patterns are newly burnished by contemporary playwrights.

This book investigates plays whose devices of non-realism seem to me to fall into certain forms. Sometimes the whole play will abjure realism, for example verse drama, Shakespeare adaptation, or a historical setting. Sometimes intrusive techniques will wrench the play from realism, for example theatre in the theatre or split characters. At the start of each chapter, I will try to justify my choice of the particular aspect of non-realism, but I cannot justify my choice of plays. Every reader will fault me for inclusions or exclusions, but at least that provokes dialogue about drama.

2

Staging England

I take it he has some kind of allegorical significance outside the framework of the play. I mean I don't know if this is right but I rather took him to signify England.   (Don in Christopher Hampton's *The Philanthropist*)

An optimist? In this country? Now?   (Ann in Christopher Hampton's *Treats*)

In this chapter of my investigation, I plunge at once into plays that may at first glance look realistic, but that radiate more or less strongly with "allegorical significance." Time has endowed the classic dramas of realism with such significance. Some of these classics are a century old, but they still summon sympathy for middle-class characters with domestic, and often domesticated, problems. These classic realistic dramas glow with the patina of the decades. No experienced theatre-goer now comes fresh to *Ghosts*, *The Father*, or *Three Sisters*, where the protagonists are not only familiar but representative individuals on whom an emblematic status is conferred by a token set, a new translation, a directorial innovation, atmospheric lighting, critical re-examination, or the gravity of time. When these early realistic plays were written, however, set far from the traditional theatre capitals of Europe (Paris, London, and Berlin or Munich), the characters were not interpreted as allegorical figures of Norway, Sweden, or Russia. A serious drama about John Bull, Marianne, or Uncle Sam sounds preposterous, but invented characters or institutions *have* been invested with national identity.

The protagonist as nation

Over a half-century after the inauguration of classic realism, John Osborne wrote *Look Back in Anger*. It is doubtful that Osborne reached

19

beyond the creation of a specific impassioned character, but the protagonist of that play was interpreted to speak, if not for modern England, at least for an energetic and voluble part of that island, newly stripped of an overseas empire. John Osborne's Jimmy Porter, the protagonist of *Look Back in Anger*, voiced feelings of the generation of Englishmen (I use the masculine noun deliberately) who came of age after World War II. Too young to recognize the sacrifices of that war, too old to acquiesce in the residual postwar privations, unwilling to accept prewar decorum, this generation wanted to be noticed.

In the very year that the English Stage Company was founded – 1956 – *Look Back in Anger* arrived in the mail at the Royal Court Theatre, and soon after that theatre opened, so did the play. Penned by an unknown playwright, performed by relatively unknown actors, the play garnered encouraging but hardly rapturous reviews. In the influential Sunday *Observer*, however, Kenneth Tynan waxed ecstatic, and his sentences have often been quoted: "I agree that *Look Back in Anger* is likely to remain a minority taste. What matters, however, is the size of the minority. I estimate it at roughly 6,733,000, which is the number of people in this country between twenty and thirty." Not even a small fraction of that number frequented the theatre, much less a theatre outside of the West End of London. Nor did Tynan's eulogy send crowds of young people to the Court, as legend would have it.[1] Only in revival did a blend of television airing, word of mouth, and an increasingly dyspeptic attitude toward England attract full houses to Osborne's *Anger*, whose emotion appealed to audiences.

No one supposed *Look Back in Anger* was formally adventurous, and the critic John Russell Taylor explains: "It is a well-made play, with all its climaxes, its tightenings and slackenings of tension in the right places, and in general layout it belongs clearly enough to the solid realistic tradition . . ." (*Anger and After*, p. 38). For all that, as Taylor also points out: "Jimmy Porter was linked in a rather improbable twosome with [the novelist] Amis's Lucky Jim as the cult-figure of the younger generation" (p. 39). Not only the cult-figure but the very emblem.

Over thirty years and many plays later, *Look Back in Anger* has acquired some of the patina of the classics of realistic drama. The very presence of an angry protagonist, however self-pitying, fuelled by a vigorous theatre production, however conventional, nevertheless

---

1 See, for example, *Drama*, no. 165: "Kenneth Tynan's famous review of *Look Back in Anger* was based on a misunderstanding of the play and has adversely affected the course of British theatre, argues Harold Hobson."

facilitated English stage departures from realism, and Osborne's later plays were sometimes viewed as images of contemporary England, e.g. *The Entertainer* (rightly), *The World of Paul Slickey*, *Inadmissible Evidence, A Patriot for Me, The End of Me Old Cigar, Watch It Come Down* (more or less wrongly). Some plays were designed for symbolic resonance, but *Look Back in Anger* had its resonance thrust upon it. For over a decade Osborne's Jimmy Porter was heard as the spokesman of young England, sensitizing critics to that voice. As late as 1986 David Edgar credits Osborne with inventing "the angry young man, the socially uprooted, existentially precarious child of the 1944 Education Act, appalled by Suez but paralyzed by Hungary" (*Second Time as Farce*, p. 227).

As the years went by, other stage voices were more strident in their blame of their country, and by 1970 reviewers were labeling a theatre subgenre, the State-of-England play. By that time some dramatists were abandoning the old-fashioned realism of *Anger* to venture forth in plays that were *intended* to stage England in microcosm. David Edgar in 1989 introduced a collection of his mid-1970s short plays as microcosm plays: "a flush of metaphors of a declining and decaying England." I propose in this chapter to examine that flush of metaphors, grouping plays by the particular metaphor, moving from individuals to larger scenic images, and within each rubric, viewing them chronologically.

A single character as a specific country is a dangerous equation in serious drama, since most audiences still want to respond to the specificity of individuals on stage, rather than peer at them through clouds of allegory. Osborne skirts that danger in *West of Suez* (1971), where the basically realistic play occasionally lurches toward allegory. In the person of the famous writer Wyatt Gillman, father of four daughters, and traveler on as many continents, Osborne creates a character who is at once witty and wily, civilized and selfish, and who dreads a "ludicrous death." Since Osborne entitles his play WEST *of Suez* (in contrast to Somerset Maugham's *East of Suez*), he points to a post-Suez England, an England aware of its dwindling power after the 1956 débâcle at Suez. Yet Wyatt Gillman preserves a pre-Suez charm, especially as played by Ralph Richardson in the original production. As Irving Wardle realized in his review, Richardson was at once "an embodiment of the England Osborne is sorry to lose, and a reason for the loss."

Near the end of Osborne's play a brash American hippie assaults Wyatt with a long tirade, climaxed by "die, die, baby." (A play about such a hippie, Jerry Rubin, was at the Court's Theatre Upstairs even while *West of Suez* played on the main stage.) However, it is not the Rubinesque American but anonymous Caribbean natives who shoot the cultured old Englishman, subjecting him to the "ludicrous death" he feared. Yet the suspicion arises that Osborne himself is not always precise about the words he cherishes, for on stage a crumpled body was sobering rather than ludicrous. Wyatt Gillman's death may be absurd, but it is not ludicrous, and neither adjective is applicable to the waning of British power west of Suez. It is only in the shadow of *Look Back in Anger* that *West of Suez* reads like another portrait of England. On stage in the original production, a seasoned West End actor as Wyatt Gillman (Ralph Richardson) recalled another seasoned West End actor (Laurence Olivier) as the Entertainer, who belongs to a patently symbolic English music-hall family. The genteel theatre tradition of Olivier and Richardson dissolved into nostalgia for an older, privileged British Empire.

David Hare's *Plenty* (1978), in contrast, stabs both at old England and at its modern avatar, an island of postwar plenty. Hare, having moved from fringe theatre through the Royal Court, presented *Plenty* on the plentiful Lyttleton stage of Britain's National Theatre. Although Hare's play opens on Easter, 1962, the body of *Plenty* flashes back to two decades in the life of Susan Traherne, from her World War II activity as a courier in the French Resistance to her emotional privation in the post-Suez British plenty. A teenager during the war, Susan afterwards turns her capable hands to civil service, business, motherhood (at least the desire for a child), diplomacy (as the wife of a diplomat) – without personal fulfillment. Hare's introduction to his *History Plays* reads *Plenty* as "a play about the cost of spending your whole life in dissent," but Susan's dissent seems temperamental rather than social. It is marked by abrupt flashbacks that resemble cinematic jump-cuts, each scene revealing progress toward national plenty, however such plenty may be restricted to Susan's class. From scene to scene Susan dresses more modishly, but she is also more isolated on stage. The darkness at the start of each scene hints at Susan's own feeling of disjunction. Theatrically, Susan Traherne's restlessness mirrors that of postwar Britain – nostalgic about a heroic past, clinging hypocritically to an eroding empire, claiming class privilege while gesturing toward workers, reacting violently when crossed, behaving both cruelly and suicidally.

Having climbed to ever greater plenty, Susan gradually abandons her dependable diplomat husband, her self-sufficient woman friend, and her considerable belongings. In a tawdry hotel-room she meets her World War II Resistance colleague, known to her only by his code-name Lazar. Symbolically resurrected from a dead past, they make love. Susan smokes marijuana and slips into its spell. She sees herself radiant at the end of World War II; in a brilliantly lit scene she predicts a brilliant future: "We have grown up. We will improve our world." In her drug-induced fantasy, a Frenchman invites her to share his soup, and, calling him her friend, she speaks the last line of the play: "There will be days and days and days like this." The irony is patent, for an early scene has bristled with wartime rivalry between the English and the French, and the main action of the drama has traced an erosion of bright promise. In contrast to Osborne's 1956 *Look Back in Anger*, Hare's 1978 *Plenty* implies: "Look back on illusion."

The movie version of *Plenty*, although scripted by Hare, presents the case history of a neurotic woman, but the more economical stage drama resonates in wider disintegration. In Kate Nelligan's edgy portrayal, we could read national insecurity in Susan's fearful but idealistic dedication to the dangerous Resistance, her postwar contempt for her own class, her thrashing about between lovers and careers, her taunts to the gentleman diplomat and her ineffectual threats to his post-Suez replacement, her manic rejection of her life in a land of surface plenty and ethical penury. Although the mercurial original actress endowed Susan Traherne with credibility as the malaise of postwar England, the resonance is written into Hare's play. By cutting swathes through time, by juxtaposing tense scenes flaming with volatile emotions, by positioning Susan at the Foreign Office before a huge drape of Britannia Mother of the Colonies, and by concluding the play in luminous irony, Hare enlarges *Plenty* beyond realism. Susan Traherne is both a poignant individual and an emblem of Britain's postwar decline.

The national extension of *Plenty* shows one way that Hare stretches the frame of realism. In an early play, *Slag* (1970), Hare relies on Shakespeare to rescue him; in *Teeth 'n' Smiles* (1975) he inserts pointed rock songs; in *A Map of the World* (1982) he introduces a movie within his play. Occasionally, too, Hare succumbs to conventional realism, with the middle-class family in its middle-class living-room rendered by a box set, but he is far harsher on them – as in *Secret Rapture* (1988) – than were the original masters of classic dramatic realism.[2]

Nevertheless, as I suggested earlier, the classics of realism have

---

2 In the original production of *Secret Rapture* Hare broke the realistic frame at the very end, when the dead protagonist appears to the sister who collaborated in her undoing. The Faber edition lacks this ghost.

acquired a resonance beyond their specific situation. Family plays in particular illuminate a broad social group – the sexual sado-masochists of Strindberg's bourgeoisie, the hypocritical pillars of Ibsen's society, the charming incompetents of Chekhov's ruined estates. In these plays the family becomes a tenacious symbol of class. Later realists also focus on the family as representatives of a class, e.g. O'Casey's urban Irish, Miller's Depression-buffeted Americans, Wesker's East End Jews, but dramatists of the second half of the twentieth century occasionally portray the family as the symbol of the whole nation.

England as a family

For comparison, it is instructive to glance at a family play that was rejected by London theatres in the climate of New English Theatre. Enid Bagnold (1889–1981) the pen-name of Lady Roderick Jones, is resolutely optimistic about Britain in *Call Me Jacky* (1968), revised to *A Matter of Gravity* (1976). As in other (and better) Bagnold plays, the protagonist is an elderly aristocrat who is pampered by an eccentric servant. Mrs. Basil lives in an old thirty-room country house, where she is quixotically served by Jacky Dubois, who can fly. Mrs. Basil's only relative, her grandson Nicky, invites his friends for a weekend in her mansion – a Jewish member of Parliament and her putative black lover Elizabeth, a homosexual critic Herbert and his lover. Nicky falls in love with Elizabeth, who accepts him as a husband because – we learn later – she has fallen in love with Mrs. Basil's grand old mansion. The weekend closes on new relationships – Nicky and Elizabeth to live in Jamaica, Herbert and Mrs. Basil to sustain a desultory friendship, and Mrs. Basil to bear witness to her servant's ability to fly.

Eight years later the main characters reassemble. The Nicky–Elizabeth marriage (with two children) is under strain, for black Elizabeth wants to live in Mrs. Basil's England, and not Jamaica. Because the servant Jacky levitates, she has been receiving special treatment in an asylum. The sanctuary seems inviting to Mrs. Basil, who deeds her house to Elizabeth and Nicky, with the hope that they will live together and cherish it. In the play's original finale the levitating servant asks Mrs. Basil to call her Jacky, but Mrs. Basil retorts: "I'll be buggered if I do." Aristocratic to the last, she can talk tougher than her servant. In the revised version, however, Mrs. Basil and her esthete friend muse about the existence of God, and the old aristocrat closes the play: "Then I must trust Him not to be careless . . . I am good material!"

24

Perhaps. Because she can tolerate blacks, homosexuals, and levitating servants? In Bagnold's preface to *A Question of Gravity* she states flatly: "Mrs. Basil was more permissive than they thought." *Call Me Jacky* was first performed in the year 1968, a year of confrontation rather than permissiveness, and by 1976, when the play opened in New York (with Katherine Hepburn in a wheelchair as Mrs. Basil) the play was a period piece. What Bagnold failed to discern in the post-*Anger* climate was the inadequacy not only of permissiveness but of static stage rhetoric. The central conceit of the levitating servant (presumably a symbol for amiable democratic ambition) remains invisible, and as such is incredible. Although the sexual and racial deviancies of Mrs. Basil's extended family *are* visible, what we endlessly hear about is the thirty-room house, which, it is intimated, is spacious and gracious enough to provide a home for all races and classes. To borrow what was written of another Bagnold play, *The Chalk Garden* (1955): "Simply stated, Miss Bagnold's subject is affirmation" (Weales "Madrigal in the Garden", p. 44). Affirmation, however, is inherently undramatic, unless earned through anguish. It is against affirmation that modern England-as-family plays react.

Although John Osborne's *The Entertainer* (1957) was less widely heralded than his Jimmy Porter as a symbol of postwar Britain, it more skillfully encompasses the family as a metaphor to dramatize the decline of Britain. Osborne's old-fashioned, well-made *Anger* was burdened with postwar disillusion (along with nostalgia for prewar simplicities), but his next play was embittered by the Suez fiasco, which confirmed British failure in international eyes.

The first sentence of Osborne's Note to *The Entertainer* reads: "The music hall is dying, and, with it, a significant part of England." Osborne does not quite enunciate the equation: "A music-hall family equals England," but the review of Kenneth Tynan virtually did: "Mr. Osborne has had the big and brilliant notion of putting the whole of contemporary England on to one and the same stage . . . He chooses, as his national microcosm, a family of run-down vaudevillians" (*Tynan on Theatre*, p. 49, from *The Observer*, April 14, 1957).[3]

---

3 A few months later Tynan changed his mind:

> At first sight I took Mr. Osborne's play to be a microcosm of contemporary England, with Billie Rice representing departed Edwardian bliss, Archie standing for useless middle-age, and his daughter Jean for crazy mixed-up youth. I am now prepared to modify my claim; I do not think Mr. Osborne meant to cast so wide a net. His object is to show us a single wrecked family, and to suggest that the clue to its disintegration lies in the breakdown of solid Edwardian values. (p. 19)

> Tynan wallows in the intentional fallacy, whereas Osborne *stages* contemporary England.

1 Max Wall in *The Entertainer* by John Osborne, directed by Osborne in Greenwich, 1974

The head of that family, Archie Rice, was originally played by Sir Laurence Olivier. It was inspired casting, and nothing in print quite explains it. Olivier admits that he failed to appreciate *Look Back in Anger* until Arthur Miller expressed enthusiasm, and yet the leading actor of the English stage requested a play from Osborne, who denies that he ever wrote with a particular actor in mind. The classically trained Olivier assumed the part of vulgar Archie Rice even before Osborne completed his script, and the actor prepared the role as carefully as he did Shakespeare. For the conventional London theatre-goer, Olivier embodied the legitimate English stage, so that his decline to a tawdry music-hall (and to the decidedly unroyal Royal Court Theatre) perfectly dramatized the decline of England. Concealing his celebrated profile, Olivier appeared with thinning hair, beetle eyebrows, and a gap between his upper front teeth. Kenneth Tynan has highlighted details of the performance: "The mechanical wink, the slapdash buck-and-wing, the compulsive gin-swilling, the infectious cynicism" (*The Observer*, September 15, 1957).

Although *The Entertainer* zigzags inventively (for its time) between a rundown music-hall and a rundown bed-sitter, the story line traces the dwindling fortunes of the Rice family – retired vaudevillian Billy, his entertainer son Archie, his successful businessman brother Bill, Archie's film-addicted wife Phoebe, his socially awakening daughter Jean, her proper fiancé Graham Dodd, her pacifist brother Frank, and her invisible brother Mick, whose arrival the family *awaits* for much of the play. (The first London production of *Waiting for Godot* was directed by Peter Hall two years earlier, in 1955.) "Thank God we're normal," Archie sings, ironically encapsulating his family, as divided as Britain itself during that period. The Suez invasion provoked the most acrimonious exchanges ever heard in the House of Commons.

The dialogue of *The Entertainer* opens xenophobically with old Billy's "Bloody Poles and Irish! I hate the bastards," and he then breaks cheerfully into the hymn "Nearer my God to Thee." He hates "the bastards," considering it self-evident that, as an Englishman, he is nearer to God than any other race or nation. The play ends on a long music-hall routine of Archie Rice, the entertainer reduced to performing with vulgar nudes, one of whom wears the helmet of Britannia: "What about her, eh – Madam with the helmet on? I reckon she's sagging a bit, if you ask me. She needs some beef putting into her – the roast beef of old England."

A sequence of scenes that Osborne designates as "turn numbers" charts the decline of Archie Rice as entertainer, family man, and human being. Archie even condemns himself: "Old Archie, dead behind the eyes, is sitting on his hands, he lost his responses on the way." In the original performance, however, Olivier was never "dead behind the eyes," even when his wrists hung limp to show his fatigue. As the embodiment of the music-hall tradition (merged, finally, with the more genteel version of Billy Rice), Archie/Olivier aroused nostalgia for a simpler, popular past. Although Osborne portrays the Rice family as a compendium of English attitudes, it is Archie/Olivier/music-hall/England to whom the audience warmed.

Even without Olivier, however, the play remains lively in performance. Osborne himself directed the music-hall star, Max Wall, in a nostalgic revival. With hindsight we can now discern Osborne's social ambivalence: on the one hand, Archie Rice is both self-destructive and destructive of his family; he virtually murders his father by forcing him to perform again; Archie allows his son Mick to volunteer for the Suez invasion where he is killed. The philandering Archie conspires to abandon his faithful wife, and he brags about his copulations – "Just like a piece of bacon on the slab"; yet he refuses to emigrate to Canada, as he sinks into professional ruin. On the other hand, Archie Rice is the most attractive performer in the play, responsive to a black gospel song, joking in the face of adversity, and addressing the audience directly in his appealing self-deprecation. Osborne implies that Britain may not be a world power after the suicidal venture of Suez, but it's still "Good Old Number One" in the only song repeated in the play. By 1975 the critic Ronald Bryden could point to the seminal importance of *The Entertainer*: "It set the generation of playwrights who succeeded Osborne – Peter Nichols, Joe Orton, Peter Barnes, Charles Wood and the rest – on the track of the popular culture and theatre Britain lost with the music-halls, and showed the way to a drama which could image the nation to itself . . ." (quoted in Page, *File on Osborne*, pp. 20–1).

Without this context of popular culture, family-equals-England plays may seem improbable equations, but the probability increases with arresting, sometimes self-conscious, theatricality. *Belcher's Luck* by David Mercer (1966) was written the year after the broadcast of his television play *And Did Those Feet*, which its director describes as "a symbolical statement about England" (Taylor, *Days of Vision*, p. 211). The stage play juxtaposes the gusto of its protagonist against the flaccidity of the family members who gain control of the old estate (England) by the end of the play. Mercer's title is ironic, for Belcher, a not uncommon if somewhat repulsive English name, proves to have no luck.[4] Man-of-all-work on the estate of Sir Gerald Catesby, Belcher is a member of a family which has served the Catesbys for generations, and he believes himself due for a reward. He is "strong and

---

4 Belcher is the name of one of Marlowe's minor devils in *Dr. Faustus*, and it is also the name of one of the authorities cited by Beckett's Lucky, working in a team with Fartov.

insolent" in the knowledge that he will inherit the estate, if only through his bastard, the effete Victor, beloved of Sir Gerald. Over-educated like Jimmy Porter, Victor is not angry at all, but indolent. Haunted by the cultural icons of an aristocratic tradition, he disdains to compete for a heritage.

Into these three generations bound by love–hate tensions stamps Sir Gerald's niece, who woos each of the men in turn. Spurred by her, Belcher is instrumental in killing Sir Gerald. When he claims his reward from Sir Gerald's niece – "I want what I been promised" – he is spurned, and Victor offers a Latin quotation for the occasion: "And the Britons completely isolated from the whole world. Virgil. Eclogue, one sixty-six."

Sir Gerald and Belcher, master and servant, mutually interdependent but "isolated from the whole world," come to disastrous ends, the one killed and the other dispossessed, having been unable to combine forces against a calculating self-seeker and her intellectual sycophant. On stage Sir Gerald and Belcher are a strikingly contrasted couple, English to their guilty feudal core, whereas Victor is an esthete who lacks moral responsibility or national identity. Although Sir Gerald's niece Helen amazingly predicts the ruthless pieties of Mrs. Thatcher, Mercer's sharpest condemnation pinions Victor (lisped by John Hurt in the original production), an intellectual like Mercer himself, and a member of a class that cherishes a tradition and erudition which nourish nobody. Far from the Victor designated by his name, the intellectual is ineffectual, and he enunciates that fact, closing the play: "don't look at me, or I'll vanish." It was Belcher's bad luck to be rebuffed by each of the others – an impotent aristocrat, an even more impotent intellectual, a hard acquisitive schemer – or by a family typifying England, as portrayed by David Mercer. It is the unrealistic isolation of this class-divided family that imposes symbolic extension upon the play.

Acquisitive scheming divides another destructive English family in Guy Hibbert's *On the Edge* (1985). And again it is the unrealistic isolation, but also the location, of an English family that highlights its representation of the whole country. Like Mercer, Hibbert came to the stage via television, and yet neither dramatist resorts to the short, shifting scenes of that medium. *"Betty's isolated and broken-down bungalow"* is oppressively visible throughout the play. The bungalow is occupied by Betty, her current lover Ted, and three of her children. There are no surnames for the members of this English family, for Betty resembles Brecht's Mother Courage in spawning offspring by different fathers, and she clings as tenaciously to her bungalow as

Courage does to her wagon. Unlike Courage, however, Betty is not a businesswoman following the fortunes of war, and she is not a devoted mother. She is, on the contrary, a cruel and capricious whore who maintains her crumbling property through selling sex at the nearby but offstage American army base.

As gradually paced as clues in a detective story, the revelations of the Gothic elements of this modern English family are horrifying. Betty has jettisoned her older son and daughter when they were children; manic Kenny is her favorite, and he alone has prevented her from killing the unwanted Cherry, who is, however, mentally maimed. Kenny boasts of murdering a black American soldier – "slicing his head off" – but although the police investigate, they can find no proof. Moreover, Betty's lover Ted swears that he was in Kenny's company throughout the day of the murder, and on the strength of that alibi Ted rules the ill-assorted roost.

Into their midst returns the eldest son Jimmy, with a black American friend Bobby, about to leave for the United States. As in many realistic plays, it is through the stranger that the audience absorbs the exposition, but this stranger Jimmy is a family member, and his friend Bobby has been a soldier at the nearby American army base. When the two friends depart, abandoning the two half-sisters, the family seems to circle back to its original maudlin condition. But Betty's lover Ted, aware of Kenny's prurience, taunts him with pornography, and in a shocking finale Kenny kills Ted before our eyes – slicing his head off with a cheese wire. Kenny then proceeds to fantasize a green and pleasant land for his beloved and demented sister Cherry.

Literally, Betty's rundown bungalow is "on the edge" of an American army base, and metaphorically each of the characters is poised on the edge of destruction; the relationship between the two edges is patent. These semi-literate, chance offspring express their desires obliquely, through popular songs, a soundscape for spiritual impoverishment. Explosive Kenny has pastoral fantasies, whereas ambitious Jimmy is enthusiastic about automobiles. One daughter is abused sexually, and the other is abused mentally. And yet this maimed family is united in its racism against Bobby, the humane stranger. No one on Guy Hibbert's stage shares the permissiveness of Bagnold's Mrs. Basil, and finally it is England that is "on the edge," selling itself to American greed for sex and drugs. Hibbert has created an English family of dangerous characters who are themselves in danger.

A more blatantly non-realistic family allegory of England has been widely popular among audiences on both sides of the Atlantic – Caryl Churchill's *Cloud 9* (1979). Linking colonial and sexual repression,

Churchill sets the first act of her play in Victorian Africa. Clive, the English paterfamilias, dominates his wife Betty, his effeminate son Edward, his infant daughter Victoria (represented by a doll), and his black servant. Oblivious alike of his family as individuals and his servants as rebels, Clive rapes his widowed neighbor and forces marriage upon his homosexual friend. Churchill's merry rhymes preclude sympathy for any of these caricatures, but through their relationships nevertheless seeps a broad equation of sexism and British colonialism. Written last, this first act of *Cloud 9* announces its serious themes through the verve of farce.

In a bold unrealistic stroke, Churchill sets her second act a hundred years later, but the nuclear English family has aged only twenty-five years. The anachronistic dominant male vanishes from the stage, and his wife Betty seeks her own identity. The effeminate Edward has a gay lover who rejects his old-fashioned monogamous (pre-Aids) values. The infant daughter has grown into a married mother who experiments with a lesbian lover. The end of empire apparently entails the end of conventional sexuality.

This act, the first to be written, reads like a realistic problem play, except for Churchill's stipulation about the casting: "The doubling [with characters in the first act] can be done in any way that seems right for any particular production." However doubled, one adult actor plays a young child with farcical charm. And however doubled, the newly independent grandmother Betty has to encounter her former self, the timorous young wife of Victorian Britain. Rejecting both sexism and imperialism, she now represents an England that can face the future with relish, humor, and confident uncertainty. The caricatured family of the first act is whittled down, finally, to the forward-looking woman of the play's end – each of her avatars emblematic of the England of her time. Nominally a critique of England, *Cloud 9* is cheerfully optimistic, although it lacks Bagnold's resolute affirmation: Betty is only hesitantly in touch with herself, Victoria wavers between husband and lover, Edward strains away from homosexual monogamy. The English family still needs self-exploration, and that exploration is vividly reflected in the theatrical doubling of any particular performance.

Unlike *Cloud 9*, most of these State-of-England plays observe the surface conventions of realism, but some skew or gratuitous detail can abruptly illuminate the nation – a woman before a painting of Britannia in *Plenty*, an apt Latin quotation in *Belcher's Luck*, a prurient murderer chanting pastoral phrases in *On the Edge*. Such details are dramatic invitations to interpret these plays as portraits of a nation as well as a family. More obstreperously theatrical than these plays are the two England-as-family plays, written a quarter of a century apart. Osborne's *The Entertainer* and Churchill's *Cloud 9* deploy, respectively, music-hall turns and presentational rhymes to enlarge their scope. Despite their common theatricality, however, Osborne and Churchill are at antipodes in their attitudes toward their country: Osborne's nostalgia strains through the vulgar present, but Churchill's optimism bounces through the permissive present.

Britain as an institution

Rather than rendering England as a family, some playwrights emblematize the whole country by a particular institution. Not surprisingly, the institution of the British concentration camp has never been convincingly staged; and not surprisingly, such staging is nevertheless attempted by playwrights who thrive on shock.

Originally conceived for television, *The Erpingham Camp* by Joe Orton (television, 1965; Royal Court, 1967) teeters uncertainly between picture-frame rooms and open spaces. In spite of the holiday camp setting, Orton specifically demands "an unlocalized area," and changes of scene are achieved "by lighting and banners after the manner of the Royal Shakespeare Company's productions of Shakespeare's histories." Orton's mordant image of modern Britain is not, however, patterned on Shakespeare but on *The Bacchae* by Euripides.

A holiday camp named for its owner-manager Erpingham (Orton's Pentheus-figure) is invaded by the Dionysian spirit of the Irishman Chief Redcoat Riley (a name with echoes of Eliot and Pinter). A working-class couple and a middle-class couple revel in holiday anarchy, which infects the whole camp. The puritanical dictator Erpingham responds with a prayer but also with "fire-hoses, tear-gas, and the boot" before he falls through the floor, bloodily smashed and smashing into a dancing couple. When wild Riley replaces Erpingham as commandant of the camp, he suddenly stiffens into decorous piety. The Pentheus spirit triumphs over Dionysos, and the holiday camp is finally indistinguishable from a concentration camp – in merry old England. Although Orton has been championed by both the political left and right, it is naive to take his anarchic lashing as social criticism.

A comparable anarchic spirit pervades the play of the resolutely non-realistic Peter Nichols. In *The Freeway* (1974), the road of our automobile civilization becomes a repressive institution. The freeway is filled with an eighty-mile long traffic jam, where the four occupants of a camper are contrasted with an aristocratic dowager and her middle-aged son in an estate car. As both groups praise democracy, class differences seem to dissolve under the stress of the road block. However, privilege tells even in a traffic jam; the aristocrats escape by helicopter, whereas the commoners are forced to abandon their camper and walk the many miles to their home. But one of them refuses to obey the totalitarian injunctions of the "free" way guards and literally goes underground. Nichols implies that only a liberation into nature can save England from turning into an automated concentration camp, even while its citizens pay lip service to freedom. Poorly received, the allegory remains a favorite of Nichols, but he does admit to a weak second part: "I should have made it about mobility, to contrast with the immobility of the first act; I should have shown the people being forced to travel up the road, seeing contemporary England, in a kind of epic" (Kerensky, *New British Drama*, p. 76). Yet epic is a form entirely foreign to Nichols' histrionic temperament.

Howard Brenton, in contrast, a politically committed playwright who has translated Brecht, is occasionally drawn to epic scope, most notably in his *Epsom Downs*. Written three years earlier, his *Churchill Play* (1974) is named for the play within his concentration camp play. In its original version Brenton set his drama in the Orwellian year of doom, 1984, when Britain is portrayed as a vast network of concentration camps. The play's action departs from realism mainly by virtue of its play within the play, *The Churchill Play*, and I therefore prefer to examine Brenton's drama in my chapter on "Framing theatre."

Similarly, Alan Bennett's *Forty Years On* (1968) converts England into the tautological Albion School, which is the setting for *two* plays within the play, to be examined in the chapter on "Framing theatre." It is nevertheless worth noting here that a decade after Olivier played the Entertainer at the Royal Court Theatre, the equally honored John Gielgud came to Sloane Square to play a fussy, musty schoolmaster, emblematic of a traditional old England. *Doubles entendres*, frequent changes of costume, and John Gielgud as a lovable, bumbling headmaster enliven a trip through English history, which oscillates between jokes and gentle satire. Lacking Bagnold's explicit affirmation, Bennett's Albion School is nevertheless the only good-natured metaphor for England on the post-Suez stage, where one can scarcely imagine a line like the one that concludes Somerset Maugham's *For Services Rendered* (1932): "This old England of ours isn't done yet and I for one believe in it and all it stands for."

In their sharply differing tones, Brenton and Bennett dip in and out of realism, but Peter Nichols exploits a panoply of non-realistic devices. Even more often than Bennett and Brenton, he revels in forms of theatre in the theatre (to be examined in chapter 5), but he also metaphorizes England – the hospital of *The National Health*, the gay music-hall in *Privates on Parade*, and the pantomime in *Poppy*, as well as his more dyspeptic *Freeway*. Although *The National Health* (1969) contains a fantasy soap opera within the play, the very title *The* NATIONAL *Health* reaches out to all of Britain. The play did not, however, begin with that title; for that matter, it did not begin as a stage play but as a television script entitled "The End Beds," which was rejected by the BBC as "too depressing" (Hayman, *Playback*, p. 157). Even in that germinal state, however, Nichols saw his work as "an impression of life in England, seen in this very specific way" (Hayman, p. 162). The "very specific way" displays how hospital patients receive medical treatment under the National Health Law passed by the Labor Government in 1948.

The National Health or Nurse Norton's Affair opens with the account of a death and closes with a double wedding; the play is a comedy both in this celebration and in its many laugh-lines. Nichols was taking no risks that his stage play would be rejected as "depressing," as was also the case for his earlier play *A Day in the Death of Joe Egg* (1967). Patients in the men's ward of a hospital are differentiated by illness and temperament, rather than by class. At one level *The National Health* exposes credible case histories – fractures, cancer, heart disease, ulcers, senility, dipsomania, diabetes – without dwelling on pain. Upon that realistic fabric Nichols embroiders a fantasy that skirts racial tension since all the patients are white males, but several of the nurses are black. The three doctors are white, but an (incompetent) intern is Indian.

Nichols' subtitle, *Nurse Norton's Affair*, refers to a dream subplot that parodies the medical soap operas of the period, such as *Dr. Kildare* and *Emergency Ward 10*. A black nurse, Cleo Norton, imagines a romance with the handsome white doctor Neil Boyd, whose surgeon father disapproves of interracial marriages. Nichols juxtaposes the coarse and sometimes funny details of hospital routine against the gaudy costumes and pastiche dialogue of the dream sequences, which are only lightly linked to the national health. Even in the realistic ward scenes, specific references to the actual England of 1969 are rare. One patient, a dour advocate of euthanasia, envisages a servile peasantry under a totalitarian order. Several other patients voice their prejudice against non-whites. At intervals we hear the

Gaumont British theme song, and a patient remarks casually: "We're all British, and the British ought to stand together against the wogs." The final scene in the hospital juxtaposes an accident victim reduced to idiocy and a chronic invalid who sings the praises of the royal family: "We need something fine to which to aspire. We want to rise, not sink in the bog." One level of the play is an anthology of illnesses, but Nichols' final scene rises to the double wedding in the nurse's dream, which is performed by a black bishop whose train is carried by an acolyte in blackface. Nurse Norton's "affair" ends spectacularly, but Nichols nevertheless risks a faint serious note when a last image freezes the patients in their beds.

Entertaining in its shifts from the racist, plaintive patients to the black–white romance of a poverty-stricken imagination (with a hospital porter as a master of ceremonies who lubricates both parts by cynical jokes), *The National Health* neither fuses its two plots nor draws sustenance from their contrast, no matter how they may have mocked television unrealities of the time. Good-naturedly fingering the flammable issues of 1969, actually providing roles for black actors, Nichols superimposes jokes and romance upon his metaphor of Britain as a hospital. Although he was praised for his "power to put modern Britain on the stage" (Wardle in *The Times*), the play might have been written a decade or two earlier, for all its cogent attention to modern Britain.

David Storey's plays conceal their national resonance so adroitly that an audience has to absorb it as if by osmosis. That this is deliberate on his part emerges from his remark to an interviewer: "The purely literal level has to work first. And perhaps work only at that level. Leave the audience to fathom the symbolic level" (Ansorge in *Plays and Players* [September 1973], p. 35). Storey nevertheless lends the audience an occasional helping hand, as in his comment on the hypnotic rise and fall of the tent in *The Contractor* (1969): "I see it [*The Contractor*] more and more as being about – or somehow related to – the decline and fading-away of a capitalist society. Or I have seen it as a metaphor for artistic creation, all the labour of putting up this tent, and when it's there, what good is it?" (Taylor, *Second Wave*, p. 145). Setting aside the jaundiced view of artistic creation, we may remark that the particular "capitalist society" best known to Storey is that of contemporary England.

Although not, strictly speaking, an institution, the capital–labor relationship – the contract – of *The Contractor* illuminates recent English social history. As William Hutchings has observed: "The characters of *The Contractor* . . . constitute a microcosm of English society"

(*The Plays of David Storey*, p. 170). The eponymous contractor has hired
a work team to raise a tent (Act I) for his daughter's wedding reception
(Act II), and to take it down after the event (Act III). Three generations
of the affluent Ewbank family are contrasted with the motley crew of
workmen who originate in different regions of Britain and Ireland.
The team achieve a purpose that is enjoyed by the privileged family
members, before they go their separate ways. The tent – its rise and
dismantling – is Storey's most pluralistic symbol, and the decline of
England is one reading, sanctioned by Storey himself.

Storey has not, to my knowledge, commented publicly on what
Home (1970) is "about," and yet a few reviewers discerned that the
play dramatizes the decline of England. Philip Hope-Wallace in *The
Guardian* wrote that *Home* was "an allegory about the whole of our
country – society being a lunatic asylum." And Benedict Nightingale
in *The New Statesman* called *Home* "a discreet allegory of the state of
contemporary Britain." Richard Findlater dismisses the equation in a
parenthesis: "(whatever social allegory might have been intended)"
(*These Our Actors*, p. 139). If it was an allegory, it was certainly discreet, since these were the only English reviewers to notice it. When
the play crossed the Atlantic to New York, reviewers Clive Barnes,
Harold Clurman, T. E. Kalem, and John O'Connor were sensitive to
the play's display of "the nether side of Merrie old England." Mike
Bygrave sneered

Home is two plays. And one of them is an entirely honest, if small-scale
examination of four people's despair. A kind of End of Everything. Dust and
ashes, if you like, to the molten rock of the previous plays (which marked a
considerable cooling off from the novels, and so on). And the other is David
Storey realizing that and thinking, this is no good, it's got to be a microcosm
somehow and these four people had better represent Britain and we'll throw
in a lot of references to history and the end of the Empire.

(*Theatre Quarterly* [April–June 1971], p. 36)

Rather than cite "a lot of references," however, most reviewers preferred to rhapsodize about the exquisite acting of John Gielgud and
Ralph Richardson.

Apart from the performance, however, *Home*, the play, is a major
work of the contemporary English theatre. Its dialogue compares
with, and was probably influenced by, that of Chekhov, Pinter, and
Beckett. *Home* resembles Chekhov in his penchant for interstitial
meanings. Like a Pinter play, *Home* embraces silences and hesi-
tations. Like Beckett's dialogue, that of *Home* is disjunctive. Most
particularly, the structure as well as the dialogue of *Home* mirrors

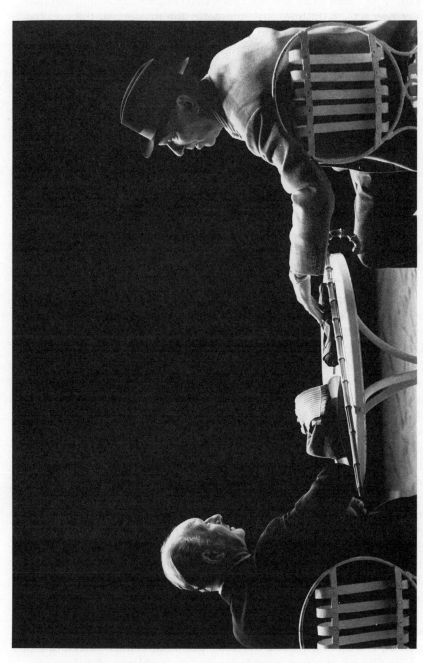

2 John Gielgud and Ralph Richardson as Harry and Jack in *Home* by David Storey, directed by Lindsay Anderson at the Royal Court, 1970

Waiting for Godot in its symmetries – two couples sustaining inaction over two acts. Both titles are enigmatic: the mystery of the awaited presence in the one play and the mystery of the designated home in the other. As in Beckett's tragicomedy, too, Storey's set is unlocalized and suggestive; mound and tree are replaced with a round metal table, matching chairs, and a flagless flagpole in the void of stage space.

That fragile setting seeded *Home*. In Storey's words:

It was the image at the end of *The Contractor* which had prompted, in the writing, the beginning of the next play, *Home*: a white, metalwork table around which the Contractor toasts and is toasted by his workmen, and which in *Home* comprises, together with four metalwork chairs, the sole 'furniture' of a play which, halfway through the writing, I discovered was taking place in a lunatic asylum.   (Findlater, *At the Royal Court*, p. 113)

Despite the unlocalized table and chairs, however, Storey's dialogue emanates from contemporary England, and it is by dialogue that Storey constructs the metaphor of England as a mental asylum.

Storey's dapper Harry and Jack are at first hard to distinguish from one another, so similar is their courteous speech. Jack prefers the expletive "By Jove," and Harry "My word" – both redolent of another age. Although each repeats the word "Really?" they are vague about concrete reality. Jack claims a past in the army, and "an ambition to be a priest"; Harry once wished to be a dancer or musician, and boasts of acting bit parts. They refer grandly but somewhat vaguely to other professions: "My friend here, Harry, is a specialist in house-warming, and I myself am a retailer in preserves." Both gentlemen glancingly mention their wives, and Jack refers to two married children. Both Jack and Harry irrelevantly introduce family anecdotes into their conversation. Although they feel at ease in one another's presence, both gentlemen "mix up" various offstage people. Both men utter fragmented slogans, and both lament the casualties of war even while approving of its camaraderie. They also approve of marriage, large families, social organization, and religion, maintaining that Adam and Eve were born in England. In each act the gentlemen chant a litany of the great men of the island, whose name they occasionally forget – "This little island." Played by those grand old noblemen of the English theatre, John Gielgud and Ralph Richardson, the "lordships" could evoke from the flick of a glove, the angle of a hat, or a trailing syllable the faded grandeur of the British Empire.

Like Olivier, the two actor-knights were emblems of a dominant culture. They had sometimes played together, most recently in a

West End disaster, Enid Bagnold's *Last Joke* (1960), about which it is all too easy to make bad jokes. In her memoirs Bagnold complained: "The knights turned author on their way to London. They were my words, but sorted out and rejammed together" (O'Connor, *Ralph Richardson*, p. 224). Thereafter both knights were reluctant to appear in new plays, but when Richardson did, he continued his sly authorship. Ill at ease as the maniacal Dr. Rance in Joe Orton's posthumous *What the Butler Saw* (1969), Richardson cleaned his text of lines he found offensive. Gielgud's appearance at the Royal Court was a much happier affair, enacting the grand old headmaster in Alan Bennett's *Forty Years On* in 1968, when the direct address to a real audience was a new experience for him.

Gielgud as nostalgic Harry and Richardson as common-sense Jack were different faces of the same royal coin, but they were nevertheless surprised to be invited to the Court together. Moreover, Lindsay Anderson, the director who cast them as the gentlemen Harry and Jack, had impeccable upper-class credentials: "My father was an Army officer, and my mother the daughter of a wool-merchant" (Masler, *Declaration*, p. 157). Anderson was therefore in an excellent position to be critical of how his class governed his country: "Britain is a country without problems, in which no essential changes have occurred for the last fifty years, and which still remains the centre of an Empire on which the sun will never have the bad manners to set" (p. 159). It was the country in which Gielgud and Richardson enjoyed their theatre careers, and it was a country they were superlatively capable of evoking onstage.

Once these two aristocrats of the theatre followed Olivier into the avant-garde of the Royal Court (Gielgud: "I thought I would like to take a chance" [Findlater, *At the Royal Court*, p. 137]), there was evidently some uncertainty as to which of them would play which role in Storey's *Home*. Then Richardson volunteered: "I'll play the one who does the conjuring tricks, because I can conjure." But of course, Storey's Jack fails in his three attempts at card tricks; he is as ineffectual as a P. G. Wodehouse aristocrat. At first the veteran actors felt ineffectual as actors: "We had fearful doubts . . . We stumbled along, saying our strange lines over and over again. I think it was very trusting of us, because you see we were all old stagers – the two actresses felt the same" (Hayman, *Playback*, p. 91). Yet the two veteran actors were grateful that the Court company did not find them "stuck-up West End Establishment figures, hidebound by tradition." They apparently did not realize that that very tradition was so telling for their roles.

In *Home* Storey offers a contrast to these patricians of crumbling phrases; their (occasional) female companions bristle with vigorous complaints and the cockney oath "Cor, blimey!" When we first see the women, Marjorie is supporting Kathleen of the aching feet. Whereas the two gentlemen bask in the sunshine, the two women expect rain. Middle-aged, the two ailing women address each other as "girl." Kathleen's feet pain her cruelly, and all Marjorie's teeth have been pulled. Like the gentlemen, the women have been married (to a bus-driver and a janitor, respectively), but they speak of that state with bitterness. They leer in sexual innuendoes about one another, about Harry and Jack, about their offstage colleagues. Not for them are the male generalizations about war and peace, art and invention. They sneer at the weeping men as "water babies," but they express concern for actual affliction: "You all right?" They intimate that Harry is in the asylum for chasing girls, and Jack for arson. Kathleen is a veteran of suicide attempts, and Marjorie is a "persistent offender," with offense unspecified. It is Marjorie who introduces the others to Alfred, the name of Britain's great king of the Anglo-Saxon Chronicles. But Storey's Alfred is a lobotomized strongman, pointlessly lifting table and chairs.

Of the five characters, it is Marjorie who is most aware of her surroundings, and whose memory seems trustworthy, and it is she who delivers the damning line: "'S not like home." Even though Kathleen retorts: "Thank Gawd," it is the only home of the five characters of the play. Despite the class and sex differences, the two couples are condemned to the same asylum, even competing for chairs and food. Their entrapment is emphasized by the paucity of movement on the stage.

When Kathleen and Harry form a brief alliance, Marjorie charges him: "I don't know what you're saying half the time." Like the governors and the governed in modern Britain. With the mutually supportive Kathleen and Marjorie offstage, the two genteel "water babies" utter a sustained eulogy of the "little island," including "Empire the like of which no one has ever seen." Alfred removes the metal table and the chairs for which the others have been desultorily vying throughout the play. Jack makes a last ineffectual attempt at a card trick. The two immaculate gentlemen mention an inmate, the sea, a relative, the church, God – "'Shouldn't wonder He's disappointed.' (*Looks up.*)" When Alfred removes the wicker chairs, each "lordship" in turn wipes his eyes. Among their sorrows is the loss of the island-controlled empire in which, judging by their comforting clichés, they did once feel at home.

Storey's mental asylum is a repressive institution whose inhabitants evoke a warm audience response – not only for knighted actors. In Nichols' hospital pain is underplayed, whereas his freeway resembles the concentration camps of Brenton and Orton who too easily exploit the horrific resonances of that setting, without credibly indicting contemporary Britain. In these three condemnatory plays, the blame is inadequately mediated through suffering individuals. The delicacy of *Home*, however, calls up a spectrum of interpretations – an actual home for anachronistic Englishmen, a lunatic asylum for opposite sexes and classes, an illusion of asylum. Storey in an interview declared: "The longer you stay bonkers the safer you are. It's that kind of fantasy in *Home*" (*Plays and Players* [September, 1973], p. 35).

A cross-section of Britain

After a century of realistic plays, only exceptional individuals can still command attention in rooms rendered stale with familiarity. Escaping from such rooms, Britain has been dramatically encapsulated in an individual, family, or institution. Although the family dramas and the institution dramas sometimes strive to portray a cross-section of Britain, an open stage is more conducive to this epic scope.

The cross-section play is usually set in a specific time and place, and yet the calculatedly various cast of characters compels resonant extension. Probably the earliest British dramatic cross-sectionalism occurs in Shakespeare's *Henry V*, where soldiers from the several regions of Britain prepare for the Battle of Agincourt. Perhaps influenced by that play, Ben Jonson presents a cross-section on holiday in *Bartholomew Fair*. As Nicholas Grene summarizes: "Jonson wants to show an image of the whole realm in holiday disorder, as Shakespeare wanted to show the whole realm assisting in the glorious victory of Agincourt" (Grene, *Shakespeare, Jonson, Molière*, p. 10).

In modern cross-section plays, however, the dramatic point lies not so much in the different regions as the different classes of the realm. In pre-*Anger* plays Shaw evidently intended his *Heartbreak House* to illustrate the plight of the several classes in the ship of England during World War I, even though most of his characters speak like Shaw. In 1937, with war-clouds gathering on the continent, J. B. Priestley tried to warn his compatriots in his *Bees on the Boat Deck*. Like Shaw's people, those of Priestley tend to speak in the lucid sentences of their creator, but they are also mouthpieces for abstract ideas – communism, fascism, capitalism, science, and of course young love.

Two true blue Englishmen (played by Ralph Richardson and Laurence Olivier in the original production) rescue their beloved ship from plots to destroy it, only to learn that the Home Office proposes to do exactly that. Like Shaw's drama, Priestley's play ends in an implied warning to England. Shaw and Priestley in their respective plays (and their respective wars) stage a cross-section of England to make a mild political statement – in rare pre-contemporary examples of the metaphorizing device.

A frankly and sometimes belligerently political playwright, Howard Brenton is refreshingly oblique in his ambitious cross-section play *Epsom Downs* (1977). Like David Hare's *Fanshen*, probably the best-known production of the Joint Stock Company, Brenton's play represents a departure from his customary "aggro" attitude. Although *Epsom Downs* was subjected to the usual workshop method of Joint Stock, Brenton began with a script, which he willingly revised according to company suggestions. A famous Victorian painting by William Frith portrays a genteel crowd at Epsom Downs race-course, but Brenton's drama depicts a contemporary population of mixed classes, enacted by nine performers in forty-nine parts (Ritchie, *Joint Stock Book*, p. 34). In his Author's Note to *Epsom Downs* Brenton pays tribute to the Joint Stock contribution: "Joint Stock has a distinctive way of working with a playwright. The final text is the writer's alone, but it is written in full view of the company's constant, questioning gaze." And that gaze relied on attendance at several horse-races, climaxed by Derby Day at Epsom Downs, largely a working-class holiday.

The Joint Stock Company objected to Brenton's first rendition of Derby Day as a dishonest event, and the director Max Stafford-Clark noted:

> It's true that it's no good simply witnessing events . . . however accurately we can do it . . . there also has to be some analysis . . . but it's also true that there's a general nastiness in Howard's play that we simply didn't see yesterday. There were no policemen beating up tramps . . . no mothers abandoning their babies, no pockets picked . . . but it's difficult to write a vibrant play about people having a good time.   (Ritchie, *Joint Stock Book*, p. 133)

A vibrant play is nevertheless what Brenton finally wrote, with most people having a good time, which was reflected in the good time of some of the actors. Tony Rohr, for example, has recorded his experience:

> I was a busker, a bookie, a trainer and the race course in *Epsom Downs* – the last in a green suit with a piece of artificial grass in my hand, smoking a

cigarette in a long elegant holder [not indicated in the published play]. I also
played a horse. I knew a lot about horses. When the company spent a day at
the Derby I backed the winner at 6 to 1 – Lester Piggot on The Minstrel.
Playing a horse was not quite so easy.   (Ritchie, *Joint Stock Book*, p. 130)

For all the elegance of the race-course, Brenton makes us dramatically aware of the class divisions of contemporary England. Yet *Epsom
Downs* sports not only a cross-section of classes – from a lord to a
gypsy, from the Aga Khan to buskers – but also a cross-section of ages
– from a child of three to her grandfather. The nine actors represent
thousands of people at the Epsom Downs races; they play not only
people, but horses, the spirit of Epsom Downs, and a ghost – of Emily
Davison, a suffragette who dramatized the plight of women by committing suicide spectacularly on Derby Day, 1913. She threw herself
in front of the king's horse at Epsom Downs.

Brenton's panoramic drama is more obstreperously non-realistic
than earlier cross-section plays, with actors playing props, horses,
and even the race-course itself. *Epsom Downs* opens in silence, as we
are introduced to three people: a seven-year-old boy flying a kite, a
fifteen-year-old gypsy sunbathing, a thirty-four-year-old man drib-
bling a ball while smoking and drinking beer. Pleasure radiates on a
fine day before Brenton shocks us with two speaking characters on
horseback – a police constable and a race-horse owner; they are
shocking (as late as 1977 in residually puritanical England) because
the horses are played by nude actors. Ignoring their human steeds,
the mounted friends voice their contempt for the "half a million
cheeky chappies" who will attend the Derby. The privileged riders
patronize man and beast. A stable boy will tell us: "The parade ring at
the Derby. Three kinds of animal, and all bred for it. The horses, bred
for it. The little men to ride the horses, bred for it. The owners of the
horses, bred for it." Among the onlookers are evangelists, buskers,
bookmakers, gamblers, lovers, families, and many drunks – "England at peace on Derby day."

For the most part these English revelers lack class consciousness.
We see a far more nuanced canvas than the rich and famous exploit-
ing the poor and vulnerable, for the heady day bubbles over rich and
poor, but not alike. Only gradually are we aware that a "red" stable-
boy has been fired, that he is desired and yet spurned by the young
gypsy, that the jockeys scorn the race-horse owners, that it is an irony
when "an old atheist, socialist life peer says – God's in his heaven and
all's right with the world." A distraught young mother is tempted to
imitate Emily Davison in suicide, even though her husband picks a
winner in the Derby. At the end of the long day, the ghost of Emily

Davison watches compassionately as lunatics are released from a nearby asylum to clean up the refuse of half a million celebrants on Epsom Downs.

Colored by an English holiday, *Epsom Downs* thrives on a company of English actors taking many roles to convey a cross-section of English society. Unlike the mainly comic doubling of *Cloud 9*, that of *Epsom Downs* energizes a panoramic canvas of performance skills; the holiday spirit is concretized in the actors' theatricality, and yet the tensions seep through – of class, sex, generations. Enactment creates contemporary England on Epsom Downs. It is not a show that can travel.

More recent cross-section plays have been more modest, housed as they were in more conventional theatres. One might not guess from the mere title *Road* (1986) that the scene is one of suburban squalor. Similarly, one might not guess from the title *Country Dancing* (1986) that the theme is one of a lost community. Yet both plays that opened in 1986 are also metaphors for aspects of England, extending the drama beyond realism. Cross-sectional, the plays call special attention to their physical space.

In *Country Dancing* Nigel Williams zigzags between 1914, when the ethnologist Cecil Sharp recorded scarcely-remembered songs and dances, dating from a half-century earlier, when the Industrial Revolution struck the English countryside. The link between the two periods is Ted Rogers, an old fiddler born in the year of Waterloo. Interwoven with his own story (of love, marriage, labor unrest, betrayal of a friend, and vengeance of that friend) are the songs and dances of rural England. As the ethnologist Cecil Sharp says: "I'd like to put all of this in a book to bottle it, you know, all of England, the way it is this evening, these fields, those trees." Fields and trees cannot be bottled, but they can form a background for the love songs as well as those of social consciousness. For example, "Forward Stations" is about a man "too damn forward in your station." With few characters, the play traces social history in the change from community dancing to waltzes or "one to one dancing," and that change is epitomized in the song "The Hard Times of England."

Williams is nostalgic for an older way of life, but he does not gloss over its hardships and brutalities. The inquisitive ethnologist has the same name – Sharp – as the country squire who can sentence poachers to death or irons, and who becomes a factory owner locking out a worker on strike. Although the two Sharps are not related, they are played by the same actor, and this forges continuity for a character who stands aside from participation in everyday communal life. In that life personal rivalries have public resonances. When Ted Rogers falsely accuses Sam Mowbray of poaching, the latter escapes hanging and becomes a rich man by trading slaves in Tasmania. One wrong spawns another of far greater consequence. Ted, who committed that first wrong, is left old and lonely, but still able to conjure up the "country dancing" of the English heritage.

There is little sense of an English heritage on the nameless road that gives a title and a metaphor to the first play of Jim Cartwright – *Road*. Benedict Nightingale's review points to the play's ancestors: "Jim Cartwright's *Road* is *Coronation Street* with vomit, excrement and used contraceptives cluttering its gutters, *Under Milk Wood* packed with blunt, despairing curse-words, *Our Town* in terminal disarray." Not only our town, but our country.

The road is an old metaphor for human life, but Cartwright's language insists on the fact that it is a contemporary English road that gradually opens up before us. That road functions credibly and metaphorically in north country dialect, where "anyroad" means "anyway." Scullery is a Brechtian narrator-guide along this epic journey "house by house," but the road also has a Beckettian circularity as we meet in Act II characters first glimpsed in Act I. As in Beckett, too, Cartwright's dialogue is full of telling repetitions. Like Osborne's Archie Rice moved by a Negro spiritual, two drunk young men on the dole respond to an Otis Redding record. Nevertheless, Cartwright's play sings out with an individual voice, in several registers.

Structurally, *Road* is divided into two acts, each rising climactically to an extended scene. Before those scenes, however, we hear several monologues – an old woman's fantasy, a professor's account of case histories, a confession of conversion from the pleasures of violence to those of contemplative Buddhism, a nostalgic recollection of a hopeful past. Weaving through these brief scenes in the several houses are Scullery's street meetings with the drunks and sex-seekers, whose companion he is. In the second act almost all the dialogue hinges – sometimes humorously, sometimes touchingly – on unsatisfactory couplings.

But coupling is only incidental to the extended scenes that terminate each act. In the first act Joey, a teenager who is already disillusioned with life, seeks a mystical vision by fasting in his own bed: "I feel like England's forcing the brain out me head." Unresponsive to his parents' pleas to unlock his door, Joey admits his girlfriend Clare, who shares his fate, without grasping his motivation. The mindless life on the road continues, and as Clare trembles into death by starvation, Joey shakes his thin fist at the audience, the sky, the door

3 *Road* by Jim Cartwright, directed by Simon Curtis at the Royal Court, 1986; the guide Scullery (Edward Tudor-Pole) is in the shopping cart

locking his family out, and then bites his fist. After a blackout Clare's face is covered, with Joey's feet next to it. His face hangs over the edge of the bed, so we see him cruciform and upside down. His dying words deny the vision he sought, and he taunts the audience: "But you're all adding a maybe, aren't you?" He winks and dies. There is no life for youth on this road.

A more extended scene climaxes the second act. Two young men, Brink and Eddie, have picked up two young women, Carol and Louise – whom we have seen separately in the first act. The young men ply the young women with drink so as to induce them to agree to sexual intercourse. When Carol resists and taunts them with their conventional conduct, they promise "something that we always do when outside gets to us." Only after they perform their three-part ritual does Brink enunciate it: "That's what you do, you drink, you listen to Otis [Redding], you get to the bottom of things and let rip." In the "rip" Eddie, conflating several American mythic outlaws, creates a heroic image of himself against England: "England's an old twat in the sea." Brink becomes a cowboy but cries real tears: "A man cry." After the girls' less vivid "rip"s, the four chant a choral: "Somehow a somehow a somehow might escape." Finally, after a last quick glance into the several rooms in the houses along the road, the guide Scullery invites us to "call again."

Several reviewers compared *Road* with *Look Back in Anger*, which opened at the same Royal Court Theatre thirty years earlier, and these reviewers contrasted Osborne's *Look Back in Anger* with Cartwright's look back in despair, making no allowance for Joey's "maybe." And yet Joey's "maybe" is highlighted by his final cruciform position, which in our culture is associated with resurrection. Moreover, there is a structural similarity in the final scenes of each act – the parallel visionary escapes sought by Joey, and then by Eddie and Brink. Joey dies in quest of a vision, without attaining it. But Eddie and Brink find a vision in Otis Redding's "Try a little Tenderness," whose chorus they finally chant – the "I" broadened to the Lancastrian "a," which sounds like "all." The individual may sing for everybody on the road in this non-realistic play.

The Royal Court Theatre, in its thirtieth anniversary season, did Cartwright proud. For all the daring subject matter and vocabulary of its plays, only miracles of design (mainly by Jocelyn Herbert) and lighting (mainly by Andy Philips) could change the appearance of the Court's deep, narrow proscenium stage. For *Road*, however, a false floor covered the orchestra, and the road became the length, breadth, and even height of the theatre, the audience moving from house to house in the style called promenade. But the word "promenade" almost trivializes the theatre tension aroused by following Scullery, then adjusting to the skillful shifts of focus on the particular actor arresting our momentary attention. Sometimes manipulated and sometimes ignored by Scullery, we too trudge along that road peopled with defiant losers who are dynamic performers.

It is fitting to close this chapter on Cartwright and Williams, two young playwrights who stretch realism in such differently inventive ways – the one moving us along a depleted contemporary "anyroad" and the other transporting us into a coherent community of the past. In England. Some of the other dramas symbolizing England will reappear in my chapters that examine more explicit devices of non-realism. None of these State-of-England dramas falls wholly within the realistic traditions of picture-frame stage, cause-and-effect plot, coherent characters, and sequential dialogue. Hare's *Plenty* juggles with time and fantasy. Violence shrieks its symbolism in *Belcher's Luck* and *On the Edge*. Churchill's *Cloud 9* plays with time, sex, and rhyme. Osborne's *The Entertainer* borrows from music-hall, and Brenton's *Epsom Downs* includes a ghost and human horses in its vast panorama. Differing in presentation style, this group of plays depict modern Britain as character, family, hospital, asylum, race-course, road, or dance, and the metaphor usually indicts the nation.

3

Shakespeare left and righted

Jokes about my play setting the house on fire?

(Shakespeare in Bond's *Bingo*)

Shakespeare is, of course, the national British icon, and one way of escaping contemporary realism is, paradoxically, to treat Shakespeare as our contemporary. The English title of an influential book by Jan Kott (published in French in 1962, but in the original Polish only in 1964), Shakespeare had already been staged as our contemporary by means of modern setting and costumes, rearrangement and abridgement of the sometimes problematic text, and unmetrical delivery of the verse, as in Peter Hall's early productions for the Royal Shakespeare Company.[1] In his own time, Shakespeare may have looked contemporary, since there was virtually no setting, and costumes were in part the cast-off clothes of aristocratic patrons. Although Queen Elizabeth apparently understood that the performance of Shakespeare's *Richard II* threatened her own stability, it is not until the twentieth century that directors deliberately manipulate Shakespeare's text to stress or strain its current topicality. In their wake contemporary playwrights who turn to Shakespeare – whether to burlesque, subvert, or modernize him – also turn away from realism.[2]

Although critics (including myself) have viewed the Shakespeare adaptations of the London-based American Charles Marowitz, as burlesque, he himself has publicized the seriousness of his inten-

---

1 William Dudley, an RSC designer, speaks for the opposition: "I don't like Shakespearian tragedies set in Fascist states with machine guns and so on, mostly because of the language. The law of weapons and steel fights it fundamentally – you lose all the personal valour of swordsmanship and hand-to-hand combat if you fight it out with Armalite rifles" (Cook, *Directors' Theatre*, pp. 29–30).

2 Cf. Ruby Cohn, *Modern Shakespeare Offshoots*, Princeton: Princeton University Press, 1976.

tions, notably in the Introduction to *The Marowitz Shakespeare*. That volume presents the texts of five of his six adaptations, omitting *An Othello*. His *Hamlet* (1965) and *Macbeth* (1969) are collages, applying scissors and paste to Shakespeare's texts. In these freewheeling derivations, Shakespeare's characters are reduced, doubled, plunged into busy and dizzy scenes, but Marowitz is faithful in his fashion to Shakespeare's dialogue, since he injects few of his own words into these collages. However, when the German State Theatre commissioned *An Othello* for the Wiesbaden Festival of 1972, Marowitz introduced contemporary language for his "Uncle Tom" Othello, who is opposed by a black activist Iago. Similarly, in successively revised versions of *The Shrew* (1973) Marowitz introduces a contemporaryy nameless Boy and Girl, who "gradually disappear into the feckless, wholly expedient, mutually exploitative morass of moddern life," while Petruchio "brainwashes" Katherine into submission. *Measure for Measure* (1975) twists Shakespeare's plot to victimize both Claudio and Isabella, with the play closing on the pious hypocrisies of Angelo and the Duke. Finally (one hopes), *Variations on the Merchant of Venice* (1977) sets a variant of Shakespeare's play in Palestine at the time of the British mandate. Conflating Marlovian lines with the best-known passages of Shakespeare's text, Marowitz emphasizes the anti-semitism of Antonio, Bassanio "and their Jew-baiting British cohorts," to explain contemporary violence in Jerusalem. From collage to variant, Marowitz contributed to manipulation of the Bard on the London fringe, so that Pip Simmons deromanticizes *The Tempest* (1977) and Cheek by Jowl place their own distinctive stamp on their Shakespeare productions of the 1980s.

Almost contemporary with early Marowitz was the first short version of *Rosencrantz and Guildenstern Are Dead*, which Tom Stoppard wrote in 1964 in Berlin where, to quote Stoppard, "the Ford Foundation was financing a kind of annual cultural picnic" (*Theatre Quarterly* [May–July 1974], p. 5). Triggered by a question of his agent, Kenneth Ewing, about which Shakespearean English king received the letter that was written by King Claudius and entrusted to Rosencrantz and Guildenstern, a one-act verse burlesque became *Rosencrantz and Guildenstern Meet King Lear* (Tynan, *View of the English Stage, passim*). Along with other Ford-sponsored plays, this sketch was performed in Berlin by the London-based Questors Theatre, who afterwards presented Stoppard's play at their own theatre. Stoppard may have written more than one version because his recollection of the single act – "a sort of Shakespearian pastiche" – differs from that of Alfred Emmet of the Questors, who maintains that the early draft "is clearly

the seed from which the full version grew," including the philosophi-
cal Player (*Theatre Quarterly* [March–May 1975], p. 95).

Stoppard expanded the single act to a full-length version:

What I do remember is that the transition from one play to the other was an
attempt to find a solution to a practical problem – that if you write a play
about Rosencrantz and Guildenstern in England, you can't count on people
knowing who they are and how they got there. So one tended to get back into
the end of *Hamlet* a bit. But the explanations were always partial and ambiguous, so one went back a bit further into the plot, and as soon as I started
doing this I totally lost interest in England. The interesting thing was them at
Elsinore . . . The chief interest and objective was to exploit a situation which
seemed to me to have enormous dramatic and comic potential – of these two
guys who in Shakespeare's context don't really know what they're doing . . .
it has the right combination of specificity and vague generality which was
interesting at that time to (it seemed) eight out of ten playwrights.

(*Theatre Quarterly* [May–July 1974], p. 6)

So successful was Stoppard's combination of specificity and vague
generality that the Royal Shakespeare Company took an option on
the still unfinished play. Dissatisfied with the ending, they let the
option lapse without performance, and Stoppard thereupon offered
the play to Frank Hauser, the artistic director of the Oxford Playhouse, who passed it on to an Oxford student group for performance
on the fringe of the Edinburgh Festival. For forty-eight frenetic hours,
Stoppard himself assumed direction of the play in August, 1966.
Praised fulsomely by Ronald Bryden in the influential *Observer*, *Rosencrantz and Guildenstern* was snapped up by Kenneth Tynan, who by
then had graduated from the *Observer* to become the Literary Advisor
of the recently founded National Theatre of Great Britain.

By far the most celebrated transplantation of Shakespeare's characters, *Rosencrantz and Guildenstern Are Dead* owes as much to Samuel
Beckett's *Waiting for Godot* as to *Hamlet*.[3] Both sources bend Stop-
pard's play far, far from realism. Except for the title and finale, Stop-
pard's characters are not dead, but, on the contrary, very lively in a
play that dovetails the modern dialogue into that of Shakespeare.
Stoppard uses and sometimes abuses lines from Shakespeare's Act II,
Scenes 1 and 2; Act III, Scene 1; Act IV, Scenes 1 to 4; and Act V.
Moreover, Stoppard stages two reported actions of Shakespeare –
Hamlet's dishevelled appearance before Ophelia, and Hamlet's

3 For intelligent examinations, see Egan, Robert, "A Thin Beam of Light," *Theatre
Journal* (March, 1979); Giancaris, C. G., "Absurdism Altered," *Drama Survey* (Winter,
1968–69); Levenson, Jill, "Views from a Revolving Door," *Queen's Quarterly* (Fall,
1971).

substitution of his own letter that will lead to the execution of its bearers, Rosencrantz and Guildenstern.

For all the residual Shakespeare dialogue, Stoppard's play is modern. "[Rosencrantz and Guildenstern] are twentieth-century agnostics, uncommitted and frightened: little men being used by those in power, and cipher characters being used by the dramatist. There is a paradoxical inconsistency here between the rootless twentieth-century man and the defined character imprisoned in his play" (Hunter, *Tom Stoppard's Plays*, pp. 136–7). Stoppard engages our sympathy for these unfortunate, loquacious, and unrealistic characters who play their lives away. "We the audience never know more than Didi and Gogo, because Beckett knows no more. We know much more than Ros and Guil because we have aborbed *Hamlet*" (Cohn, *Modern Shakespeare Offshoots* p. 217). We know, as Ros and Guil do not, that the entertaining metaphysical questioning will come to naught.

Stoppard's further forays into Shakespeare were not developed into full-length plays. For the fringe director Ed Berman, who adopted the pseudonym Dogg, Stoppard in 1972 devised a Wittgensteinian language game *Dogg's Our Pet* (an anagram of Dogg's Troupe). For the same intrepid director, who produced theatre in a double-decker bus, Stoppard abridged *Hamlet* to a fifteen-minute performance. In 1979 Stoppard conflated these two sketches into *Dogg's Hamlet*, which he paired with *Cahoot's Macbeth*, to last about an hour in performance. Beneath the double burlesque lie serious ideas: Stoppard's *Hamlet* teaches an audience to understand Dogg language, as well as to accept radical reduction of an iconic play, from which, incidentally, Rosencrantz and Guildenstern are absent. Stoppard's *Macbeth* pays tribute to the censored Czech playwright Pavel Cahout, and to Czech actors who, barred from theatres, performed in their own apartments.

Thus toying sporadically with Shakespeare, Stoppard does not shake the foundations of a quasi-sacred tradition, which is nourished rather than undermined by burlesque. Two of Stoppard's three Shakespeare offshoots began as burlesque, and yet the final plays reach out for serious import. Inventive as the two brief plays are, and noble as their purpose may be, *Dogg's Hamlet* and *Cahoot's Macbeth* are little more than pastiche. *Rosencrantz and Guildenstern Are Dead*, in contrast, rises above its burlesque beginnings and static residue to evoke sympathy for the little men (as opposed to the common men) of this world and this theatre.

When in the mid-sixties Marowitz invoked Artaud for his Shakespeare manipulations, and Stoppard emerged from pastiche, they initiated a minor trend of non-realism which continued into the 1970s. The first generation of new playwrights – John Arden, John Osborne, Harold Pinter, Arnold Wesker – wrote in part against Shakespeare's dominance of the London stage, and none of them turned in immediate urgency to the Bard. In 1973, however, John Osborne diluted *Coriolanus* into the contemporary prose of a self-involved articulate protagonist in *A Place Calling Itself Rome* (1973), and in 1975–6 Wesker rewrote *The Merchant of Venice*.

In contrast to the first generation of dramatists, those born in the 1940s were weaned on the ideals of a postwar Labor government, and when they came of writing age, they lashed out at the social, sexual, and cultural corruption beneath a Conservative veneer of peace and prosperity, summed up in the title of David Hare's *Plenty*. University men – Howard Brenton, David Edgar, David Hare – they occasionally bent Shakespeare to their purpose. In a public forum of 1986 David Hare criticized Edward Bond (his senior by thirteen years) for adapting Shakespeare, an endeavor he pronounced "absurd." Nevertheless, one of Hare's own earliest plays *Slag* (1970) derives – consciously or not – from *Love's Labour's Lost*. Hare's title not only spells "gals" backwards but is also a pun; the *OED* defines slag as "a piece of refuse matter separated from a metal in the process of smelting," but the word is also Cockney slang for worn-out female flesh. Both meanings might have been in Hare's mind, even though his three characters are *young* women.

The structure of *Slag* inevitably recalls that of *Love's Labour's Lost*, subverting its surface realism. As Shakespeare's three courtiers follow the King of Navarre into monastic seclusion, Hare's three woman teachers staff a girls school.

Ann owns the school where she employs Elise and Joanne as teachers. Both *Love's Labour's Lost* and Hare's echo begin with a separationist oath, but Shakespeare eventually contrives the happy heterosexual ending of comedy (albeit delayed for a year), whereas Hare contrives comic deflation of his female trio. Sooner than in *Love's Labour's Lost* the women chafe against their oath of celibacy; indeed they do so almost as soon as they have sworn. Far from the courtly address of Shakespeare's comedy, insults and lies pour forth from Hare's trio. Ann desires "a tight-knit community" of women, so she tolerates Joanne's barbs and obeys Elise's pregnant whims. While we witness feminine anarchy onstage, the offstage students withdraw or are withdrawn from the school. Thrown upon themselves, the three women teachers engage in a series of two-against-one alliances. Ann and Elise start a lesbian love affair, Elise addressing Ann as

Desdemona, and Ann Elise as Ophelia (two docile women on Shakespeare's roster, as feminist critics would soon point out). By the end of *Slag*, there is neither community for Ann, radical feminism for Joanne, nor birth for Elise: "There was a great wet fart and it had gone." The play ends inconclusively, with the three women circling the stage and Joanne murmuring: "Well then –."

David Hare was twenty-two years old when he created these three women aged twenty-three, twenty-six, and thirty-two. He may well owe a debt to Sartre's *Huis clos*, as well as to Shakespeare, for the trio is in hell much of the time – a hell of their own making. Hare's titular slag, the refuse of the melting process, may, as he has hinted, refer to the academic institution rather than three female misfits, but no student appears on stage. Hare mocks his academic trio less affectionately than Shakespeare does his would-be monks. Although Hare has claimed that his women were portrayed more roundly and comprehensively than was then usual, *Slag* sounds oddly misogynistic for the beginning of the 1970s. *Slag* does, however, presage Hare's predilection for women protagonists who live a lie, and thus represent contemporary Britain.

Hare may have borrowed unconsciously from Shakespeare for this early play, but other left-wing adapters were quite consciously refuting Shakespeare. David Edgar came to fringe theatre by way of journalism, and he wrote short agitprop skits for the theatre collective General Will before graduating to longer, subtler plays. To attract inhabitual theatre audiences, Edgar wrote rapidly and topically. *Death Story* (1972) belongs to this early period of his work, and it hovers uneasily between agitprop and deeper exploration. Patterned on Shakespeare's tragedy of young love, *Death Story* is necessarily non-realistic. Edgar has pinpointed his simultaneous admiration for and rejection of Shakespeare at that time: "I'd seen the Zeffirelli film of *Romeo and Juliet* and walked out of the cinema shaking with fury, because I'd always been fascinated by the original play. So the first half of *Death Story* is me saying, I think the original is about this, and the second half of the play is me saying, I don't think the original is relevant" (Marowitz and Trussler, *New Theatre Voices*, p. 165).

Nominally set in Verona, like Shakespeare's *Romeo and Juliet*, Edgar's revision is intended to comment on the British armed presence in Northern Ireland. Edgar distinguishes between native (presumably Irish) craftsmen, the Montagues, and foreign (presumably British) capitalists, the Capulets. Romeo Montague is an insouciant youth in love with love, who is oblivious to the industrial unrest that pits his class against its exploiters, who are vaguely modeled on

54

the British in Ireland. Nevertheless supporting his kinsman Mercutio against the insults of Tybalt, Romeo shoots the latter, and that triggers his political education. After his night of love with Juliet, he informs her that political differences must sunder them. Distraught, she turns to a priest, who formulates a quasi-Shakespearean plan to unite the lovers: Juliet will pretend to be dying (a suicide), and Romeo will visit her in the hospital, where family feuds will melt in the warmth of young love.

In the hospital, however, Verona's military commander seizes Romeo who is, in turn, suspicious and armed. Stabbing the commander, Romeo leaves the hospital without a backward glance at Juliet, who thereupon flirts with suicide in her grief, striking her head on the wall, cutting her wrists, and finally screaming: "I wish we were dead." "We" is problematic: the young lovers of Shakespeare's legend? Her selfish family and class?[4]

In either case Edgar's "death story" is social as well as personal. He himself has characterized it as a retort to those who believed "that problems in Northern Ireland could all be solved if people just got a little friendly with one another. And the play was trying to make the point that life doesn't work like that. The rather melodramatic qualities about the play have made it extremely popular with young performers" (Marowitz and Trussler, *New Theatre Voices*, p. 165). The play may also be popular because young people enjoy ridiculing a major myth of our culture.

Edgar does not end his *Death Story* on the separated lovers; instead, ne returns all characters to the stage to mock the Bard's tragic finale. That end is a virtual prelude to Edgar's frankly parodic stabs at the Bard, which follow *Death Story*. In 1973, again for the fringe group General Will, Edgar collaborated with Howard Brenton on *A Fart for Europe*, twisting *King Lear* to oppose Britain's membership in the European Economic Community. In 1974 the small Bush Theatre commissioned Edgar to write a sequel to *Tedderella*, his parody of *Cinderella*, but Edgar, an erstwhile journalist and avid newspaper-reader, suddenly connected the headlines about President Nixon with another villain, Shakespeare's Richard III. *Dick Deterred* (1974) foists the Watergate scandal upon Richard III. "I didn't," Edgar has confessed, "actually read *Richard the Third*, check whether it was going to fit, until the statutory five weeks before the play was due. In fact, it does fit, and it was mainly a mathematical task of fitting the

---

4 In Swain's book on Edgar she quotes: "I wish I were dead," and I do not know whether this is her error or an earlier version.

two components together. So essentially form preceded content there" (Marowitz and Trussler, *New Theatre Voices*, p. 166).

Form and content merge in the surreptitious taping of conversations of the audience as they enter the theatre – so apposite to the form and content of the illicit Watergate tapes. In the play itself Edgar pilots seven actors (with frequent doubling) through two acts that trace the Watergate conspiracy from the 1968 Republican National Convention to Richard's battle with ghosts in Camp David. Moving swiftly, the scenes are punctuated by variants of well-known Shakespeare lines from several plays. Richard enters while Johnson is still President: "Now is the winter of our discontent / Made glorious summer by this Texan bum." Crowned, Richard addresses his supporters: "Friends and Republicans, lend me your ears . . ." More germane to the conspiracy, Richard worries: "To bug or not to bug, that was the question." And having decided to bug, Richard closes the first act: "If I am bugging you, then doubtless you are bugging me," in a happy pun.

As Act II traces Richard's successive betrayals of his supporters, he rhymes: "A greater love hath none, in time of strife / Than laying down his friends to save his life." Richard in battle yearns: "A goat! A goat! My kingdom for another scapegoat!" Slain by Richmond (Sam Ervin), Richard rises from his coffin, dons his crown, orders police to point carbines at the audience, and the performance ends with the audience tape that was recorded before the play began. The audience realizes it has been bugged.

Edgar's political parody is truer to the chronology of Watergate than to the scenic sequence of Shakespeare's history play. Wittier than Barbara Garson's *Macbeth* parody, the comparably political *MacBird* which preceded it by nearly a decade, *Dick Deterred* was scheduled, after a run at London's Bush Theatre, for an off-Broadway opening, when Nixon resigned, and the whole project was abandoned. Edgar then abandoned Shakespeare, to undertake serious plays of private and public morality. At a 1987 benefit for the Bush and Tricycle theatres I heard him read with spirit from *Dick Deterred* – to an appreciative audience that looked too young to remember Watergate. Some English theatregoers must be studying United States history, for background knowledge is the prerequisite of burlesque.

Of the left-wing playwrights born in the 1940s Howard Brenton has been most vituperative against mainstream culture: "The situationists showed how all of them, the dead greats, are corpses on our backs – Goethe, Beethoven – how gigantic the fraud is" (Marowitz and

Trussler, *New Theatre Voices* p. 97). For a postsituationist British play-wright, Shakespeare would seem to be "THE dead great," and yet Brenton has been quixotically loyal to him. Having read English literature at the university, Brenton and other "refugees from Cambridge" formed a fringe company called the Combination, for which he wrote and acted, but his first professional production was *Revenge* (1969) in the Royal Court Upstairs. The play took three years to write, and its seed was Shakespeare:

It had very literary beginnings in that it was going to be a rewrite of *King Lear*, no less, and there still are the *Lear* elements there, in that the criminal [protagonist] has two daughters and he gives up his kingdom and tries to get it back and fails. And they never mention the mother, which is one of the oddly crucial things about *Lear* . . . It first had a formal scene with [the criminal] giving up his gangster kingdom and then going to gaol – that's how the play began.   (Marowitz and Trussler, *New Theatre Voices* pp, 89–90)

But *Revenge* departs from *Lear* when the criminal and the Police Commissioner, played by the same actor, square off in a duel to the death. Brenton depicts two faces of the same coin; in a totally corrupt British society, both transgressor and policeman are anachronisms in their petty quests for vengeance: "The whole country on the fiddle, the gamble, the open snatch, the bit on the side." The Shakespearean residue is scarcely detectable without Brenton's instruction, and yet it serves to slant the play's ethic away from causally probable realism.

Brenton has also claimed, perhaps with a mischievous tongue in his cheek, that the ferocious play within the play of his *Churchill Play* (1974) was modeled on the Pyramus and Thisbe play of *A Midsummer Night's Dream*, but it escapes my search. Over a decade later Brenton's *Greenland* (1988) draws title and Utopia from Shakespeare's "green" comedies where a magic forest is the setting for a pastoral idyll.

These oblique Shakespearean borrowings were preceded by an adaptation of *Measure for Measure* (1972), which marked Brenton's graduation from fringe and studio theatres to his first commission for a major professional theatre, the Northcott of Exeter. Brenton invested *Measure for Measure* (1972) with the shock or "aggro" effect that became his signature. Specifying "The play is set in England, now," Brenton colors Claudio and Isabella black, whereas the rest of the cast remain white. Color is the only similarity between brother and sister, since Claudio is a rock star and Isabella a Bible sister. In the list of characters the Duke and Angelo are both designated "dictators," but in William Gaskill's Exeter production the Duke was intended to resemble Conservative Harold Macmillan while Angelo was modeled on racist Enoch Powell. The cynical Lucio becomes Jerky Joe, "the Cecil B. De Mille of the blue movie trade."

Brenton kept Shakespeare's intricate plot, but he deliberately simplified and caricatured the characters. He excised much of Shakespeare's blank verse, and played the residue against the vigorous contemporary idiom of the low comedy characters. The problematic Shakespearean ethic is displaced by a demonstration of the hypocrisy and brutality of those in power. The occasional verse underlines the official lies – a rhythmic counterpoint that Brenton may have learned from *St. Joan of the Stockyards* or *The Resistible Rise of Arturo Ui* by Bertolt Brecht, whose *Galileo* he later translated for the National Theatre.

As in Shakespeare, Brenton's Duke relinquishes power to Angelo, who initiates an anti-pornography cease-and-arrest act. In Piccadilly Circus, despite the screams of rock fans, Claudio is arrested. When Jerky Joe's movie is impounded, profit as well as friendship prompts him to enlist the aid of pious Isabella. More or less on the advice of his psychiatrist, the Duke arranges Angelo's fornication with Mistress Overdone, but Jerky Joe is to film their copulation, leading to Angelo's downfall, for the aristocratic Duke regrets empowering Angelo, the commoner.

But the wily Angelo circumvents the Duke's plan, actually decapitating Claudio. Ignorant of that dire event, the rest of the cast meet in the brothel to view the movie of Angelo's disgrace. The Duke accuses his deputy: "You traded a brother's head for a sister's disgrace. You went too far, and England abhors a man who goes too far." Angelo's retort is Claudio's head, before he destroys the incriminating film and sentences everyone to jail, except the Duke who is sent to a nursing home: "Let him decay quietly, among the other wrecks of his kind." Angelo finally reigns diabolically supreme. In an improbable aside, he utters Brenton's lesson: "The old order, unchecked, will bring forth a new and far harsher form of itself."

The Exeter production of Brenton's *Measure* made liberal reference to London with its Piccadilly, Hyde Park, Soho sex shops. London, however, is not Boston, where scandal often spells box office success. Lawsuits apparently loomed in the capital, one newspaper screaming: "Inquiry into Disgusting Exeter Play." Softening the disgust, Brenton finally sends his cast (including Claudio) to sea aboard the SS Political Utopia. Seeing them off, Angelo pushes the Duke in a wheelchair. The cast wave and shout gaily: "Goodbye England." Brenton means that farewell to be a leave-taking from English democracy, once the new order is entrenched.

The following year, 1973, Brenton collaborated with David Edgar in another Shakespeare derivation *A Fart for Europe*, but that manuscript is apparently lost. The *File on Brenton* describes its beginning as a parody of *King Lear* "casting an anti-EEC Labour MP . . . in the role of poor Tom." More seriously, but still politically, Brenton returned to Shakespeare in *Thirteenth Night* (1981). Blending connotations of after-the-festive-comedy (*Twelfth Night*) into the bad luck associated with the number thirteen, Brenton's play adapts *Macbeth*. In his words: "Its title is a code for the play's theme – this is the play for when the celebrations have to stop" (*Plays*, Vol. 2, p. xi). Subtitled "a dream play," Brenton's drama owes little to Strindberg, except perhaps for the sexual attraction/antagonism of its principals, but then that is already present in Shakespeare's *Macbeth*.

In *Thirteenth Night*, middle-class, married, well-educated Jack Beaty works in the left wing of England's Labor Party, along with his activist lover, Jenny Gaze. Attacked by fascist thugs, Beaty falls unconscious, and in his delirium sees himself as a Macbeth-figure. Brenton's subtitle, *A Dream Play*, designates a left-wing politician's nightmare, which arises from a question of the Labor Party leader: "If a socialist party really came t'power in Britain . . . what do you do, eh?" What Jack Beaty does is emulate Macbeth, and that emulation was not played like a dream in the original production at the small Donmar Warehouse. Some spectators thought that the Beaty actor Michael Pennington resembled the Labor leader Neil Kinnock; others saw an analogy with the dissident Laborite Tony Benn. Brenton has said that the play is about Stalinism or "the blood in the revolution's cradle" (*New Theatre Quarterly* [August 1987], p. 200).

In his dream Jack Beaty is spurred by his lover, Jenny, to kill the Labor Prime Minister, a father-figure. With the help of the Secret Service Chief Ross, Beaty imprisons his best friend Feast, releasing him to be murdered by thugs, who are in turn slated for execution. The Macduff and Malcolm figures coalesce into a single character, Murgatroyd, who flees, not to England for an avenging army, but to California, where he and Feast both die. Beaty's lover, the Lady Macbeth analogue, takes the poison proffered by the three witches, who appear intermittently in several disguises. In a last soliloquy Beaty tries to justify himself to the ghosts of his victims, but the *Macbeth* adaptation ends with the three witches shining flashlights on Beaty's throne-like chair; they illuminate a grinning skeleton.

The dream is over in the final scene of *Thirteenth Night*. Beaty and Jenny, wounded heroes of the Labor Party, stroll on a beach. Each admits to having a dream about peace, and as Jenny picks up a stone,

Beaty muses: "Peace is not a personal matter, is it?" "No," she replies, and the two actors freeze, Beaty in a limp, and Jenny's arm
raised to throw the stone into the sea. The nightmare has not taught
them that peace and politics *are* personal matters. In a catch-phrase of
the day: "The personal is political," Jack Beaty has dreamed *Macbeth*,
but it is the audience who must appreciate Shakespeare's warning
against ruthless ambition.

Although Arnold Wesker is a decade older than the Brenton–
Edgar–Hare group, he was their contemporary in adapting Shakespeare. Not until the mid-1970s did he attempt a passionate rebuttal of
The Merchant of Venice. In earlier English theatre, several actors and
authors occasionally reacted against the devastating portrait of Shylock the Jew (for example, the actor Macready's sympathetic Shylock
and the playwright St. John Ervine's 1924 *Lady of Belmont*), but after
the Nazi holocaust, opposition to Shakespeare's portrait has been so
intense that performance of *The Merchant of Venice* has sometimes
been prohibited, e.g. in Israel, Hungary and certain United States
schools. This has never been true in England, and an English Socialist
Jew, Arnold Wesker, describes what provoked his own play:

Once again *The Merchant of Venice* is on school syllabuses. Productions are
being mounted around the country. The Royal Shakespeare Company has
transferred its version from Stratford to London, though not without some
anxiety . . . I revere Shakespeare, am proud to write in his shadow . . . and I
would passionately defend the right of anyone anywhere to present and
teach this play. But nothing will make me admire it nor has anyone persuaded me the holocaust is irrelevant to my responses . . . [*cf.* Ryan, *Shakespeare*, pp 14–24] I ceased finally to be a "forgiver" . . . in 1973, watching
Laurence Olivier's oi-yoi-yoi portrayal of Shylock in Jonathan Miller's production [of *The Merchant of Venice*] at the National Theatre.
(*Theatre Quarterly* [Winter 1977–8], p. 21).

Wesker continues: "When Portia suddenly gets to the bit about having a pound of flesh but no blood, it flashed on me that the kind of
Jew I know would stand up and say 'Thank God!'" Wesker conceived
a play to give voice to that "kind of Jew."

Wesker investigated the nature of contracts in Renaissance Venice,
and his fascination with that time, place, and culture drenched the
eventual drama. Wesker retained Shakespeare's three plot strands:
the casket choice of a husband for Portia, the runaway daughter of
Shylock, and, preeminently, the pound-of-flesh contract between
Shylock and Antonio. But even while retaining these matters, Wesker
modified them. In Bassanio's choice of the lead casket, he is cool and
calculating; Jessica comes to despise Lorenzo and does not marry

him. Most importantly, the pound-of-flesh contract is a defiant joke suggested by Shylock in scorn of the Venetian law that forbids Jews to lend money to Christians unprotected by contract.[5]

Wesker's Shylock is not only a scholar but a humanitarian: he provides asylum for Jews fleeing from Portugal and the Inquisition; his home is open to the many refugees who pass through and into Venice, although the actual burden of caring for them falls on his daughter and sister. Insensitive to the women in his own household, Shylock nevertheless admires Portia when she saves Antonio in the court scene patterned on that of Shakespeare. Wesker's Shylock is not, however, condemned to be a Christian; instead, his life is spared, but his books are confiscated. An embittered sage with no further desires, Wesker's Shylock leaves Venice for Jerusalem.

In the last scene in Belmont, Jessica spurns Lorenzo, and Portia views her husband Bassanio critically. In the finale,

Portia, Antonio, and Jessica "move away to different corners of the garden . . . three lonely points of a triangle" which enclose and contain but cannot silence the arrogant prattle of three willfully ignorant young men in whom history . . . has actually placed the future of Venice. So Nerissa, who must serve them, like it or not, ironically observes: "And heroes you are, sirs, true. No denying it. True, true, heroes indeed. True. True, true, true. Heroes!"

(Alter, "Barbaric Laws," p. 545)

Wesker steeped himself in the climate of Renaissance Venice, but modern London theatre directors were wary of the long learned speeches and the static first act. *The Merchant* was premiered in Stockholm in 1976, but the National Theatre of Britain refused it because "every character was articulate and expressive of every single point of view that Wesker might take about every aspect of the situation" (Leeming, *Wesker the Playwright*, p. 131). John Dexter, the director of earlier Wesker plays at the Royal Court, was enthusiastic about *The Merchant*, and he undertook to direct it in New York, with Zero Mostel as Shylock. Rehearsals were evidently troublesome, climaxed by Mostel's death after a single performance in Philadelphia.

Further rehearsals became acrimonious, and during Wesker's absence in England the director imposed cuts. An unfavorable review in *The New York Times* effectively laid the play to rest in the United States, but a British premiere took place in Birmingham. The Methuen text of the play is Wesker's eighth version of *The Merchant*. Noble in intention, it is still burdened with long speeches, and the

5 For a learned explication of "bond" versus "contract" see Iska Alter, "Wesker's *Merchant*," *Modern Drama* (December, 1988).

documentary evidence of Venetian anti-semitism is spelled out in undramatic detail. The play also sounds a faint feminist note, since Wesker's Shylock is not perfect, but exploits the women in his household, his sister Rivkah and his daughter Jessica. Moreover, Portia and Jessica are wiser and kinder than the young men they love. To this day Wesker's *The Merchant* has had no professional London production, but it is occasionally taught in English schools.

Only two years separate Arnold Wesker from Edward Bond (b. 1934). Autodidacts, both playwrights take pride in their plebeian origins, discovering Shakespeare on their own, rather than through set texts in national examinations. Bond even finds that Shakespeare is a kindred spirit in this respect:

> *A further Poem on Shakespeare*
>
> He is not an academic
> His written words
> Are the echoes of speech
> His learning is prefaced
> By experience
> He does not come from school
> He goes to it.

As opposed to Arnold Wesker's single revision of Shakespeare, Edward Bond has engaged during the 1970s in a sustained dialogue with Shakespeare. Bond's early plan for the arc of his own career was modeled on Shakespeare's actual career – beginning with tragedy in *The Pope's Wedding* (1962) and reaching hopefully toward comedy in *The Sea* (1973). Somewhat extraneous to this large design, *Early Morning* of 1968 recalls *Henry VI* in royal familial strife, and that Bond play also echoes *Hamlet* when a ghostly father appears to his son, with the injunction to avenge his death.

Specifically, it is with *Lear* (1971) that Bond begins to offer dramatic rebuttals to Shakespeare – in Brecht's term for his own adaptations, "counter-plays." While Bond's *Lear* was still in an embryonic stage, he linked it with Shakespeare's *Measure for Measure*: "[Shakespeare] knew that the political model he had in *Measure for Measure* didn't work, couldn't work, so he had to write *King Lear*, which is the same programme on a much more basic, much more fundamental and much more less self-deceived level" (*Gambit*, no. 17, p. 26).

Before launching into his own *Lear*, Bond cooperated with Keith Hack, then a Cambridge University undergraduate, on a translation of Brecht's *Roundheads and Peakheads*, paying close attention to the way the German playwright had adapted *Measure for Measure* for that epic play. Hack describes the process:

First we made a very literal translation where Bond insisted that every nuance of the text be rendered. Then we decided to do our own version of the play – really a new play, loosely based on the Brecht play but modernized and set in England, with many new scenes and a total shift of emphasis . . . he then spent three months doing a more faithful translation and adaptation, setting the play in Enoch Powell's England. (Scharine, *Plays of Edward Bond*, p. 166)

Even as Howard Brenton was to set Shakespeare's *Measure for Measure*. Bond, however, scrapped this work, salvaging only an essay for the program note to Keith Hack's Cambridge production.

Bond continued his dialogue with Shakespeare. Although Bond scribbles verses in connection with all his plays, the poems are most numerous and intense for *Lear*. Begun soon after the completion of. *Lear*, *The Sea* echoes several facets of *The Tempest*, obliquely countering its characters, but spurning magic staff and book. Bond's *Bingo* (1973) dramatizes discord rather than harmony in the last days of Shakespeare at Stratford. When the contemporary playwright directed his *Worlds* (1979), he drew upon Shakespeare's Timon for the character of his protagonist Trench (Hay and Roberts, *Bond*, p. 180). In essay and interview, Bond mentions Shakespeare, sometimes admiringly and sometimes scathingly. The shadow of the Bard hovers over his non-realistic drama of the 1970s.

Lear (1971) is Bond's most sustained homage to and critique of Shakespeare, as he himself was well aware:

Shakespeare's *Lear* is usually seen as an image of high, academic culture. The play is seen as a sublime action and the audience are expected to show the depth of their culture by the extent to which they penetrate its mysteries . . . But the social moral of Shakespeare's *Lear* is this: endure till in time the world will be made right. That's a dangerous moral for us. We have less time than Shakespeare.
(Bond, program note for Liverpool Everyman Theatre production, October, 1975; quoted in Hay and Roberts, *Edward Bond*, p. 53)

In Bond's drama King Lear has built a wall to isolate his kingdom from its enemies, who are led by his two daughters, Bodice and Fontanelle. Bond's Cordelia is not Lear's daughter, but the wife of his Fool-analogue, the Gravedigger's Boy who is killed in the civil war, but whose Ghost accompanies old dethroned Lear for much of the play. The old king suffers blindness, madness, and emotional dislocation in the civil war that installs a vengeful Cordelia as ruler of the kingdom. After luring Lear to the pastoral retreat of his former home, the Ghost shrivels visibly as the old man gradually acquires self-knowledge and public responsibility. Lear dies nobly in an attempt to unbuild Cordelia's wall, which he as ruler once built. As James

4 *Lear* by Edward Bond, directed by William Gaskill at the Royal Court, 1971; Cordelia (Celestine Randall) admonishes a blind Lear (Harry Andrews) but does not see the Ghost of the Gravedigger's Boy (Mark McManus)

Bulman succinctly observes: "Together, Cordelia and the Grave-digger's Boy represent the Scylla and Charybdis, married in opposition, of political defensiveness and private retreat between which Lear must sail if he is to become a genuinely moral man" ("On Bond," p. 63).[6]

The critics Malcolm Hay and Philip Roberts cite Bond's debts to Shakespeare's *King Lear*:

Both . . . show a king and father acting arbitrarily and being opposed by two daughters whose sole concern is to acquire power. Both Lears move from autocratic behaviour into a kind of insanity and come towards some understanding and pity. Incidents to do with the partition of the kingdom, blinding, the imprisonment of father and daughter and the general deployment of animal imagery are common to each of the versions.   (*Bond*, p. 116)

Bond thrusts his Lear into Shakespeare's horrors – war, prison, torture, madness – and Lear's suffering softens his passion into compassion. As Shakespeare's Lear carries Cordelia's corpse, Bond's Lear cradles the dying Ghost of the Gravedigger's Boy.

Like Shakespeare, too, Bond risks grotesque comedy to intensify the tragedy, and he also bases specific scenes on Shakespeare: the partition of the kingdom, a mock trial in a hovel, and a father–daughter imprisonment. More limited than Shakespeare in his several rhythms, Bond suffuses his contemporary prose with similar imagery of vision, of animals, and especially of the maimed human body. Bond's Lear is finally a man of action. Climbing the wall that was rebuilt by the order of Cordelia, Lear begins to dismantle it, and is shot. He nevertheless grasps his shovel and gasps: "One more" before he dies. The two syllables close Bond's drama on a note of optimism, for "one more" is one defiant shovelful of wall, the *un*digging of a symbolic grave, but it may also be the one more person who will free the country from any walls at all. In the words of its first director, William Gaskill:

Unlike Brecht, who creates a mythical fairy-tale world to draw a political parallel, Bond makes a dream world in which the reality of rifles jostles a Shakespearian myth. The poet and the political thinker are trying to co-exist, a struggle that has gone on in Bond ever since. But the play, as far as it is polemical at all, is pacifist, against violence, and sceptical of political change by the masses. It is finally the action of one man that counts.

                    (*A Sense of Direction*, p. 122)

6 *Cf.* James Bulman, "Bond, Shakespeare, and the Absurd," *Modern Drama* (March, 1986).

Bond's creation of an activist Lear was followed immediately by *The Sea*, his only play specifically subtitled *A Comedy*. Together, the two Shakespeare derivations reflect what Bond has called "a whole vision of life . . . if one's going to write a play like *Lear*, in order to give oneself the courage to write that, one must also have in one's mind, 'Yes, but there's also *The Sea*'" (*The Times*, May 22, 1973).

The Sea reflects on *The Tempest*. Both plays open on a tempest, and both plays close on a young couple who will found a more ethical society. Bond wrote to the director of an amateur production: "Like the young couple in *The Tempest*, Willy and Rose [the young couple in *The Sea*] have to create their own personal maturity" (Hay and Roberts, *Edward Bond*, p. 57). Aside from the young couple, however, Bond's Shakespeare-analogues are only approximate in *The Sea*. The Prospero-figure is an upper-class Mrs. Rafi, who rules the turn-of-the-century seaside English town authoritatively. The Caliban-figure is a lower-class draper, Mr. Hatch; the physical deformity of Shakespeare's creature becomes mental deformity in Bond's comedy. Unlike the Caliban who is "read" as a revolutionary hero in recent anti-colonialist discourse, (e.g. *Une Tempête* by Aimé Césaire, *Prospero and Caliban* by O. Mannoni, *Prospero's Magic* by Philip Mason; *cf.* Brown, "*The Tempest* and the Discourse of Colonialism,"), Bond's Mr. Hatch is a paranoid fascist who schemes against invaders from outer space. And Ariel is absent.

Like *The Tempest*, *The Sea* is centered on the locus of authority. Shakespeare stages two conspiracies – the Antonio–Sebastian plot against the usurping Alonzo, and its grotesque mirror in the Caliban–Stephano–Trinculo plot against Prospero. Bond renders both his abortive rebellions grotesque – the Hatch-led vigilantes and the Rafi-dominated townswomen who scatter mere verbal barbs. Shakespeare exempts none of his characters from taking a position on legitimate authority, but Bond invents a character who abhors the rigid class structure of turn-of-the-century England, yet does nothing to change it. Bond's Evens drinks his life away by the sea; he describes himself as "a wreck rotting on the beach," and that wreck, drunk, fails to aid a drowning man. His passivity is murderous.

The Sea is a quiet play after the opening storm, but Bond dramatizes the cruel price of social harmony – a rigid and oppressive class structure, which the young couple must reject if they are to found a new and just society. In Shakespeare's play the highest-ranking character commands an entertainment to celebrate a nuptial; in Bond's play the highest-ranking character organizes an entertainment to commemorate a burial, but both plays within the play rest on a classical legacy – the harvest gods of Prospero's "insubstantial pageant" and Mrs. Rafi's original drama of Orpheus and Eurydice. (Bond himself has written a ballet and a sequence of poems on the Orpheus theme.) Dreams and drunkenness hover at the edge of both plays, and Bond at least once echoes Shakespeare's phrases:

FERDINAND: This music crept by me upon the waters
            Allaying both their fury and my passion
            With its sweet air.
MRS. TILEHOUSE: Something terrible is going to happen. I know it. A
            thing brushed past me through the air.

In Shakespeare's *The Tempest* mysterious forces are benign, but Bond banishes them from his self-styled Rational Theatre.

Bond's *Lear* and *The Sea* are counter-plays, arguing against their respective models, but *Bingo* sets Shakespeare himself on stage in an inquiry into the meaning of art: "Art has very practical consequences. Most 'cultural appreciation' ignores this and is no more relevant than a game of 'Bingo' and less honest" (Bond, *Sunday Times*, November 25, 1973). Although Bond avoids the dramatic trap of eulogizing Shakespeare's art, aspects of that art inevitably nurtured *Bingo*:

. . . the imagery of that situation is extraordinary. Welcombe . . . was a sort of open heath. And he'd written this play about Lear, who went mad on the heath, and standing on the heath insisted on certain moral insights, certain moral priorities for conduct, and you did those things even if it meant *your* death and even if it meant the destruction of your family. You did these things because there was no other life that is bearable . . . And when it came down to his own business transactions he did exactly the opposite.

(Hay and Roberts, *Bond*, p. 59)

Prematurely aged and retired to Stratford, Bond's Shakespeare finds small comfort in his comfortable home – New Place, which was Bond's working title for his "Scenes of Money and Death." Aware of the cruel greed of the rising capitalist class, Bond's Shakespeare will not imperil his own income by protesting against injustice to the underprivileged. Specifically, Shakespeare acquiesces to the land enclosures that starve out poor farmers and force them to migrate. By the end of *Bingo*, an insignificant numbers game, Shakespeare cannot live with himself: "I could have done so much . . . I was a hangman's assistant, a gaoler's errand boy." In self-contempt and condemnation, Bond's Shakespeare swallows poison.

Bond's public plot about Shakespeare, Money, and Death is balanced by a private plot with the same triangulation, since Shakespeare's family, financially greedy, await his death. Shakespeare's dying wife (not seen on stage) and his daughter Judith are passionate only about property – an obsession that reflects Shakespeare's own conduct. In the parallel pattern that Bond learned from the playwright Shakespeare, he invents a lower-class family for contrast. As in Shakespeare, these commoners are nameless – the Old Man, the Old Woman, the Son. Although Shakespeare's wise old servant owns nothing, she loves her mentally deficient husband and their radical Puritan son, and indeed her master, William Shakespeare.

The only Shakespeare play mentioned (by Ben Jonson) in Bond's *Bingo* is the significantly titled *A Winter's Tale*, but Bond's winter's tale recalls the heath scene of *King Lear*. As Shakespeare's king stumbles toward self-knowledge, Bond's landowner stumbles through the snow toward self-blame. Fallen, Bond's usually taciturn Shakespeare finally indulges in a soliloquy that bares his guilt in the cold. Unlike Bond's Lear, who finally acts responsibly, his Shakespeare can only moan the rhetorical Da Vinci question that he will repeat some dozen times before he dies: "Was anything done?" The passive mode reflects the social passivity of Bond's Shakespeare; even grammar condemns him. (In the poems that were written along with *Bingo*, however, Bond is less severe on the Bard.)

Although Bond's *Summer* has been interpreted as another *Tempest* (by the novelist Eva Figes, *Times Literary Supplement*, February 5, 1982), Bond's last published debt to Shakespeare appears in *The Worlds* (1979). The action juxtaposes a corporate world against that of the workers and also against that of terrorists. When Trench, a self-made man who owns a company, is kidnapped by terrorists, his administrative staff institute the changes he has resisted. Like Shakespeare's Timon of Athens, Trench lashes out against the friends who have betrayed him, and like Timon he withers into a half-crazed hermit. But unlike Shakespeare's Timon, who dies, Trench kills an innocent hostage seized by error. Finally, the corporate victimizer and the terrorist victimizer are the same man, and were played by the same mercurial actor Ian McDiarmid. It is an anticlimactic end to a decade during which Bond engaged in a dialogue with Shakespeare, from decreasingly hesitant adaptation to the bold staging of Shakespeare himself.

And I come to an anticlimactic end to this chapter with Howard Barker's *Seven Lears* (1989). Through a characteristically convoluted plot threads Barker's preferred theme of a quest for goodness in a world lacking ethical guides. A more accurate title for Barker's play would be "The Seven Ages of Lear," which serve as a prequel to the Shakespeare play. During Lear's growth through time we witness his sexual initiation by Prudentia and his marriage to her daughter Clarissa, with both names too pointedly meaningful. The Fool, Gloucester, and Oswald join Barker's invented characters. Unable to bear Clarissa's unflinching honesty, Lear drives her into Kent's bed. Goneril and Regan are Lear's daughters, but Cordelia is fathered by Kent. In a final scene, the stage is bare of women and of the verse-chanting Chorus of the Gaoled, as Lear and Kent, two old friend/enemies, play chess. Although Kent has cuckolded Lear and cheated at chess, he finally takes the King's hand in love. Goodness is perhaps relative.

From the merry rhymes of Edgar's *Dick Deterred* to Bond's anguished *Lear*, from Wesker's *Merchant* in the Renaissance Venetian Ghetto to Brenton's *Measure* in modern London, contemporary English drama-tists intermittently respond to Shakespeare, and some familiarity with his plays is mandatory to appreciate these adaptations. An edu-cated audience feels amused suspense, wondering how the modern plot will be tailored to the Shakespeare play. Although Tom Stoppard began his *Rosencrantz and Guildenstern Are Dead* as a parody of *Hamlet*, his admiration for Beckett enabled him to vivify the attendant lords, and polish the witty Player King. That play is the main Shakespear-ean string for Stoppard's deft bow, but Brenton surprisingly turns Shakespeare into shock effects, and Barker subdues his imagery to impose his own favorite theme on *King Lear*. Bond views Shakespeare at times as a tutelary deity and at times as an antagonist. During the formative years of his writing life, Bond engages in dialogue with Shakespeare – in poem, preface, and several major plays. Unshavian, however, Bond does not debate with the Bard. On the contrary, he is often in Shakespeare's debt – for image, structure, and tensions that theatricalize different strains of our time. From Stoppard's conflation of Shakespeare and Beckett to Bond's deconstruction of an icon, Shakespeare adaptation has proved surprisingly tough ground for departures from realism.

4

Diversities of verse

A poet? Really? Well, if he'd like to send me some examples of his work, double spaced on quarto, with copies in a separate folder by separate post in case of loss or misappropriation, stamped addressed envelope enclosed, I'll read them.   (Spooner in Harold Pinter's *No Man's Land*)

Poetic is a treacherous adjective for drama. Long a term of praise, "poetic" by the late twentieth century hints at escape from reality. But reality itself has disintegrated into a problematic concept that is barely represented by familiar surface detail. It is against, or below, or above that surface that several turn-of-the-twentieth century playwrights wrote, for example Strindberg, Hofmannsthal, Yeats, Maeterlinck.[1] Each of these poets of the theatre broke the picture-frame stage to penetrate to what he felt was a deeper level of reality, but their depths do not connect. Poetic drama is elusive of definition; does the poetry lie in the lexicon, the stage image, the reach toward myth or mystery? I investigate the more limited terrain of poetic as verse, and yet I do not quite avoid these questions since verse drama seeks resonance beyond surface detail (even when it is frankly parodic). Through rhythm, the playwright tries to impose depth, mystery, or mythic connection and thereby estranges his work from the everyday quality of realism.

Modern English playwrights who are attracted to verse as an antirealistic device have to find a rhythm to dislodge prose habits of theatre. Blank verse lies in the shadow of the perennial performances of Shakespeare in England. Aware of this, T. S. Eliot invented a looser three-beat line, but no one else danced to his rhythm. Even within his own chapel poets reverted to blank verse – Ronald Duncan, Norman Nicholson, Ann Ridler, and especially Christopher

1 Cf. Eric Salmon, "Verse Versus Poetry," in *Is the Theatre Still Dying?*, New York: Greenwood Press, 1985.

Fry. In the next theatre generation John Arden is partial to ballad rhythms, but he is a lone singer in that form. More usually, free verse lines of varying beat and length become instruments by which several recent English dramatists reach beyond realism, but the printed line is rarely recognizable as verse in the theatre. Such recognition may be a mere academic problem, but it becomes a theatre problem when the spectator/auditor cannot enjoy the tension between the grammatical sentence and the verse line.

The heritage of European drama is formed and informed by verse, where language is constrained within recurrent rhythms. Although classical Greek drama may have sounded like our opera, the music was lost so early that later playwrights quarried both classical tragedy and comedy for dialogue in verse. Like these classical ancestors, the earliest plays in modern European languages were written in verse, although the metrical line differs with the language. In the great ages of European drama verse was the norm – Elizabethan English, Golden Age Spanish, Classical French, Storm and Stress German. Comedy usually preceded tragedy in shifting to prose, and by the eighteenth century prose commanded the English stage. But in the early nineteenth century both poets and actors throughout Europe paid homage to Shakespeare, the former imitating him disastrously, and the latter performing him in melodramatic fashion. Especially in England, their separate failures produced closet dramas, on the one hand, and swashbuckling drivel, on the other. It is true that the popular actors Charles Macready and Henry Irving espoused new plays in verse, and that Irving's favorite role was that of the titular hero of Tennyson's verse play *Becket*, but we search in vain for a single inventive verse play written in English during the nineteenth century. (With ruthless cutting, Shelley's *Cenci* and Byron's *Manfred* and *Cain* are sporadically performed, mainly by amateurs.)

Despite the dominance of realistic drawing-room drama on the London stage of the first half of the twentieth century, there were occasional calls for a revival of poetic drama. More or less inept verse plays were produced by Lascelles Abercrombie, Clifford Bax, Gordon Bottomley, John Drinkwater, T. Sturge Moore, and especially John Masefield. During the 1930s Ashley Dukes' Mercury Theatre welcomed verse plays. Not only did T. S. Eliot's *Murder in the Cathedral* alight at the Mercury between Canterbury Cathedral and the West End of London, but the Mercury also housed Rupert Doone's Group Theatre productions of plays by Auden and Isherwood, Stephen Spender, and Louis MacNeice, which were at least partly in verse. In 1946 the Mercury Theatre's new director, E. Martin

Browne, announced a season of verse drama – by Christopher Fry, Ronald Duncan, Norman Nicholson, Ann Ridler, and Donagh MacDonagh. Although Fry alone transferred to the West End, it seemed as though verse would sound the clarion call for experiment on the post-World War II English stage, threatening the supremacy of realism.

Almost every generation of English writers since the Romantics espoused the return of poetry to the theatre, but the time did seem propitious after World War II. With the war dead fresh in memory, with bombed-out ruins in daily view, and with rationing still in force, but with a whole populace anxious to begin a new life, many of the English urged a new spirituality in the theatre, to be conveyed by verse. In 1950 T. S. Eliot's (1935) *Murder in the Cathedral* was revived by Peter Brook for a successful run in the West End, and in its wake came Eliot's new verse play, *The Cocktail Party*. Actors, writers, and critics engaged in lively dialogues about verse in the theatre.

When the English Stage Company was formed in 1954, some members of its Board of Directors – above all Ronald Duncan – were fond of verse plays, and perhaps this was the spur to the anti-verse stance of the critic Kenneth Tynan: "The powers of the line that stops short of the margin are again being hymned and its mysteries celebrated" ("Prose and the Playwright," in *Tynan on Theatre*, p. 330). Tynan turned his own irreverent prose against such mysteries. At the same time, the artistic director of the English Stage Company, George Devine, wooed novelists for his Royal Court theatre, but he kept a discreet silence about poets. Irving Wardle's book about George Devine portrays a director who was careful not to reveal his distaste for Ronald Duncan's verse plays, but two of those plays fell to Devine to direct – by default, since the other director, Tony Richardson, was busy with *Look Back in Anger*. Wardle writes: "It is superbly ironic that the architect of the demotic writers' theatre [Devine] should have received his brief from the high priest of the poetic drama movement [Duncan]" (*Theatres of George Devine*, p. 168).

Instead of choosing one of the two plays offered by Duncan, Devine cut large chunks from *Don Juan* and *The Death of Satan* in order to present them as a double bill. Attendance at the Court fell to eighteen percent, and Duncan's plays were withdrawn after eight performances. Wardle pointedly compares Duncan's hero and Osborne's angry protagonist:

Don Juan and Jimmy Porter are both men of passion invading the territory of good manners. The message is the same. England has gone to sleep behind its mask of respectability; it would be better to wake up and feel something, even if that means treating your wife badly or being sent to hell. The all important difference between the two is language . . . this contrast was the most crucial in defining the Royal Court's identity. It was a writers' theatre: it was not a literary theatre." (*Theatres of George Devine*, p. 183)

In the context of subsequent visual and physical theatre, "writers" and "literary" do not seem far apart, but Devine's production of Duncan virtually smothered the verse drama movement.

Since the Duncan plays were produced soon after Osborne's *Look Back in Anger*, the Royal Court was the setting for a brief duel of theatre idioms, as Duncan bitterly realized: "the convention of Shaftesbury Avenue duchesses fiddling with flower vases was replaced by Jimmy Porters picking their noses in public" (Introduction to *Collected Plays*). In pluralizing the Osborne hero of *Look Back in Anger*, Duncan seems deaf to his highly individual articulacy, and to the realistic frame for both duchesses and Jimmy Porter. Realistic or not, vitriolic monologues remained Osborne's dramatic strength, but language was also on the mind of other playwrights, as John Russell Brown implies when he entitles a book on Osborne, Pinter, Wesker, and Arden *Theatre Language* (even though that book is not limited to verbal language). Not only was Jimmy Porter's articulate anger publicized as the emotion of a whole decade, but Wesker's regional dialects – Jewish East End and Norfolk – seduced the London theatregoer. Pinter's lower-class lexicon, scrupulously rhythmed, gradually etched his characters into audience memory. Of the first wave of new playwrights, only Arden, with his epic scope, was attracted to verse in drama, and since he sustained that attraction over the years, I break chronology to examine two major non-realistic Arden plays that often lilt in verse.

Even in his plays of the 1950s, before finding his stage legs, Arden swerved away from realism by means of verse-studded dialogue. As early as 1960, Arden declared his love of the ballad meter, having preceded that declaration with practice. Arden enfolded ballads (as well as freer rhymes) into the *Waters of Babylon* (1957), *Live Like Pigs* (1958), and *Serjeant Musgrave's Dance* (1959), which played to empty houses at the Court. For all his allegiance to verse in the theatre, Arden rejected aspects of Eliot's practice: "It is not necessary for dramatists to write in verse – and if they do, there is no reason for them to involve themselves in Eliot's laborious theories of sprung rhythm and so forth – ordinary verse that rhymes and uses an iambic beat or a ballad stanza will do just as well" ("A Plea for a Poetic Drama," quoted in Page, *Arden on File*, p. 77). It will do especially for a dramatist who still admires heroic action within a socially nuanced context. Like playwrights before and after him, Arden defends what he sees as his own practice: "So in a play, the dialogue can be naturalistic and 'plotty' as long as the basic poetic issue has not been crystallized. But when this point is reached then the language becomes formal (if you like, in verse or sung), the visual pattern coalesces into a vital image that is one of the nerve-centres of the play" ("Telling a True Tale," in *Encore Reader*, p. 214).[2]

Arden's plays in print do not, however, reveal these points clearly. In *Armstrong's Last Goodnight* (1964) the eponymous hero's free-ranging ballads are subdued to Lindsay's smooth diplomatic prose, and over a decade later in the radio play *Pearl* (1978) Arden not only distinguishes a play within the play by verse, but he also depends upon verse to highlight intense moments of the frame play. However, in Arden's more ambitious endeavors for the stage, like *The Island of the Mighty* (1972, about one-quarter in verse) or *The Non-Stop Connolly Show* (1975, about one-third in verse) it is not always evident that calculated rhythm intensifies the crystallization of the verbal and the visual, but it *is* always evident that the drama reaches beyond the familiar contemporary surface of realism. As in other matters, both dramatic and political, Arden preserves his independence; he alone of the New Playwrights has defended and exemplified the bardic tradition. Unlike Bond, however, Arden rarely writes about writers. It is all the more remarkable, then, that three poets play significant roles in his *The Island of the Mighty*.

Arden devoted many years to drama about King Arthur. While still at Cambridge University he penned an Arthurian play in verse, which he later declared "pretty ponderous and pretentious" (Preface to *The Island of the Mighty*, p. 12). In 1962 he presented an Arthurian play to the Royal Court, where it was rejected, but the British Broadcasting Corporation requested that he reshape the material for television, evidently curtailing the amount of verse: "When the poets in the plays recited their works I wrote verse for them, but otherwise the dialogue was as naturalistic as the settings."

In the published version of *The Island of the Mighty*, about a quarter of the dialogue is in verse, and another eighth in songs. (Although both Ardens are listed as the authors of *The Island of the Mighty*, I assume that the verse passages were written by Arden alone, since Margaretta D'Arcy told me that that was generally true of their work.)

2 Andrew Kennedy enfolds a pointed discussion of Arden's verse into the larger analysis of his stage dialogue in *Six Dramatists in Search of a Language*.

More often than not, Arden's verse rhymes, and the beat may vary from two to six accents per line. Boldly, Arden mixes prose, verse, and song; colloquialisms rub shoulders with ceremonial declamations; wrenched syntax can be climaxed by a simple declarative sentence. Free both in metre and placement of rhyme, Arden's dialogue relies on rhythm rather than image.

Several readings (but, unfortunately, no viewing) have not furnished me with the key – if there is one – to the verse/prose divisions of *The Island of the Mighty*. The three poets speak verse, but not all the time. In Part I of the play King Arthur's poet Merlin alternates between patriotic song and unctuous prose: "As Chief Poet to the General my first responsibility is to praise him by means of verse and music." When Merlin goes mad, however, he shifts to ballad rhythms and fills them with images drawn from nature – birds and plants. The conservative poet Taliesin begins with stiff martial prose, but near the play's end he curses Merlin in short sharp verse lines. The third poet, Aneurin, having no official function, speaks and sings pithily. Although inclusion of the contrasting poets offers Arden the opportunity for contrasting rhythms, he allows events rather than characters to determine the beat.

Flouting the decorum of the Elizabethans he loves, Arden does not award verse to the nobles and prose to the commoners. Often, but not consistently, he distinguishes the sexes rhythmically. The Pict women speak more lyrically than Arthur's warriors. Gwenhwyvar, the bride kidnapped by Arthur, utters long lines of free verse, which are linked by assonance and colorful images. Arthur's sister–mistress Morgan, grown old and isolated, breathes gnomic dimeters, which rhyme irregularly. Thus the two loves of Arthur are rhythmically differentiated, contributing to their mythic dimension.

More usually, however, it is situation rather than character that seems to demand verse; that is to say, no character "owns" a particular rhythm, and some tense moments tend to fall into verse lines of varying length. This is particularly true in early and late scenes of *The Island of the Mighty*, whereas prose carries the action in the middle. Part III highlights the consciousness of Merlin, so that a major theme of the play becomes the function of poets in society. Finally, Merlin is drawn to simple ballads, a compelling rhythm, but it is hard to know whether Arden's freer rhythms are audible as verse in the theatre. Reviewers of the Aldwych production of *The Island of the Mighty* occasionally mention "blank verse" but not in conjunction with specific scenes. Moreover, the several rhythms of Arden rarely fall into blank verse – neither pentameter nor unrhymed.

My few generalizations about the verse of *The Island of the Mighty* – dictated by events, unconfined to specific characters, clearly differentiated from prose but varying in metre and placement of rhyme, with imagery drawn from nature or everyday life – are also true of *The Non-Stop Connolly Show* (1975). For a play whose performance would take twenty-six hours, variety is sought in the blend of verse, song, and prose. In this mammoth play the prose includes quotations from Connolly's writing, as well as from that of historical figures who are devalued by the Ardens. Aware of their innovations, the Ardens summarize one difficulty of their epic saga:

> My name it is James Connolly
> I neither smoke nor drink.
> Come to the theatre for twenty-six hours
> And watch me sit and think.
>
> (*To Present the Pretence*, p 96)

Yet their work coheres through the exemplary (but not infallible) figure of Connolly. The coherence of the sprawling play reflects the cohesion of the working class, for both work and class are dominated by small, undernourished Connolly. Although he was shot in 1916, the Ardens imply that his revolutionary action continues non-stop, including an unprecedented "Dramatic Cycle of Continuous Struggle."

Given the unusual (perhaps inordinate) length of *The Non-Stop Connolly Show*, it is helpful, before examining the verse, to quote a few sentences from the authors' preface:

These six plays have . . . taken the form of not so much a straight biography of Connolly, as a series of digressive stage-presentations of the events of his time which influenced his political views and consequent actions. They were written to be shown as one complete connected sequence, and have been so produced, both in Dublin and in London . . . Despite the apparent complexity of *The Non-Stop Connolly Show*, the staging need not present any very difficult problems. The approach should be "emblematic" rather than "naturalistic"; and ideally a number of stages should be used, arranged around the audience, and connected perhaps with gangways at various levels . . . The large cast can be contained by a basic company of about a dozen actors, who will each have to play many different roles, not necessarily of their own sex: but stylised, easily-changed, strongly-defined costumes, and possibly stock-masks for recurrent social types (i.e. bourgeois politicians, employers, military officers, etc.) would greatly assist this technique . . .

Essentially the plays need *speed* – and close attention to *rhythm*. Each scene or episode should be understood as a self-contained combination of voice, movement, colour and music, with precise dramatic momentum of its own, which makes its point as sharply as possible and is then withdrawn from the stage, as sharply as possible, to be replaced by the next grouping. We would emphasise finally that the play will work only if the actors are more concerned with understanding the political arguments and implications of the story than with "creating character" in the normal theatrical sense.

It is easy to cite Brecht for the self-sufficient scenes, Mnouchkine for the connected stages, and the agitprop tradition for affixing masks to the "recurrent social types." Yet the blend is unique. The Ardens allegorize the spirit of capitalism in an invented character named Grabitall, whose function is to oppose Connolly wherever he may be, in whatever he may endeavor to do.

More pointedly than Brecht with his summarizing signs, the Ardens print summaries not only of the action of their six plays, but also of each of the three acts of the last four plays. Probably these summaries are intended for projection in the theatre, so that the audience will not wonder *what* is happening but can concentrate on *why* it is happening – as in Brecht's theory. To summarize the summaries: in 1868 James Connolly is born in Edinburgh into a working-class Irish family. Unable to find work, he joins the British army but deserts when he awakens to Irish nationalism in Ireland. Vaguely a Protestant, Connolly marries Lillie Reynolds, a Catholic who supports him both literally and figuratively for the remainder of his life. Producing a large family, Connolly needs to be paid while he works for Irish socialism. Founder of the Irish Socialist Republican Party, he is in constant conflict with the English who flout Irish nationalism, and with various international socialists who do not recognize the special problems of the Irish. Invited to the United States, he joins the Socialist Labor Party; then, frustrated by its sectarianism, he joins the Industrial Workers of the World (Wobblies) and participates in the electoral campaign of the socialist candidate Eugene Debs. Urged to return to the Irish Labor movement, which is undergoing a crisis, he and James Larkin organize a general strike, but it fails when British labor denies its support. With the declaration of World War I, international socialism collapses, and Connolly seeks other allies, notably Padraic Pearse. Knowing that the Dublin Easter 1916 uprising is doomed, Connolly nevertheless marshals his forces heroically. Wounded but indomitable, he is summarily executed by a British firing squad.

The Non-Stop Connolly Show is particularly generous with verse toward the beginning and end. Its rhythms vary from dimeters to heptameters, but are usually iambic and usually rhymed. As in *The Island of the Mighty*, no character "owns" the verse, which is spoken alike by Connolly and his allies, but also by his enemies, as by imaginary characters. Moreover, there are no sustained poet-figures to provide a rationale for the verse, although a Narrator makes sporadic appearances in the late scenes. Yeats, appearing briefly in Part III, wonders at Connolly's mandate in an echo of his own line: "Who is this dangerous man / Slouching, as it were, towards Bethlehem to be born?"

Since poets are scarce in this class struggle, the question of rhythm is rarely raised within the play, as it is in *The Island of the Mighty*, but there are nevertheless references to the language. When Connolly's brother John incites Edinburgh workers to rebel against the union leadership, he admonishes Jim: "Dear goodness, man, that kind o' thing is not what politics is all about! Indeed there is poetry in it, or I'd not be in it myself: but the entire art of the business is to find where and when the poetry has a function to pursue." That is what the semi-literate Jim Connolly will slowly learn:

> So local Secretary I was made
> Of the Scottish Socialist Federation –
> And at once I must begin to write and to read
> The multifarious meticulous precise documentation
> Appertaining to such an office in such an organization.

The Latinate lexicon reflects Connolly's own bewilderment before he masters the passionate vocabulary and oppressive facts that will make him a leader of the working class. In his embryonic phase he shifts rhythm to address his beloved Lillie in Belfast:

If I am an oak tree my fingers are blunt twigs on the ends of knotted
  branches
For the first time in my lifetime a regular pen they must wield –
Lillie, they would be happier grappling with your soft haunches,
Lillie, for Godsake help me, there are so many thistles in this field –
I am not a bloody donkey: I don't know how to eat them:
Lillie, you must come in with me and show me how to cut them!

The Ardens' play traces Connolly's development as a forceful speaker and leader. When Connolly initiates his eldest daughter Nora into socialism, he requests her to address the women millworkers. Instead of repeating her father's initial timidity, the Ardens allow a Narrator to describe Nora's feelings, much as the Narrator does that of Grusha and Simon in Brecht's *Caucasian Chalk Circle*:

> Her mouth, she said, was very dry,
> She stammered as she spoke
> She knew what she wanted to say
> It came out as a kind of croak:

But in the end she got through with it and brought it to an end:
She said she felt that they felt that like her father she was their friend.

Somewhat comic in its clumsiness, the verse rises to achievement without didacticism. At another point it is witty. Of the militant Maud Gonne, Connolly says: "She paid for the doctor / She paid the rent / She did almost everything for me it was possible to resent."

Occasionally in *The Non-Stop Connolly Show*. Arden's verse soars expressionistically. In 1916, abandoned by socialists in other countries, Connolly still hesitates to join forces with the bourgeois, mystical Pearse. The Ardens stage his Dark Night of the Soul in the form of a verse debate with a Bird who utters some of Connolly's own hard-learned lessons. Although Connolly is shaken, the figure of his wife strengthens his resolution:

> 9th Shape (Lillie)
> In order to provide for six children in a small dark flat
> Lillie Connolly must take in washing, mending clothes, and that's that.
>
> Connolly
> See the slave of a slave taking orders from her boss
> So that *his* boss may be toppled with the minimum of loss . . .
> Very well: I am a man who will hazard his whole life
> And those of his friends, because he knows his wife
> Has got from him alive such little good.
> Very well, perhaps I do shed blood
> Perhaps I do make war
> For no-one else but her –
> What's wrong with that: she is a legion, I can't count
> How many of her there are, and what they want . . .

Believing himself to be in Wolfe Tone's mould, Connolly decides to join forces with Pearse. When Countess Markievicz, the Irish champion, taunts Connolly with succumbing to Pearse's mystical Easter, he retorts in verse that she utters "Too much poetry," but he shifts to prose when he hopes that the Germans will arm the anti-British rebellion. It is a vain hope, and when it fails, Connolly is captured and shot. But even dead, Connolly is hopeful of the future, and his last post-mortem lines are forcefully monosyllabic:

> We were the first. We shall not be the last.
> This was not history. It has not passed.

Although the long saga was read over a week of lunchtime theatre in London, it is unlikely that professionals will mount a full production of one of the most ambitious dramas of postwar Britain.

Compared with Arden, other contemporary English poets and playwrights only occasionally resort to verse, among them the poet laureate Ted Hughes. He adapted Seneca's *Oedipus* into a rhythm based on the phrase rather than the foot; it has been printed mainly as prose with blank spaces separating the phrases. Another poet, Adrian Mitchell, often translates foreign verse plays into English verse; he also writes verse plays for children, but these have not been published. *Tyger* (1971), "A Celebration Based on the Life & Work of William Blake," is Mitchell's first full-length play. It is set at once in Blake's lifetime and the current period of Philistinism. Mitchell interlards Blake poems (set to music) with his own, but most of the play is in prose. Like Hughes and Mitchell, the poet Tony Harrison has been adept in adapting verse classics of other languages into English verse, but Hughes alone has published *contemporary* English verse plays – for children. These children's plays might be considered a *violon d'Ingres* of this usually dark and brooding poet. Written for radio (and published collectively in 1970), they can easily be staged.

As announced by the title, *The Coming of the Kings* is a Christmas play. Warned by a Fortune-Teller that kings will descend upon his inn, an ambitious inn-keeper relegates Joseph and Mary to the stable. When the three kings arrive, they pass right by the inn and proceed to the stable, and the play closes on a minstrel's benediction: "Every snowflake is an angelll. / The angels are settling on the world. / The world will be white with angels. / The world will be deep in angels." In a resplendent and silent finale a golden light from a bright star beams down on the manger. The short play sparkles not so much in the seasonal ending as in the townspeople at the inn, who erupt in Hughes' vigorous, deftly rhyming lines.

The Tiger's Bones is a science fiction fantasy. After several adventures that burlesque scientific "objectivity," the verse play is climaxed by a contest between two sages, who vie to reassemble the scattered bones of a tiger. Since both sages can clothe the bones with flesh, the sly non-scientist challenges his rival to breathe life into those bones, and the latter succeeds, only to be eaten by the tiger. The handyman Dully, who provided the labor for the satirized scientific cogitations – "If you ask me, they're all brains and no sense" – is left to tell of the demise of the scientist, in lines of uneven length, rhythmed by rhetorical parallels and repetitions.

The last two plays in Hughes' volume borrow fairy-tale motifs. The very title *Beauty and the Beast* says it all; in this play the beast is a bear, but upon the maiden's declaration of love, he becomes the proverbial swain: "He's a remarkably handsome fellow, for a bear." Again, rhythmic charm rests upon rhetorical parallelism and frequent repetition.

Sean, the Fool, the Devil and the Cats is more intricately plotted and more densely populated. We follow Sean through a series of adventures, climaxed by his union with the heroine-cat. But Hughes adds a delightful coda. The Fool, envying Sean's luck, repeats his adventures, but, forgetting to feed stew to the cat, the Fool is attacked and mauled by the slighted feline: "I got back to my crossroads torn to tassels." And he enunciates the moral: "When you deal with the devil, never forget his cat!" (Could this be a prediction of the prosperous career of T. S. Eliot's *Cats*?) Hughes has as strong a sense of drama as had Eliot, and his poems have been adapted for the stage, but he himself has turned all too rarely to the theatre.

Committed political playwrights also turn rarely to verse. Howard Brenton's first (unpublished) produced play *Ladder of Fools* has been described as "a violent, allegorical, operatic dream play about a holy fool," couched in ornate verse (Mitchell, *File on Brenton*, p. 11). Another socially committed playwright, David Edgar, has occasionally experimented with verse. He condemned Romeo and Juliet to prose in his *Death Story*, but he sported couplets when matching his *Dick Deterred* with Shakespeare's *Richard III*. Aside from parody, however, Edgar hazarded verse in an intricate play within a play, *O Fair Jerusalem* (1975).

In that ambitious drama Edgar attempted a comparison and contrast of cross-sections of English society, separated by six hundred years. The prose frame play is set in 1948 in a church, where actors rehearse a play set in 1348, the year the Black Plague reached England. Divided into three acts, Edgar's play opens on a medieval church service at Easter, the day that William chooses to break his feudal bond and leave his oppressive village: "Best day to go." Edgar then swiftly presents representatives of different medieval social classes – noblemen, clergymen, soldiers, actors – but it is mainly William who threads the story-line with his matter-of-fact prose. The clergy and nobility speak in verse – in accord with Elizabethan rather than medieval convention. As in *Hamlet* the actors of a play within the play emote in old-fashioned verse, but in Edgar's *Jerusalem* there are also sketches within the play within the play. Short rhyming lines serve the Actor, Actress, and "Ham" in swift scenes that reveal the dog-eat-dog manner of survival in medieval society, but the players do not survive, falling dead of the plague at the end of their performance.

Only in Act II, Scene 1 are we informed by a prose exposition that in

1948 Edmund Wolfe has written a play for amateur actors to present in a church, with the enthusiastic support of the vicar. When the rehearsal continues, prose replaces the earlier verse, as we witness the spread of the plague, but on Christmas the actor Ham makes a pathetic effort at a play within the play within the play, in which he takes all the roles, couched in short rhyming lines.

Act III is framed by modern scenes, but the bulk of the action (six scenes) is medieval. The characters speak prose, as though drained of ceremony. Ham the actor, in his madness, cherishes the dead bastard of the dead Knight and the Lady. Only William offers hope for the future: "We don't know what the world is, no better. But there's no more plague." However, mad Ham retorts: "Mebbe it's waiting." Abruptly, the modern clergyman surprises his cast with a prose sermon against that modern plague, the atomic bomb. Tutored by the visiting doctor, the modern actors realize that for the first time "it" is not waiting, since science today permits the eradication of disease and poverty.

"The architecture of *Jerusalem* . . . is built on metaphorical rather than strictly realist foundations," and the metaphor is elucidated by one of the actors in the frame play: "the plague as a symbol, of the war . . . in which 360,000 Englishmen died." That metaphor is complicated rather than reenforced by the varied verse rhythms of the dialogue of the inner play. In Act I the Knight, Lady, and Clerk address one another in rough pentameter couplets. The priests speak in lines of uneven length, linked by assonance. Of their ritualistic rhythms, William remarks: "I didn't catch a word of it." And the soldier Diccon retorts: "No more should." The Knight vows devotion to the Lady, who responds formally; rhyme and rhetorical parallelism embellish their quatrains, but the ceremony is a lie, for their desire for each other is merely sexual.

Since the frame play actors speak in modern prose, Edgar relies on verse to invigorate the inner play, and even the plays within that inner play, as enacted by the pointedly named Ham. Despite a rudimentary skill in the several meters, however, Edgar never gives the impression that the verse-speaking characters are naturally rhythmic; rather, the verse formalizes and distances them, like figures on a frieze. Even if one did not know Edgar's political stance, it is clear that his sympathies are with those who suffer in the rigid feudal structure, and especially with William, who expresses himself in economical prose, nude of imagery or special rhythms. Such prose is the vehicle of Edgar's subsequent plays.

O Fair Jerusalem has never had a London production, and it is easy to guess why: intricate plot with little action, large cast, dense language that is difficult to absorb. Yet a comparable drama of another mainly prose playwright *was* performed in London – Edward Bond's trilogy of *War Plays* (1985). The man who was noted for the harsh realism of his early Court plays began in the 1970s to annotate each of his productions with poems, but not until his 1985 *War* trilogy did he publish a whole drama in verse.

The first play of the trilogy, *Red Black and Ignorant*, traces the life story of an unnamed monster. Bond's title seems at first to designate the Monster-protagonist, who may be a "uniform black" or "uniform red," and who is innocent in his ignorance. In long irregular verse lines, the Monster comes to social and moral consciousness, as we watch him develop from childhood to fatherhood. When every soldier is ordered to shoot a civilian, the Monster's son, unwilling to murder an old invalid, shoots his own father, and his mother inveighs against "rulers with redness on their hands, blackness in their hearts and ignorance in their minds." Presumably, the violence perpetrated against an individual is the kernel of war in this trilogy of *War Plays*. The main rhythm of the first play is a long free verse line, but this contracts during tense disagreements between the Monster and his wife, or the Monster and his son. Dense allusive imagery fills the speech of all three characters, confusing their viewpoints in the theatre.

Of the three plays, it is the second, *The Tin Can People*, that most effectively links Bond's verse rhythm to the dramatic event. In the post-holocaust dust a few survivors nourish themselves from tin cans while the long, uneven lines of their dialogue describe the recent atomic war. Into their midst comes a wanderer from afar, expressing his wonder in short vigorous lines. At first the tin can people welcome him joyously, plying him with food. But when one of them dies, and then another and another, they condemn the wanderer to death. Only one nameless woman refuses to accept their verdict, and at the last she, the man from afar, and another woman refuse the tins, resolved to found a new society that is organically linked to the earth. They voice that resolution in prose.

It is not clear whether the title of Bond's third play *The Great Peace* is ironic. We now meet the only character with a name – Pemberton – who subsumes the cruelties of unnamed soldiers. In an army-ruled city, each soldier is ordered to kill a child. That barbaric command parallels the scene in the first play, where each soldier was to kill a civilian. At the same time, the order recalls the stoning of the baby in Bond's early realistic play *Saved*, which first brought him to public attention. Pemberton not only obeys the murderous order but accepts a bribe to substitute the dead baby's body for a rich man's child. Like the Monster's son in the first play, Pemberton's nameless comrade, unwilling to kill a neighbor's child, murders his own sibling. But the deed drives him mad, and he is shot for insubordination.

Seventeen years later his mother, tending a bundle as though an infant were alive, wanders distraught in the wilderness. She meets a pregnant woman – the companion of the newcomer in *The Tin Can People* – and helps her give birth, but when the new mother dies, she abandons the infant so as to save the bundle she believes to be her own child. Soon she improvises a cart for the humanized bundle, a prop that recalls Brecht's Mother Courage. As the latter profits from the war, the former profits emotionally by endowing a bundle with the life of her murdered child. The soldier Pemberton arrives, leading his derelict squad, as once in life – "Dead livin' off the dead" – and confronts the woman with the bundle. In a scene derived from Goya's painting "Third of May, 1808," Pemberton shoots his men and speaks nostalgically of army discipline, but his verse lines are uneven. He fantasizes the presence of his squad, as the woman has fantasized the presence of her infant.

When she meets her old neighbor with her daughter, the woman nurses the former while the latter goes in search of other living beings. Upon their arrival, the mad mother thinks a young man is her murdering son. In blame and guilt, she refuses his help, but, accepting his padded coat, she will brave the winter alone. In the final wordless scene of the long, intricate drama, the young man finds the woman's bones on the coat *"lying roughly in the human shape. In the stomach: tins, some open and empty."* Presumably, we have seen the last of the vengeful tin can people, a barbaric residue of a barbaric military rule.

Less densely imaged than the first two parts, the language of *The Great Peace* is crisp and colloquial. In tense scenes the characters exchange short, stichomythic lines, but often, too, they indulge in long, free verse soliloquies, as when the nameless woman recounts her seventeen years in the wilderness, or when another woman explains that her unborn child was fathered by the newcomer to the tin can people. From the printed page Bond's lines can be read aloud to emphasize recurrent phrases or shifts in rhythm, but in the theatre the dialogue was unrecognizable as verse.

In a letter of 1982 (Roberts, *Bond on File*, p. 74) Bond acknowledges: "I have some skills that would enable me to 'write well' . . . But you ought not to use your skills to write well. Use them to struggle . . ." In a context – mine – which still values good writing, i.e. dramatic writing that probes, inflames, exposes, arouses, but does not preach, the *War Trilogy* stretches out too long to sustain a drama. Seeing the three plays in succession, I was one of the few diehards to remain in the uncomfortable RSC Pit through nearly five hours of performance. As intransigent in the direction as in the writing of his recent plays, Bond makes no concessions to the theatre habits of the admittedly bourgeois audiences. A master of colloquial speech and inventive imagery, Bond robs his recent plays of passionate characters and visual images. Especially when he himself directs, his drama suffers for lack of a critical eye – or critical ear to temper the verse rhythms that do not modulate dramatically.

Verse on today's stage demands such unusual attention that each of these playwrights presents problems to the critics. Arden's rationale is most apparent in his epic dramas, and yet he too can be puzzling in his rhythmic shifts. Edgar and Hughes contrast sharply; the poet laureate left-handedly dabbles in children's plays, whereas the political playwright has a single if extended verse fling. Bond's turgid verse is confined to recent work, and it is not often recognizable as verse. The same is true of Charles Wood. He spurns not only meter, but also the secondary embellishments of verse – rhyme, image, and any seduction by sound. One of his directors, Geoffrey Reeves, spoke to me of his dialogue as "poetic prose," and John Russell Brown writes of the dialogue of Wood's *Veterans*: "It is printed in short lines that indicate the phrasing and rhythms which control the *prose* with revealing exactness" (*Short Guide*, p. 94, my emphasis). However, phrasing and rhythm might also define free verse, in which Wood occasionally indulges.

Wood is the son of itinerant actors, and he spent his formative years, from the age of eighteen to twenty-three, in the British Army. A civilian again, he worked backstage in the theatre – including Stratford East under Joan Littlewood – before writing his first plays about army life, three one-acters in a prose that is both colloquial and economical, to reveal the savagery beneath the imposed military discipline. Moving from the one-act to the three-act structure in *Dingo* (1967), Wood hardens his portrait of soldiers, trained to kill and be killed. He insists that "he is anti-war but pro-army" (Taylor, *Second Wave*, p. 63). Wood's tough language screens a covert admiration for human beings denied the luxury of humane sentiments.

Wood's sharp military idiom was forged in these early army plays, and in 1969 he shifts to slash-marked lines of verse for *H or Mono-*

5 *H* by Charles Wood, directed by Geoffrey Reeves at the National, 1969;
action before a front-cloth

logues at Front of Burning Cities. Drawing upon S. H. Jones Parry's *An Old Soldier's Memoirs* (London, 1897), Wood dramatizes the 1857–8 Indian mutiny against Britain. *H* theatricalizes the slaughter that led to burning cities, as the rebellion is quelled by General Henry Havelock, nicknamed H. Toward the end of the first act (of three) H addresses his officers, but they are so battle-weary that, standing at attention, they fall asleep, and H permits himself a moment's reflection: "There it is, / it is the fate of Generals to have / no conversation other than / monologues at front of burning cities. / Have I a report of casualties?" The wry generalization, the archaic "at front of," the snap of attention to the military matter at hand, are typical of the officers' idiom, which is also laced with pious, slightly ungrammatical platitudes about service to God and country.

86

In the course of the epic Indian campaign, we differentiate the officers: neophyte Ensign Mullett, proselytizing H, his troubled son, bloodthirsty General Neill, barbarous Surgeon Sooter, acquisitive Captain Jones Parry. Constantly in the background, visible in stock poses on front or back cloths, are the nameless British soldiers and Indian mutineers.

Wood may declare himself to be anti-war but pro-army; yet his drama indicts the army's wanton cruelty in quelling the Indian rebellion. When Lieutenant Havelock, the son of H, cannot bring himself to order the mass hanging of the mutineers, he and his father pray for strength for him to do so. Captain Jones Parry is aroused sexually by battle, as revealed in his words to his far-off wife: "I has more dreams of you on the / field of battle than ever in my / bed at night when I can do / something about it." At the end of Act II, Captain Jones Parry embarrasses his fellow officers by the sanctimoniousness of his vengeance: "India shall be pacified this time for / all time, and the shrines of our / suffering shall always be holy. / Yes./" A pattern emerges for officers' speech: verse lines tend to end on insignificant words such as articles or prepositions, but the new line begins with an important noun. In an ironic climax, orders are given to shoot a native officer, who is *"blown into the auditorium of the theatre, and the red rose petals are hurled into the expensive seats and faces."*

Without ever sentimentalizing the Indians, Wood draws them more sympathetically. Their short verse lines are often wrenched in syntax, but still couched in courtesies. Near the end of the play a defeated Indian sergeant addresses a British ensign who has been "hideously disfigured":

HAVILDAR: The bugle blown for parley sahib, we / wish to carry our dead and wounded / from the field.
MULLET: You may do that. How is your health Havildar?
HAVILDAR: Well sahib, and the health of you our father?
MULLET: Well.
HAVILDAR: And of the Colonel our father?
MULLET: The Colonel is dead.
HAVILDAR: I am sorry. / You should not have stopped speaking / to us sahib.
MULLET: I never knew what to say.

Ensign Mullet may never have known what to say, but General H and Captain Jones Parry brim with patriotic rhetoric, which fails to confess their cruel profit from a rich continent.

After the carnage, the play closes on a pastoral family scene. That family is composed of Captain Jones Parry, his wife, and her son.

Unknown to her husband, Mrs. Jones Parry was raped by a rebel bombardier of mixed race, and her son, the apple of the Captain's eye (who believes him to be his own), is "very brown." The Captain, in free tetrameters, pays his lengthy respects to "Havelock's lonely grave beneath the / scorching Eastern sky," but Mrs. Jones Parry tells her son: "Timothy, here is where your father / Was shot and died in agony" (misprinted as prose in the Methuen edition). Although she tells the boy the truth, it is a truth beyond the knowledge or sympathy of the proper Victorian lady, who has been caricatured by Wood (including enjoyment of rape). Endings are not Wood's forte; nor are women. But for the tough masculine world of war, Wood creates an arresting demotic idiom, in lines that are printed as verse but sound like stylized prose.

Wood's *Veterans* (1972) stages a movie company on location in Turkey, filming his *H*. Since Wood himself had scripted the movie *The Charge of the Light Brigade*, starring John Gielgud, *Veterans* was interpreted as a reflection of that experience – an interpretation rejectd by Wood. Virtually plotless, the play consists of the peccadilloes of the two eponymous actors who have played together on stage and in film for some forty years. The one behaves like an adolescent, and the other cringes through his role while wounding the rest of the cast in their most vulnerable spots. In contrast to the slashed lines of free verse in *H*, both dialogue and scenic directions of *Veterans* are printed erratically as verse lines. Only occasionally do the line-breaks provide guidance for the actors' phrasing, and yet the unexpected pauses prevent absorption of Wood's play as a realistic drama of a movie company on location.

Veterans portrays movie soldiers, and the dialogue weaves sexual badinage into professional rivalry. Lacking the urgency of actual warfare, "the line that stops short of the margin" – to quote Tynan's euphemism – is inaudible as verse. In spite of the presence of Gielgud as one of the veterans, no reviewer mentions that he subdued verse rhythm to his notorious disciplined voice.

We hear a speech from *H* in *Veterans*, and we also hear a few parodic lines from a script that the veteran actors agree to reject. Disdainfully, the Gielgud veteran remarks:

> What is it, two
> characters, two old men on a beach somewhere
> during the war.

It is also a summary of *Veterans*.

In Kenneth Tynan's 1954 defense of prose he suggested: "it may be
. . . that poetry in the theatre should be confined to comedy, where its
potency still lingers" (*A View of the English Stage*, p. 140). Tynan
names Auden, Isherwood, Eliot, and Fry as masters of bathos, but he
could scarcely prophesy the comic potency of Caryl Churchill.
Although her early stage plays were sombre, Churchill first achieved
widespread acclaim with *Cloud 9* (1979), which I have described in
the chapter "Staging England." Although doubling and a startling
time shift are Churchill's main weapons against realism, she also
deploys parodic verse in that play. After a rousing patriotic song,
rhyming couplets introduce a nuclear British family and their faithful
black servant, "in a British colony in Africa in Victorian times." The
long act ends on a wedding between a gay man and woman, which
has been engineered by the *paterfamilias*, who blesses the happy
couple in an eight-line stanza – before he is shot by the faithful black
servant. In that prose play the rhymed verse is the rhythm of
hypocrisy.

In Churchill's *Serious Money* (1987) everyone is a hypocrite, and
rhyme is ubiquitous. Subtitled "a City Comedy," *Serious Money* opens
with a scene from *The Volunteers or The Stockjobbers* by the seventeenth-century English playwright Thomas Shadwell. "City comedy"
is thus perpetuated from the seventeenth to the twentieth century,
although the Shadwell play is not actually an example of the genre.
An exploitative capitalist economy is alive and thriving in the contemporary City, that square mile in central London where commodities
are traded and mis-traded. Like older seventeenth-century city comedies about the rising bourgeoisie, Shadwell's play is written in
prose, but Churchill whittles verse to her purpose. Jacobean city
comedies predate realism, of course, but they offer the cause-and-
effect specificity of later realism. Churchill, in contrast, wittily caricatures stock types (pun intended) of international finance.

The play originated in a Joint Stock workshop on material with
which Churchill was unfamiliar – the machinations of the very rich –
and she therefore found the writing difficult. "The big thing that
really helped with writing was when I decided it should be in verse
. . . It made me able to get my head above the documentariness of it
. . . I wrote some chunks in prose, and during the rehearsal period I
went back and reworked them into verse" (*New Theatre Quarterly*
[February, 1988], p. 14). With rhyme her watchword, Churchill points
it in pentameter couplets, distributes it in tetrameter quatrains,
sprinkles it freely in lines of uneven length. The London performance
emphasized the rhyme-words toward the end of each act, punched

through with obstreperous flair. No character "owns" any particular verse form; nor is any given metre draped around such stereotypical scenes as confession, narration, or flashback.

The plot of *Serious Money* is hard to follow, although it was evidently clear in Churchill's mind: "The order of the last scenes was something that was very much thrown together at the end . . . There are lots of flashbacks, but the main action is the day when Jake Todd was found dead" (p. 15). Churchill was perhaps not conscious of her debt to two modern plays: the thuggery of capitalism derives from Brecht's *Resistible Rise of Arturo Ui*, where blank verse mocks those who murder for money. As in David Hare's *Knuckle* (1974), a natural concern for a missing (or murdered) sibling twists into the hunter's compliance with a vicious system. Churchill's protagonist Scilla knows no Charybdis; finally hungry not for revenge but for her dead brother's money, she leaves England: "Scilla's been named by Business Week as Wall Street's rising star."

The revenge plot wrenched into a quest (for serious money) does not of course explain the play's popularity. Rather, the money-making frenzy of the 1980s has been theatrically translated into energetic acting and choreography. With a slight change of costume, the actors play multiple roles, scene skipping swiftly into new scene. Occasionally the dialect changes, as when Scilla of the Sloane-Rangers drawl transforms into Biddulph, a clipped schoolmarmish White Knight (originally played by Linda Bassett); or when Jake the charming inside trader dons a derby and an interrogative tone to become the feared securities inspector.

The international nature of high finance is centered on the greedy Cockney Corman, his back-slapping American aide Zac, a New York-based American Southerner Marylou Baines, and an ermine-robed, beringed Peruvian businesswoman Jacinta Condor, each spouting rhymes in the caricatured ideolect. Their bone of contention is a company named, as in Bennett's *Forty Years On*, Albion (or England). But whereas Bennett is nostalgic about the old school tie, Churchill is scatological about the new City noose. And about the government that aids and abets corruption. Finally, no one cares who killed Jake Todd, because everyone is happily wallowing in her or his own greed. Almost as an afterthought, the occasional Narrator Zac ruminates: "Who wanted him out of the way? / The British government, because another scandal just before the election would have been too much fuss. / So I reckon it was MI5 or the CIA." However, this revelation is incidental; what ends the play is the minatory result of the election: "We're crossing forbidden frontiers for five more glorious years / pissed and promiscuous, the money's ridiculous / send her victorious for five fucking morious / five more glorious years."

It is churlish to sound a sour note about a play of such demonic energy, and yet *Serious Money* is hard (for me) to take seriously as satire. Geraldine Cousin praises the variety and functionalism of Churchill's verse: "The loosely sprung, lengthy verse lines which characterize Zac's speech merge with Jacinta Condor's snappy, jazzy rhythms, or the forceful driving language of Corman, the corporate raider . . . The varied rhythms of the language lead to changes of pace in the forward momentum of the play" (*Churchill the Playwright*, pp. 100–1). I argue, on the contrary, that the energetic rhymes pound home the repetitive quality of corruption, unredeemed by any direct or honest statement. Churchill's deft cabaret turns and inventive rhymes comment cleverly on recent headlines about Guinness and Boesky, but even if the money is serious, the verse is not.

More roughly scornful of corruption than Churchill, Stephen Berkoff often pours forth verse. London born and Drama School trained (Webber Douglas), Berkoff entered theatre as an actor, spending ten years in regional repertory before escaping to Paris to study mime with Jacques Le Coq. There Berkoff declared his allegiance to the theatricality of Artaud, and on his return to England began to write by way of adaptation – from Kafka, Strindberg, Poe – directing those sallies with enormous, even manic, physical energy. Nevertheless, Berkoff considers his theatre verbal: "My theatre is verbal, it isn't physical at all" (*Plays International* [July, 1988], p. 15).

Berkoff's first original play was *East* (1975), subtitled "Elegy for the East End and its energetic waste." The tone, however, is not elegiac but energetic. Although nominally set in the East End of London, the stage is bare of local color. Centered on two friends, Les and Mike, the drama consists of a series of vignettes: a gang war, a shared mistress, murder of a magistrate, homicidal yearnings of a fascist father (of Mike), separate fantasies of a weary mother and of an abandoned young woman, enactment of a gleaming (human) motorbike; all scenes are suffused in an undercurrent of violence. Far from a specific rendition of East End squalor, however, Berkoff's plays are intended to be mythic in dimension, and the language strives to soar. The critic Ned Chaillet has described Berkoff's language in *East* as "a Cockney corruption of Elizabethan-styled verse, with sexual and aggressive prose speeches." The dialogue of *East* is printed as prose, liberally punctuated with the three dots so dear to Pinter, but Berkoff's dots are devoid of Pinteresque nuance; rather, they indicate phrasing to the actor. Instead of "Elizabethan-styled verse," the dialogue is sprinkled with distorted quotations from Shakespeare, occasionally rhymed with obscenities. Archaism and vulgarity rub shoulders, especially in soliloquies. Here is Mike: "so I said to him 'fuck off thou discharge from thy mother's womb before with honed and sweetened razor I do trouble to remove thy balls from thee.'" When read, this blend sounds like pastiche, but young audiences accept the marriage of these two idioms.

When spoken, the rhythms of *East* are indistinguishable from those in Berkoff plays that are published as verse, with slashes indicating line-ends in the dialogue. Berkoff's earliest play to exhibit this technique is his adaptation of Aeschylus' *Agamemnon* (1971), whose poly-rhythmed verse has challenged such major poets as Robert Lowell. Berkoff, however, innocent of knowledge of the complexity of the Greek, varies his own free verse lines between a single syllable and as much as two lines of print. Only occasionally does he introduce rhyme, but his triumphant Clytemnestra closes the play in a quasi-quatrain: "Ignore the mob / they quake and quell / you and I are in power darling / we shall order things well . . ."

After founding his own company, the London Theatre Group, "To express drama in the most vital way imaginable; to perform at the height of one's powers with all available means. That is, through the spoken word, gesture, mime and music. Sometimes the emphasis on one, sometimes on the other" (*Theatre Quarterly* [Autumn, 1978], p. 39), Berkoff toured his adaptations of Aeschylus, Kafka, and Poe. (*The Fall of the House of Usher* fascinated Artaud before Berkoff.)

In 1979 appeared his most popular adaptation, *Greek*, based on Sophocles' *Oedipus*. Berkoff's decade on the Fringe had habituated London critics to an energetic play by Berkoff, directed energetically by Berkoff, with Berkoff in the energetic main role, but in the first performances of *Greek* he limited himself to adapting and directing. (In a 1988 revival he played Laius.) Berkoff's Eddie, like Mike of *East*, thrives on fighting and fornicating. Not unlike Oedipus and his vast theatre progeny, Eddie leaves his (putative) parents to avoid the fortune-teller's prophecy. Quarreling with and killing a restaurant manager, Eddie absconds with his wife. In Eddie's answer to the riddle of the Sphinx, the third leg is not a stick but an erect phallus of man at the height of his virility. After cutting off the head of a bored Sphinx (a proto-feminist), Eddie and his new wife prosper in the catering business – both in sensuous sexuality and conspicuous wealth. When the happy couple invite Eddie's putative parents to bless their prosperity, the son learns the truth. Eddie is briefly contrite at his incestuous love, but Berkoff explicitly rejects the Greek conclusion: "it is healthier to love your mother than expiate your alleged sin by self-mutilation" (program note to 1988 production).

Berkoff's published text designates his uneven verse lines with slashes; again Berkoff blends archaism and obscenity, with an occasional Shakespearean reminiscence – "this sceptic isle." Whereas *East* lamented the waste of heroic energy, *Greek* portrays a heroic Eddie who scorns conformity and mindless violence, even before he scorns the incest taboo. Eddie closes the play in defiant affirmation of his love for Jocasta: "for your belly twice known / for your hands twice caressed / for your breath twice smelt, for your thighs, for your cunt twice known, once head first once cock first, loving cunt holy mother wife / loving source of your being / exit from paradise / entrance to heaven." For all the lexical poverty, and the wavering rhythms, repetition lends a certain force to the lines, especially in Berkoff's staging, which has gained in precision over the years. In 1988 Berkoff's sixth staging of *Greek* depends less on manic energy and more on music, lighting, choral effects, and inventive enactment of properties. Whiteface stylizes the four characters, and striking choreography establishes rhythms absent from the printed verse.

Having enfolded his East End hero into a cultural icon of the Western world, Berkoff next turned to *Hamlet* in *West* (1983). Not only are we again, despite the title, in the East End of London, but earlier characters return. Mike/Hamlet is aided in heroic exploits by Les/ Horatio. Despite initial reluctance, Mike fights the leader of the opposing gang, is badly but not mortally wounded, and is disowned by his respectable, acquisitive father. Berkoff presents Mike as a hero of radical impulse against conformity everywhere. In Berkoff's habitual fashion of publication, slashes set off the uneven lines, punctuated by an occasional Shakespeare reminiscence, almost always in Mike's speech: "Unhand me / by heaven I'll make a corpse of him that lets me / I say away! I warned you what did I say! /" Or: "I'd rather be bounded in a nutshell and count myself king of infinite space."

Not only does Berkoff look backward for his two heroes, but he satirizes contemporary targets in a series of actors' transformations. *Decadence* (1981) displays decadence in two couples, played by only two actors. Berkoff's program note announces *Decadence* as "a study [*sic*] of the ruling classes or upper classes, so called by virtue of strangulated vowel tones rather than any real achievement." In a lovers' triangle, an upper-middle-class married man couples with an upper-class married woman; his abandoned wife urges her working-class lover to murder the adulterer. Subject to the fashion of the hour, seeking easy thrills, each couple is sensually self-indulgent.

However, the working-class lover of the upper-class wife demurs at murder. Finally, the bloodthirsty upper-class wife with "strangulated vowel tones" is abandoned. In this play Berkoff's verse lines tend to be more iambic than usual, and the rhymes more comically pointed, to expose the decadent caricatures, writhing in the rigid meter.

Satire is again the mode for *Sink the Belgrano!* (1986). A furious reaction to the Falklands War, this play caricatures Margaret Thatcher and her ministers, whom Berkoff blames for the death of Argentine sailors on the warship *Belgrano*, and of British sailors on the ships sunk in reprisal. The Chorus and all the characters speak in loose tetrameters (occasionally rhymed): "Britannia does not rule the waves / She simply waives the bloody rules." Maggot (Thatcher), more preoccupied with menus than with foreign affairs, nevertheless hesitates to sink the *Belgrano*. She finally rallies and gives the order, ending the play: "I would do it again." Politics reveals Berkoff's weakest side, lacking the personal energy of the tough scenes about the East End of London.

I am tempted, like most critics, to dismiss Berkoff as lexically imprecise, rhythmically faltering, and naively monotonous in his 1960s-type message of love, couched in obscenity: "Those four-letter words are part of the bawdiness and colour of our language" (Berkoff in *The Guardian*, July 7, 1988). What Peter Kemp writes of *Greek* is often true of Berkoff's work: "Greek archetypes and Cockney stereotypes are juxtaposed throughout" (*The Independent*, July 1, 1988). Toward the juxtaposition, Berkoff has trained and drilled his own company, the London Theatre Group, for well over a decade, and he has attracted such supple (but not subtle) actors as Georgina Brown, Linda Marlowe, Gary Oldman, Bruce Payne, Tim Roth, Mikhail Baryshnikov, and Antony Sher. He has a cult following in several cities, and his texts have served as the basis of opera. Though heavy-handed, his satire does snarl against complacency. Rooted in his native East End of London, Berkoff inflates the dialogue of his drama with very free, obscenity-studded verse, in his determination to soar above realism. It is ironic that English verse drama, idealized after World War II for its spirituality, should belch forth in Berkoff's indiscriminate demotic energy. As a weapon against realism, verse functions most pointedly in the comic mode. Of the several poets and playwrights who have summoned verse to serious purpose, only Arden elevates the line to his epic eye.

5

Theatre framing theatre

My little people in a row
Sit on the stage and watch the show.
The show they watch is rows and rows
Of people watching them. Who knows
Which is more alive than which?
(The Narrator in John Arden's *Bagman*)

Non-realism in the theatre has several synonyms – expressionism, presentation, theatricalism. Since Expressionism is a particular Central European movement about the time of World War I, its indiscriminate extension promulgates confusion. During the second half of the twentieth century, realism was submerged under the more general term "representation," and its opposite became "presentation." Another antonym for realism is theatricalism, the foregrounding of theatre in performance, which embraces styles from Aristophanes to Ayckbourn. In postmodern critical theory theatricalism has been both anathemized and valorized, depending on the theorist. Steven Connor summarizes the basis for this: "Theatricality stands for all those falsifying divisions which complicate, diffuse and displace the concentrated self-identity of a work of art, and so encompasses a number of different effects, including self-consciousness of the spectator, the awareness of context and the dependence upon extension in time" (*Postmodernist Culture*, p. 133).

Whichever antonym one chooses for realism, however, it is subverted by one principal device popular since the Renaissance – the play within the play.[1] Whittled down to parody in the eighteenth

1 This device is the subject of several studies: Lionel Abel, *Metatheatre*, New York: Hill and Wang, 1963; James Calderwood, *Shakespearean Metadrama*, Minneapolis: University of Minnesota Press, 1971, and *To Be or Not To Be*, New York: Columbia University Press, 1983; Robert Egan, *Drama within Drama*, New York: Columbia University Press, 1975; Sidney Homan, *When the Theatre Turns to Itself*, Lewisburg: Bucknell University Press, 1975; Robert Nelson, *Play within a Play*, New Haven: Yale University

century, the play within the play has reclaimed terrain in the second half of the twentieth century. Critics with a literary bias tend to synonymize "theatre in the theatre" and "play within the play," but some recent English playwrights are not so narrowly bound. Along with many formal plays within plays, popular forms of theatre have also functioned as insets into the main frame play, both spurning realism.

Popular theatre in the legitimate theatre

Popular theatre was the mass medium of the nineteenth century, but my subheading announces a late twentieth-century trend of incorporating popular theatre into serious plays. Biographical shows like *Noel and Gertie*, *Re-Joyce*, *Judy*, and *Piaf* nod toward stars of popular genres, but serious drama has also been spiced by music-hall, pantomime, standup comedy, and film. Since English theatre tends to be insular, it looks almost exclusively to English popular forms.

The indigenous English genre of music-hall or variety show (called vaudeville in the United States) dates from the mid-nineteenth century, but it was most widely applauded in the decade before World War I. "Variety" was quite literally the substance – jokes, songs, dance, impersonation, pantomime, parody could draw audiences of two thousand, but the legitimate drama rarely admitted it. In the first half of the twentieth century, however, music-hall was appreciated by a few playwrights. T. S. Eliot dedicated an appreciative essay to Marie Lloyd, and music-hall gave him jazz rhythms for his Sweeney fragments of 1926. W. H. Auden, too, admired popular theatre, and charades infiltrated his *Paid on Both Sides* (1930). The Pierrot war-turns of his *The Dance of Death* (1933) predict Joan Littlewood's *Oh, What a Lovely War* thirty years later. Auden and Isherwood borrowed from musical comedy and pantomime for *The Dog Beneath the Skin* (1935), but more recent drama embraces popular forms far more warmly.

As described in Chapter 2, John Osborne's *The Entertainer* (1957) depicts the fading glory of postwar Britain in the waning days of

Press, 1958; Anne Righter, *Shakespeare and the Idea of the Play*, London: Chatto and Windus, 1962; June Schleuter, *Metafictional Characters in Modern Drama*, New York: Columbia University Press, 1979; and Manfred Schmeling, *Métathéâtre et intertexte*, Paris: Les Lettres Modernes, 1982.

For Richard Hornby (*Drama, Metadrama, and Perception*, Lewisburg: Bucknell University Press, 1986), "Serious drama . . . always moves toward the metadramatic," which he views with what seems to me semiotic astigmatism. Hornby also classifies plays within the play as "inset," where the inner play is secondary, and "framed," where the inner play is primary. This distinction does not serve my purposes.

music-hall. What I did not mention in that context was the careful rendition of the music-hall turns. Although Laurence Olivier originally preferred the part of the retired performer, Billy Rice, he nevertheless prepared the titular role with gusto (Findlater, *These Our Actors*, p. 26). Once the play was accepted by the English Stage Company (over the objections of the artistic committee), the author John Osborne and the director Tony Richardson piloted Olivier through the few remaining music-halls of London. (They are gone today.) An expert was engaged to teach Olivier tap-dancing, and another expert to introduce a rasp into the famous mellifluous voice. With skill and diligence, and his habitual approach to character "from the outside in" (Melvin Bragg interview), the regal protagonist became a seedy entertainer. As Olivier recollected: "I learned to dance, I learned to sing like I thought Archie would, and I learned the loneliness of the standup comic" (*On Acting*, p. 157). In the opinion of the Royal Court director William Gaskill: "[Olivier] had a complete understanding of the role. In an odd way he knew it was about him" (Findlater, *These Our Actors*, p. 36).

What was new about Osborne's *The Entertainer*, aside from the appearance of the most eminent English actor in an inhabitual role, is the interdependence of Osborne's dramatic structure and texture. In spite of the conventional two intermissions, the play moves through scenes rather than acts, and each scene is presented as a music-hall number, sometimes accompanied by song. As Osborne specifies in his scenic directions: *"The scenes and interludes must, in fact, be lit as if they were simply turns on the bill."* Katharine Worth has recorded the effect:

we are Archie's audience now, reacting with him to the larger-than-life nudes and the inscription "Rock'n Roll Newd Look" plastered across the front cloth and to the nude Britannia with the bulldog and trident. We can choose to laugh or not to laugh at her and at Archie's jokes in the vein of "Madam with the helmet on is sagging a bit." But either way our response is prepared for and taken into the play. The feeling of being *really* in it together is uncomfortably communicated. *Revolutions in Modern English Drama*, p. 76

Although music-hall duets had bounced on to the legitimate London stage over a year before *The Entertainer* – in Peter Hall's production of *Waiting for Godot* at the small Arts Theatre – Osborne's version was pitched to the star turn of Olivier as jaunty, raunchy, fantasizing, wise-cracking Archie Rice "'avin' a go," with three songs, intermittent dance-steps, and *doubles entendres*. His performance has been described as a blend of "fake bonhomie, seedy bounce and mechanical randiness; the slurred, rasping voice, mixing Cockney and posh accents; the instinct for the wrong onstage emphasis" (Findlater, *These Our Actors*, p. 101). Olivier's performance was in part *about* performing, but it is Osborne the playwright who depicts Archie as crass and disloyal to his human family, and yet perversely loyal to his own art, the music-hall.

Although Osborne etched a crueller portrait in Archie Rice than in angry Jimmy Porter, Olivier aroused admiration, even from his colleagues on stage: an old music-hall performer, George Relph, huffed and puffed as a Billy Rice of dignified bigotry; Richard Pasco as Archie's son Frank pierced a Brando-like toughness with affection for his father. Neither of the successive Jean Rices was "plain," as demanded by Osborne's text – not Dorothy Tutin's pert poignancy nor Joan Plowright's tender tolerance. A superb actor's vehicle, *The Entertainer* was directed in 1974 by Osborne himself with the music-hall comedian Max Wall dancing through the part of Archie Rice, "leaning on his cane like a reflective, startled ape" (*The Independent* May 27, 1990, p. 6). Whether Olivier, Wall, or less famous performers played Archie, audiences of *The Entertainer* were flattered, amused, and touched by Archie Rice's final direct address: "A very GOOD audience. Let me know where you're working tomorrow night – and I'll come and see YOU." Osborne poured his nostalgia into that one play and did not again introduce music-hall into theatre, although he has portrayed actors in *Time Present* and *The Hotel in Amsterdam* (both 1968).

Probably influenced by *The Entertainer*, Joan Littlewood's *Oh, What a Lovely War* (1963) proclaims itself "a pierrot show of fifty years ago," and upon that format she projects World War I newsflashes. Laced with nostalgic melodies, the text of her musical comedy is too slender for close scrutiny, however radical its verve in performance.

In contrast, the savage condemnation of popular comedy as troop entertainment expands into an execration of World War II as a ghastly comic turn in Charles Wood's *Dingo* (1967, later adapted for the John Lennon film *How I Won the War*). Like the American Kilroy, Dingo is the unheroic ubiquitous British soldier of World War II. His human feelings are eroded by the inhuman scenes that make up his daily routine. Those who numb his emotions are not the enemy Germans, but his fellow-countrymen.

In the first scene Dingo is determinedly impervious when Chalky burns to death in his tank. But after Dingo's friend Tanky rescues Chalky's charred corpse, realistically staged war horrors are punctured by the Comic, who treats the theatre of war as a theatre for our entertainment: "Leave the first three rows for the officers will you?" While the British soldiers are bombed and strafed, the Comic parodies mindless entertainments and equally mindless morale-building: "I do not believe troops can succeed unless they are infected with that optimism that comes from well being." Dingo remains resolutely uninfected: "The best place to be in a battle is in the thick of it only with your head down and a look of eager bloodlust in your eyes."

Relieved to find themselves prisoners of war, Dingo and Tanky fantasize about working as surgeon and lorry-driver, respectively. On the beaches of Normandy the Comic exhorts Sergeant Mogg to act heroically: "I will let you wear my funny hat." When Mogg joins Dingo and Tanky in prison, he subjects them to his mania for following rules. While the Comic MCs a "tit show," with British officers in drag as the buxom beauties, Dingo befriends the German guard Willie. Far less friendly, the British Sergeant Mogg is "going to make this the smartest Stalag in wherever," and he therefore kicks Tanky's head to pulp. After "persuading" Tanky to escape, Mogg floodlights the attempt, and Tanky is bayonetted by Willie. Tanky's effort is applauded as a music-hall act. Before his grinning corpse, each character in prison assumes a stereotypical military role in further music-hall turns. The Comic manages to disappear: "Old Kriegies never die – they simply spade away."

Toward the end of *Dingo* the slaughter accelerates because of Anglo-American rivalry, which is revealed by the Comic's ventriloquist turn between Churchill and Eisenhower. In the play's final scene, the dead Tanky charges Sergeant Mogg repetitively: "He killed me." Tanky's rancorous attitude contrasts sharply with that of the dead Blonde, an officer in drag, who was also killed when urged to escape. Praised by the Comic for heroic (and murderous) exploits on the battlefield, the Blonde receives the DSC – on his panties. The Comic continues to spout his blend of stale jokes and stale clichés, against background wailing that will continue to the end of the play.

Throughout the caricature music-hall turns of the suddenly announced peace, Dingo stubbornly enunciates his desire to go home. He knows that the war was fought "for all the usual reasons." At the last the Comic joins Churchill in urinating against the German West wall: "*The* COMIC *faces upstage and hitches his coat for pissing.*" That posture (rather than any assumed by Dingo) sums up Dingo's attitude toward the war. His last words promise a radical vote in forthcoming British elections: "I have not come all this way to be pissed on twice by Mr. Churchill." But the dead Tanky closes the play with his echoic line: "He killed me."

Dingo has not garnered the appreciation I believe it deserves, perhaps because of Wood's unsparingly detailed authenticity of depiction of the brutalities of war – an authenticity that also colors his television drama *Tumbledown*. But whereas the teleplay is documentary in its realism, *Dingo* stages a hackneyed Comic who provides no comic *relief*, but who does lend distance to the atrocities. Shifting his stance without warning, the Comic pours out patriotic clichés of wartime performers, but he also adopts a Brechtian distance from the war in order to point out its unnecessary slaughter: "The second battle of Alamein was a political battle you know, Churchill wanted an all-out British victory before the Americans came in." The Comic tells stale and sexist jokes, but he also superintends the performance of a scene from Wilde's *Importance of Being Earnest*. Present both in battle and in prison, he directs the officers in drag, but he also urges them to suicidal escape. As a ventriloquist, he manipulates puppets of Churchill and Eisenhower: "My generals say I'm the best general the British ever had." During the ceremonies of peace, he parodies journalists, ministers, women belching forth their patriotic clichés, and yet his last speech is (I think) serious: "Your freedom is in danger. Will you vote?" Two decades after the close of World War II *Dingo* was the first play to damn the whole enterprise as a catastrophic series of music-hall turns, and Wood's major instrument toward that end was the popular variety show.

Charles Wood and Peter Nichols are Bristol neighbors who started writing for the stage at about the same time. In the same year as *Dingo*, Nichols' first play reached London – *A Day in the Death of Joe Egg* (1967). Each of the five main characters addresses the audience directly, as in a variety show. Each of the parents of a spastic child enacts scenes of the past – the birth of the child, the awareness of her hopeless condition, the fruitless quest for medical help – but these are actor's turns rather than popular theatre embedded in the very structure of the drama, as in later Nichols plays.

A fantasy explains the play within the play of *The National Health or Nurse Norton's Affair* (1969). As already described in Chapter 2, the frame play is a realistic depiction of male patients in the ward of a National Health hospital. What is resplendently theatricalized, however, is the fantasy inner play announced by Nichols' subtitle – *Nurse Norton's Affair*. A hospital orderly of the frame play, Barnet (originally played by acrobatic comedian Jim Dale), provides narration in the inner play, and in that sentimental fantasy the characters shift to a different register of dialogue that parodies soap operas of the time. Nurse Norton's purple prose is matched by elaborate costumes, garish lighting, and loud music in the five intercalated scenes that draw upon the vocabulary of popular romances or soap operas: "In the submarine strangeness of the night ward, young Doctor Neil Boyd's fingers had fleetingly touched hers. And his usually stern features had crumpled into a yearning smile. Their eyes had met and ricochetted away."

Despite the ludicrous phrasing, the inner play masks a social problem drama: race separates the two lovers, for the old Scottish surgeon refuses his consent to the marriage of his son and a black nurse. Temporarily, as in romance. When Nurse Norton sacrifices a kidney to her lover (romance is innocent of immunology!), and her rival falls in love with the widower father, obstacles dissolve, and both frame and inner plays end in a final scene of an extravagant double wedding – "the grooms in kilts, the brides in white." The whole cast, "quick and dead," throw rice and confetti, but also wave the Union Jack at this happy integration. The final line of the play is spoken by the orderly Barnet in black-face: "It's a funny old world we live in and you're lucky to get out of it alive." In stage fact, however, three of the patients were not so lucky; or perhaps they were luckier than the chronic invalids who do remain "alive." Predictably, the play was praised for avoiding depression, in spite of its subject. Toward that end, Nichols introduced his parody of romantic soap opera, a popular genre here imbued with a muted plea for racial integration.

In *Privates on Parade* (1977) Nichols turns to music-hall, but the punning title exposes the sexuality of the display – in his words, "a sustained metaphor on the phallic symbolism of weaponry" (*Plays*, p. 295). The opening scenic direction delineates setting and structure: *"The sets more or less alternate front-cloth and full-stage, in the manner of the variety theatre. Lee and Cheng sometimes move furniture and props, to the accompaniment of percussion, thus suggesting the popular Chinese opera."* As in variety shows, too, characters address the audience directly. Sprinkled through *Privates* are a dozen songs, both individual and choral.

The play's plot ambles through the adventures of an entertainment unit of the postwar British Army in Malaysia. Improbably, most members of the unit are gay, headed by the irrepressible Acting Captain Terri Dennis (originally played by Denis Quilley with high camp swish) who speaks as though the English language were surreptitiously gay – Bernardette Shaw, Matelot matelot wherefore art thou matelot, I was only being the good fairy. Intricately threaded through the variety numbers, the plot blends the sexual and military education of young (heterosexual) Steven Flowers, the blind piety of the commanding officer, the cruel corruption of the supply sergeant, the English clichés of a half-caste prostitute, and the mysterious movements of two silent Chinese, who remain behind when the unit departs for England. As in musical comedy the plot strands are familiar and subsidiary to the melodies. As in music-hall, Nichols' dialogue gravitates between one-liners and monologues.

Strictly speaking, Nichols' *Poppy* (1982) does not depict theatre framing theatre. However, it draws its form from that distinctively British popular genre, pantomime, and should be viewed in the context of Nichols' dramaturgical taste for popular forms. As early as 1935 Auden and Isherwood leaned lightly on pantomime for their *Dog Beneath the Skin*; humans in animal-skins are a staple of panto, and the very title of the Auden/Isherwood play emphasizes that beneath the skin of a ubiquitous dog is the missing Sir Francis Crewe. Nichols enlarges the Auden/Isherwood dog to two horses and he considerably enlarges the debt to panto, while also reveling in other devices of popular genres. Not only do actors play animals (appropriately named Randy and Cherry) who leer and gesture, but they engage the sympathies of the audience more than the putatively human characters. In the RSC production, the animals were a triumph of the property-makers' craft: "You pressed the right hand or the left hand to make [Randy] wink or blink and open his mouth and you pulled down to make his ears erect and then we had an enema syringe for making smoke come out of his ears. The female horse, Cherry, had to be able to cry as well so we incorporated the kind of pump used in motor cars for windscreen washers" (Cook, *Backstage*, p. 42).

From pantomime Nichols also draws the Principal Boy played by a beautiful young woman, the Principal Girl played by a girl, the Dame played by a male comedian, direct appeals to the audience, and a panoply of special effects. For the traditional Good and Bad Fairies, Nichols substitutes the Emperor of China and the British Empress Victoria, costumed in their respective regalia.

Nichols' plot is amusingly complicated, juggling the upwardly mobile squire Dick Whittington (a traditional hero of panto), his servant Jack Idle, a schoolmistress Sally Forth who loves the former and is loved by the latter, and various pious but unprincipled Britishers reaping a tidy profit from the Chinese opium trade. Poppy is not only the source of opium, but also Cockney slang for money. Since *Poppy* is a pantomime, the ending is tuneful, with the curtain falling on a dance to "The Good New Days." But Nichols sounds a faintly sour note in the traditional final walk-down of pantomime. All the characters appear in modern clothes, the Chinese wearing Mao tunics and trousers, the lower-class couple Jack and Sally equipped as American tourists, the upper-class couple Dick and Lucy garbed as City-of-London professionals, and Queen Victoria resembling Elizabeth II *"waving in the royal way."* The subtext implies that poppy still thrives, but the text wavers between nostalgia for a Victorian genre and condemnation of Victorian commerce. The satiric intention was evidently submerged in Terry Hands' lavish RSC production of 1982, and an irate Nichols threatened to cease writing for the stage. Fortunately, this witty and inventive playwright changed his mind, and fortunately, too, he tightened the text of *Poppy* for a 1988 production.

Less fortunate were Nichols' plot changes that underline what the 1988 program lists as "hypocrisy, drug dealing, racism, money worship and sexual repression" of the Opium Wars. Heroic Dick Whittington becomes a charmingly villainous capitalist, and his Lucy disappears until her wedding. Since Sally is in love with Dick, she takes to drugs when she learns that he is her half-brother, and she ends the play as a junkie, trundled in a wheelchair by Jack Idle, who has shot his lovable horse Randy rather than follow orders to send him to the slaughter-house. The Chinese Emperor becomes an inept magician, and the traditional sing-along of pantomime is led by the nefarious characters, Dick's mother and his/her instructor in the opium trade. Nichols' central problem with *Poppy* is unresolved in revision: how to reconcile his affection for a popular art, pantomime, with his condemnation of the society that fostered it.

Nichols is faithful to popular theatre within a formal play, from the 1967 *A Day in the Death of Joe Egg* to the 1988 revision of *Poppy*, but its forms enter only sporadically into other plays of the 1970s and 1980s. The meaning of popular comedy nevertheless becomes the subject of Trevor Griffiths' *Comedians* (1975), a play that originated in a conversation of comedians who played in the television series *The Comedians*, who admired a teacher of comedians while they deplored their own performance to earn money. Griffiths quarried the popular art of standup comedy, and the first actor to play Eddie Waters, the teacher of would-be comedians, was Jimmy Jewel, a seasoned music-hall performer. The play also ignited the searing performance of Jonathan Pryce as Gethin Price, which helped form a new English taste for class-conscious, alternative humor.

Comedians is plotted simply: a liberal humanist comedian teaches his craft to six working-class students, divided in neat symmetry: two

Irishmen, two brothers, a self-seeking Jew, and a class-conscious radical. One half of the class of comedians betray their teacher's ideal of comedy, and the other half are faithful in their fashion. What engages the attention is the texture of their performances.

Griffiths pored over joke-books to select those that supported his thesis, but the thesis changed during the course of writing. He has explained: "The question why we laugh at certain things becomes a metaphor for the question why we live the way we do. Originally I saw the play as a conflict between Waters and Challenor, between integrity and commercialism. But after six or eight pages of the first draft, Gethin Price came through and superseded that confrontation making it a conflict between liberal humanism and proletarian revolution" (Kerensky, *The New British Drama*, p. 204). The play gradually grows in complexity, with jokes paced too swiftly for us to ponder their prejudices of race, sex, class, and religion. Whatever Griffiths may have intended, we are attracted by both the self-critical humanist teacher Waters and the mordantly accusatory student Price.

In Griffiths' skillful pacing of *Comedians* the students begin with exercises – limericks, spoonerisms, sound play, and jokes, before they are permitted to perform a complete routine in the second act, with us as the audience they directly address. The individual skits lead to the climactic performance of Waters' favorite student, Gethin Price. His sketch (indebted to the Swiss comedian Grock) is shockingly theatrical, and appreciation depends upon a rather intimate knowledge of British social divisions. The "comic" skit ends on blood staining the heart of an elegant cardboard lady. However, Waters has the last word as he welcomes an Indian to his next class. Neither teacher nor student, humanist nor revolutionary, emerges as Griffiths' messenger-boy in this serious drama which is spun around the popular art of standup comedy.

Other popular arts feed other contemporary plays. Dotty Moore engages in play-long charades in Tom Stoppard's *Jumpers* (1972). Rock songs are heard in David Hare's *Teeth 'n' Smiles* (1975), Peter Flannery's *Heartbreak Hotel* (1975), and Stephen Poliakoff's *The Summer Party* (1980). Poliakoff enfolds radio quiz shows into *City Sugar* (1975), and Alan Ayckbourn pirouettes around a television interview in *Man of the Moment* (1990). A historical pageant is farcically treated in Alan Ayckbourn's *Ten Times Tables* (1977) and is seriously portrayed in David Edgar's *Entertaining Strangers* (1984; revised 1988). Richard Harris' *Stepping Out* (1984) circles around tap-dancing, and Peter Terson's *Strippers* (1984) around strip-shows. In these plays such popular forms of theatre are representational background, rather than the

6 *Comedians* by Trevor Griffiths, directed by Richard Eyre at the Nottingham Playhouse, 1975; the comedian Gethin Price (Jonathan Pryce) satirizes the cardboard upper-class figures (Donald Cooper)

structural fulcrum of the drama, but they all serve to undermine surface realism.

In *Country Dancing* by Nigel Williams (1986), English folk songs and dances trace both the social and emotional life of nineteenth-century England, as indicated in Chapter 2. At the same time the dancing is a metaphor for social history, as the community life of the village dances is atomized to the one-to-one couples in the waltz. Williams' introduction of country dances is slightly exotic in today's London, but the other popular forms within contemporary plays belong to only yesterday, or even today. Except for Wood's *Dingo* and Griffiths' *Comedians*, the introduction of popular forms – variety, jokes, soap opera, and even country dances – into legitimate drama casts a golden glow over the play, preventing astringency.

Self-conscious and self-reflexive plays

In contrast to this delight in the popular arts, contemporary English playwrights have merely skirted another form of theatre in the theatre, the self-conscious or self-reflexive play, which is nominally about itself.[2] Beaumont and Fletcher's *The Knight of the Burning Pestle* is the fountainhead of the few English plays in this mode, and Pirandello's *Six Characters in Search of an Author* is the best-known example of this subgenre, but because that self-reflexive play proposes a clear story-line in staging two of its key scenes, it is usually labeled a play within the play.

Ideally, self-reflexive plays are plotless; they are their own subject matter; tending toward actual theatre reality, they subvert the socio-logical and psychological conventions of realism. The post-Pirandello French theatre never achieved this, but it often inserted into drama reflections on its own nature – examples are Giraudoux, Anouilh, Ionesco, Genet, and especially Beckett. With less literary sophistica-tion, amateur groups of the theatrically effervescent 1960s staged their self-conscious gropings toward performance – more often in the United States than in England, but also in that bastion of theatre tradition. "Process" was the watchword as young, cocky, and often self-indulgent actors intimated that what you saw was all there was. So far as I know, however, these attempts did not reach print.

In that same decade James Saunders dramatizes the composition of the play we witness in *Next Time I'll Sing To You* (1962). A playwright and actors are charged with a subject for performance – the life of an actual hermit, Jimmy Mason (1857–1942; the life of Mason is also the springboard for Edward Bond's realistic *The Pope's Wedding*, also 1962). Saunders' fictional playwright Rudge has penned the begin-nings of a script which indulges in long descriptive or meditative passages rather than dialogue. For the actor who plays the Hermit, and who is known to us only as the Hermit, his character is a saint, in whose soul he buries his own individuality. The other three actors play minor roles in the Hermit's life, and they fill stage time by meandering into their own ruminations, not unlike Vladimir in Beckett's *Waiting for Godot*. Finally, one actor sums up the essential

---

2 Raymond Federman, "Self-Reflexive Fiction," in Emory Elliot (ed.), *Columbia Literary History of the United States*, New York: Columbia University Press, 1988, distinguishes between self-conscious fiction that "deals with the reading process" and self-reflex-ive fiction that "relates to the writing process." He acknowledges that these are "not always distinguishable, for they both use the same tools – parody, irony, digression, playfulness – to demystify the illusionary aspect of the story" (p. 1145).

solitude of each individual; another actor sums up the irony of events, concurrently tragic and comic; the one actress, who has been as lascivious as women in medieval fabliaux, affirms: "One thing about us – at least we're not dead." At the last, the playwright Rudge picks up the Hermit's diary and snaps it shut. The written word cannot capture living experience, and Saunders has tried to dramatize the tension between even the most rudimentary life and the task of "not dead" actors conveying it to an audience.

John Osborne's *A Sense of Detachment* (1972) is at once self-reflexive and parodic of self-reflexion. Again, this play is about the making of a play. No plot intrudes into a two-act performance by six nameless actors who are only distantly related to the six titular characters of Pirandello – "I suppose we needn't ask if there's a plot or not!" Left to their own resources, a Girl and a Chap, his Father and Grandfather, an unrelated Older Lady, and a Chairman interact fitfully, complain about their predicament, address the actual audience rudely, and parry the thrusts of a Shifting Planted Interrupter, and of a Man in a Stage Box. Soon they settle into stereotypes: the Grandfather is a crosspatch of quotations, and the Chap a series of affairs with women; the Older Lady salivates over pornography, and the money-conscious Girl is the irritant who needles the other characters, mainly the Chap. With rhyme but no reason, the Chap and the Girl abruptly fall in love, the Chairman admits his inadequacy, and the cast leaves the stage. The performance has included song, dance, dialect, jokes, quotations, projections, classical music, TV chat shows, improvisations, sermons from an onstage pulpit, and passing references to Harold Pinter, Arnold Wesker, David Storey, Edward Albee, Charles Wood, Christopher Hampton, Edna O'Brien, and "Old Uncle Sammy Beckett." Like Beckett's tramps two decades earlier, Osborne's actors disparage the audience as well as the action in which they participate.

A compendium of theatre clichés, *A Sense of Detachment* substantiates its title by detaching us from its characters who resemble cardboard cutouts manipulated in a toy theatre, even while reflecting wryly on the process of playing plays. In John Elsom's felicitous summary: "The word 'detachment' is the key to the production. The author is detached from the actors, for whom he supplies no roles: the actors are detached from the audience, for whom they offer condescendingly strips of old routines" (Page, *Osborne on File*, p. 68). In spite of the considerable talents of Nigel Hawthorne and Rachel Kempson, the audience remained detached.

Quite dissimilar is the barely self-conscious form of Nigel Williams' *My Brother's Keeper?* (1985). On the surface a tense realistic drama of two recriminatory brothers at their father's deathbed, the familiar realism dissolves into a metaphor for English theatre, as other families are a metaphor for the English nation. In *My Brother's Keeper?* the father *"is, or was, a classical actor, a man born a little too late to be as successful as he should have been, and the extravagance of his gestures and the deep thrill of his voice should be still perceptible, even though he is paralysed down one side, having suffered a cerebral stroke."* The elder of the two brothers is a businessman, and the younger a left-wing playwright. After not meeting for years, they are face to hostile face at the bedside of their father, who, lacking the will to live, has refused any nourishment. Several times their mother affirms that they are an ordinary English family, and the younger brother twists her plaintive refrain into a condemnation of their repressed emotions.

Finally, the old actor, having fought off food, falls asleep, his loveless wife and their two sons silent beside him. A jocular male nurse utters a few mindless clichés; the patient in the next bed thrashes once, then is silent. There is no resolution to the cross-conflicts of this English family, where father and son symbolize the invalidism of the English theatre. The old actor with the rich voice *refuses* nourishment, bringing on his own death. Although each of the brothers is successful, they despise one another's way of life – the pious hypocrisies of the businessman and the self-indulgent excesses of the radical dramatist. Moreover, Williams punctuates his title with a question-mark, *My Brother's Keeper?*, hinting at other questions: can business and radical drama share the same theatre? Focused on their own family problems, the two brothers show little concern for the mute bandaged man in the neighboring bed, a Mr. Pittorini, who dies under their very eyes. Revolving around theatre, the play is necessarily self-conscious about itself. At the same time *My Brother's Keeper?* contrasts the ready rhetoric of the younger theatre generation with the faltering words of a dying progenitor.

Although Peter Nichols' *A Piece of My Mind* (1986) contrasts two generations by the very casting of actors in their forties against actors in their twenties, the self-reflexivity of theatre takes another form. At the start of play the fictional playwright Ted Forrest is in his coffin, and his rival Miles Whittier (punning on "miles wittier") begins to write a play about his life. That play is putatively and intermittently enacted on stage by the four actors, who take many parts and comment on their author: "his attempts to hide the mundane naturalism of the early scenes with tricks and gimmicks put me in mind of the dreary solipsisms of Pirandello."

We follow the Forrests (named mischievously after Nichols' friends, the Charles *Wood* family) – Ted, Dinah, and their two children – from their impecunious beginnings through Ted's first success: "And so we welcome a new playwright whose way of making us belly-laugh one moment and cry the next might well be called Funny Boo-Hoo." We hear a roll-call of Ted's playwright colleagues and rivals, but, smitten with envy of Miles, the dramatist shifts to a novel, upon which he makes small progress. He closes the first of two acts: "Laughing always come to crying? Not bad. It's like what happens in my plays after the interval."

After the interval, however, Ted addresses the audience in wholly laughable blank verse, while his writing block looms so large that it figuratively makes him cry. His children mature, his father dies, and the critics bury him alive. Like the Players in *Rosencrantz and Guildenstern Are Dead* by Tom Stoppard (surely one of the clues to Miles Whittier), the actors debate about possible deaths for the protagonist, but they find that ending banal, and Ted warns them: "None of you leave this three-sided room till you help me end the play." The actors offer makeshift suggestions, and one of them eulogizes Ted: "We can't expect a meat course every time and may have to make do with a trifle, a *jeu d'esprit*, a promissory note, a piece of his mind." Which gives Nichols' play its title.

Nichols' first play in seven years, *A Piece of My Mind* deftly intertwines Ted's writer's block with Nichols' familiar autobiography to compose an apparently self-reflexive play, in which every one-liner is nicely calculated, to the last words of the play: "I'll see." In the event, we all see. But do not hear. Imaginary double-glazed windows separate the audience from the actors on stage, who break into song and dance. In a variant on the old comic gag of trains or planes drowning out speech, the audience sees the actors singing, but hears only the baaing of sheep, which have already been equated with themselves – sheep which have been feeding on the piece and peace of Nichols' mind.

Familiar plays within plays

Outnumbering these somewhat laborious forays into metatheatre are traditional plays within plays. The few critics who have analyzed this device divide them into (a) plays in which the actors of the inner play differ from those of the outer play, with *Hamlet* as the celebrated paradigm; (b) plays in which certain characters of the outer play perform in the inner play, with *The Knight of the Burning Pestle* as a tasty example (Nelson, Schmeling, Righter). Modern dramatists build exclusively on the latter form, which I subdivide into inner plays that are familiar to a sophisticated audience, and fictional plays invented for the circumstances, both far from realistic drama.

Tom Stoppard is a flamboyant craftsman in both areas. He concocts plots that draw freely upon *Hamlet, Macbeth*, or *The Importance of Being Earnest*. In two Shakespeare manipulations he allots fifteen minutes to *Hamlet* (and one minute for an encore) and a little longer to *Macbeth*, within their respective outer plays, intended for performance on a single program. In *Dogg's Hamlet* (1976, an amplification of *Dogg's Our Pet*, 1971) Stoppard's characters answer to the code-words of the alphabet (Able Baker Charlie Dog Easy Fox) and teach the audience an invented language – Dogg, based on Wittgenstein (see Levinson's account). Having triumphantly accomplished this, the same actors speed through *Hamlet* in fifteen minutes. The title of the second, more serious play *Cahoot's Macbeth* puns on the name of the Czech dissident writer Pavel Kahout, but we are also in cahoots about a drama of usurpation which is set in a private home, as Czech dissidents contrived to put on plays in private homes when they were forbidden to work in theatres. *Macbeth* becomes politically relevant in this context, but the radical abridgements inevitably parody these plays within their slender plays.[3]

Stoppard's gamesmanship is more telling in his best-known play *Rosencrantz and Guildenstern Are Dead* (1967). Stoppard's debts to *Hamlet* (as well as to *Waiting for Godot*) were noted in Chapter 3, but I want now to situate the play within the structure of metatheatre. In zigzagging between the outer and the inner play, Stoppard works in the wake of such English masterpieces as *The Knight of the Burning Pestle* and *The Critic*, but he has the temerity to do so with *Hamlet*, probably the best-known play in the English language. Stoppard's own dialogue often strays so far from any plot that we can be grateful for the summary of his Ros:

We, Rosencrantz and Guildenstern, from our young days brought up with [Hamlet], awakened by a man standing on his saddle, are summoned, and arrive, and are instructed to glean what afflicts him and draw him on to pleasures, such as a play, which unfortunately, as it turns out, is abandoned in some confusion . . . we, in consequence, are escorting [Hamlet] for his own good, to England.

The names of Stoppard's characters immediately reveal their

3 For opposing views *cf.* Diamond, Hunter, and Whitaker.

Shakespearean provenance, and the pair meet other characters besides the prince: the Player and his company, a welcoming Claudius and Gertrude, a silent Ophelia. Closing Stoppard's Act I, Polonius and Hamlet speak Shakespeare's lines.

Teasing the audience, Stoppard's Hamlet opens Act II: "S'blood, there is something in this more than natural, if philosophy could find it out." It is something less than natural, too, since excerpts from *Hamlet* in Acts II and III of Stoppard's play speed us so swiftly through Shakespeare's last four acts that it seems with hindsight a preparation for *Dogg's Hamlet*. Aside from the feverish pace, Stoppard manipulates *Hamlet* in two main ways: (1) He dramatizes the Hamlet–Ophelia scene, which Shakespeare confines to a report by Ophelia, and, similarly, he dramatizes Hamlet's adventures at sea, which Shakespeare confines to Hamlet's report to Horatio (by letter and by narration); (2) Stoppard ends his play with a stage full of corpses and the penultimate speeches from Shakespeare's tragedy, but the lines are spoken as prose, and there are *two* ambassadors from England.[4] It is thus implied that there are an infinite number of perplexed couples who will move through their repetitive lines and lives until they "disappear from view."

Strictly speaking, *Rosencrantz and Guildenstern Are Dead* is not a play within a play, but rather a play dancing within the structural frame of the most celebrated tragedy in the English language. In the context of theatre framing theatre, Roger Sales has written: "[Rosencrantz and Guildenstern] have been watching a rehearsal for the dumb show which will precede the performance of *The Murder of Gonzago* at the court. *Gonzago* is the play within the play of *Hamlet*, which is in its turn the play within the play of [Stoppard's] *Rosencrantz*" (*Tom Stoppard: Rosencrantz and Guildenstern are Dead*, p. 44). But this is not quite accurate, for Stoppard's play winds in and out of *Hamlet* rather than framing it firmly.

Played in London about a decade after *Waiting for Godot*, Stoppard's reminiscent ramble seemed to some critics to echo Beckett's absurdism, but each member of Stoppard's pair, particularly Guil, struggles to free his will in a way inconceivable in Beckett. What Stoppard learned from Beckett (as Beckett learned it from Shakespeare) was a grave philosophic ground under verbal pirouettes. All three plays – *Rosencrantz*, *Godot*, and *Hamlet* – are distinguished by

4 In the 1967 Faber edition of the play the two Ambassadors converse in music-hall rhythms and then "walk off together" before the house lights come up on the empty stage.

their protagonists' vulnerability to mortality, and by a pervasive sense of mystery – along with an antic disposition.[5] And all are leagues away from realism.

Travesties (1974) dances even more gracefully around a familiar play, *The Importance of Being Earnest*. Stoppard himself has called attention to the structure of *Travesties*: puzzling prologue, long funny monologue, scenes in which people play intellectual games, and final monologue (Hayman, *Tom Stoppard*, p. 12). Relying on biographies of famous foreigners in Zurich during World War I, Stoppard situates Joyce, Lenin, and Tzara in the Central Library of that Swiss city. It is a matter of record that James Joyce persuaded a minor British consular official, Henry Carr, to act Algernon Moncrieff in an English language performance of *The Importance of Being Earnest*. After the performance, the two theatre dilettantes quarreled, so that Carr sued Joyce, who counter-sued.

In Stoppard's *Travesties* an elderly Carr (dynamically enacted by John Wood, to whom the play is dedicated) recalls high jinks in wartime Zurich, while he careens in and out of Wilde's comedy. Even before *Earnest* is mentioned, however, two identical manilla folders containing manuscripts are exchanged by error, in the Zurich library; *"it is not important how this transference is achieved, only that it is* SEEN *to occur."* A few minutes later, in his own room, Carr twice refers to his triumph as "not Ernest, the other one." And from that point on, Wilde's play hovers over all other travesties in Stoppard's farce, rationalized as Carr's failing but grandiloquent memory of his theatre triumph.

Stoppard's bluestocking heroines are named for those of Wilde – Cecily and Gwendolyn – but Wilde's Algernon and Ernest become Carr and Tzara. Carr is romantically entwined with Cecily, who helps Lenin with a work in progress on imperialism. Tzara is enthralled by Carr's sister Gwendolyn, who helps Joyce with his work in progress, *Ulysses*. Stoppard condenses the two Wilde butlers into the repeated appearances of Bennett (the actual name of the British ambassador to Switzerland), and Stoppard's Joyce has affinities with Wilde's Lady Bracknell. Manilla folders parallel Wilde's offending handbags.

In so far as Stoppard's Act I has any plot, it is patterned on that of Wilde, even to direct quotation, while it pivots on Carr's acceptance of the role of Wilde's Algie. Stoppard thus plays a mischievous arpeggio on *Earnest*, which is at once an event in Carr's wayward memory

---

5 Sales' book is full of insights, but he does not convince me that *Rosencrantz and Guildenstern Are Dead* is a parody of *Waiting for Godot*.

in the frame play and Stoppard's structural fulcrum for that reminiscence.

Once the crucial folders (belonging, respectively, to Joyce and Lenin) are exchanged, and the character parallels are established in Act I, Stoppard indulges in language games, dialectical confrontations, and ebullient pastiche. As Andrew Kennedy notes: "*Travesties* is not content to use Wilde pastiche as the 'new material' of its dialogue; it swallows up Joycean parody, Tzara's Dadaist language, Shakespeare fragments and Lenin's speeches" (Kennedy, *Dramatic Dialogue*, p. 230). (It also juggles the chronology of actual events.) For all its verbal fireworks, Act II sags when Cecily becomes overtly political, even though Stoppard might be ridiculing pretty young women obsessed with politics, and particularly Leninist politics. But the playwright retrieves the finale when the folders are restored to their rightful owners, and romance raises its rosy head with "appropriate embraces." At the last Stoppard's *Travesties* returns us to the frame play of postwar Zurich, the home of the old couple, Carr and his wife. But the Wildean aura lingers in Mrs. Carr's name – Cecily.

Stoppard in general and *Travesties* in particular demand some sophistication in the audience, whereas such sophistication is the butt of Edward Bond's ridicule in *The Sea* (1973). Rather than plays within the play, Edward Bond tends to stage writers within his plays. As mentioned earlier, Shakespeare, John Clare, and Basho appear in, respectively, *Bingo*, *The Fool*, *Narrow Road to the Deep North*, and its revision *The Bundle*. In Chapter 3 I cited analogies between Shakespeare's *The Tempest* and Bond's *The Sea* (1973), including a play within the play, derived from Greek mythology.

To review Bond's plot briefly: Willy, the friend of a man drowned during a tempest, calls upon Mrs. Rafi, the town's leading citizen, in whose home a rehearsal is under way. Except for the Vicar as Pluto, god of the Underworld, the inner play has an all-female cast. Mrs. Rafi is playwright, director, and leading actor of *Orpheus*, and Bond indulges in parody at her expense – "Eurydice, let me clasp your marble bosom to my panting breast and warm it with my heart."

At the same time Bond makes a telling point through the familiar myth. As Orpheus rescued Eurydice from the realm of the dead, so the aptly named Willy rescues this Eurydice, played by Rose, the dead man's fiancée. And this young couple will not look back. Parody on the surface, the play within the play pillories the pious, patriotic bourgeoisie, which has driven one man to drink and the other to fascist fantasy – the two people on the beach who might have prevented the drowning. As Shakespeare's *The Tempest* reclaims

Europeans from their island interlude, Bond's *The Sea* reclaims a young couple for life. As Eurydice left the realm of the dead, Rose will leave the turn-of-the-century town with its deadening class demarcations. At the last, Bond subdues parody to his social purpose; Mrs. Rafi-Orpheus remains in her Underworld, whereas Rose-Eurydice embarks for the land of the living. By syncopating classical and Shakespearean echoes, Bond augments the resonance of his *The Sea*.

In contrast to Bond, who has never had a box-office success in England, Alan Ayckbourn thrives both at home and abroad. Although Ayckbourn toys with stage time, space, and viewpoint, he rarely indulges in any device so blatantly theatrical as a play within the play. The exception is *A Chorus of Disapproval* (1985). Set in the amateur theatre of a small Welsh town, *Chorus* is plotted around a production of *The Beggar's Opera* by John Gay. (The film of *Chorus*, scripted by Ayckbourn, is set in Scarborough, where he was Artistic Director of the theatre.) The avid Welsh director Dafydd cajoles his recalcitrant cast toward performance even though he is ironically aware: "Here we are, playing around with pretty lights and costumes held together with safety pins. Out there it's all happening." Specifically, what is happening is the embroilment of Guy Jones, the one stranger in town, in intrigues amatory and monetary, while he ascends the cast ladder to the lead role of Gay's Macheath.

Ayckbourn's play opens on Gay's final song, when Jones as Macheath is surrounded by an adoring cast, but after the curtain falls he is shunned by his colleagues in a silent "chorus of disapproval." Ayckbourn's play then becomes a flashback tracing Jones' naive entanglements. Although there are no beggars among the comfortable citizens of Ayckbourn's Wales, they too are professional thieves – through speculation, implied bribery, and sexual pressure – and Ayckbourn leans on Gay to underline the durability of chicanery, or simply to entertain us. For example, the cast in the pub sing Gay's drinking song. After the lawyer Dafydd sounds Guy out about his company's land, a cast member sings Gay's song about lawyers stealing your whole estate. Two different Macheaths bask in the rivalry of two women: Lucy and Bridget vie for Crispin, as do Hannah and Faye for Guy. By the end of *Chorus* we again hear the end of Gay's opera (slightly modified), but this time the whole cast embraces Macheath/Guy Jones. As Gay's Player imposes a happy ending upon the Beggar's play, so the writer Ayckbourn accommodates his ending to the genre of farce.

Credibility does not sully this farce, but John Arden, like Edward Bond, commits serious concerns to familiar material in a play within a play. One might expect Arden to scorn the baroque form of the play within the play, given as he is to strong and direct action. Yet he is perhaps the English playwright most consistently and insistently aware of the artifice of theatre, so he hints at plays within plays in *The Royal Pardon* and *The Bagman* (with its playwright-hero called John Arden), but he wrote his most complex treatment of the form in *Pearl* (1978), which was intended for the stage but was enacted on radio for the BBC. The action opens on Shakespeare's *Julius Caesar*, shifts backstage, and gradually situates us in a Renaissance English theatre at the time of Puritan objection to royal privilege. *Pearl*, an illicit actress of Irish–Indian descent, conspires with the playwright Tom Backhouse to create so strong a theatre piece that it will seduce the Puritans both to theatre and to an alliance with the oppressed Irish Catholics.

Toward this end they dramatize the familiar story of biblical Esther, whose actions toppled Haman, the King's Deputy. During rehearsals, however, Backhouse's radical script is gradually subverted; the play tilts toward Haman, a tragic hero who succumbs to his fatal flaw. At the premiere, Pearl is forced to dance naked, alienating the Puritans at the very time that the Scots Presbyterians have won their first battle against the army of the autocratic English king. The English Revolution has begun, but it is not the democratic revolution envisioned by Pearl. Shifting sharply to the past tense, that anachronistic actress describes how she was slashed across the face by the Royalist mistress of the theatre's patron. "After that, they wrapped rags around me; they kicked me out at a back door." Pearl is cast out by the swine – a metaphor for theatre in a world of power politics.

Written in 1978, the same year as Arden's *Pearl*, but not produced until 1985, Peter Barnes' *Red Noses* is set in an earlier historical period, the plague year of 1348. The titular Red Noses are a company of clowns who travel through France, entertaining the sick and dying. Although the chronology is unscholarly, the plays – for there are two of them – within this framework do belong to the Middle Ages. In Act I of *Red Noses* the company perform *Everyman*. At first paraphrasing a few lines of the medieval morality play, Barnes' comedians proceed to deviate from its spirit. Rather than a psychomachia at death's door, the clown-play trounces Death, and urges the populace to resist him. Everyman bests Death and proclaims: "Death doesn't count, and probably doesn't read or write either." The act ends in a joyous chorus of clowns.

By Act II of *Red Noses* the plague has subsided, and customary privilege has reassumed its power. Insouciantly, the Red Noses continue their entertainments, and, unseasonably, they present a nativity play for Easter. This time there is no departure from the familiar tale of the stable birth and the journey of the three Magi. In a kind of flashback, however, the Red Noses dramatize Herod's edict that condemns all infants to death. The intelligent but unscrupulous pope recognizes his own indictment in Herod, and he condemns the Red Noses to death. It is a typical Barnes irony to subvert an inner play of birth and peace with the power politics of death.

In 1988 two quite different familiar plays within plays were performed on the narrow stage of the Royal Court. In a rare utopian mood, Howard Brenton intrudes a miniature version of Christ's passion into *Greenland*. On election day in London in 1987, a lesbian street theatre troupe adapt the crucifixion for a female Christ.[6] The actress of the female Christ is the thirty-three-year-old daughter of a fanatically religious mother. In the second act of the frame play, seven hundred years later, the daughter disappears, and the mother conceives of a cathedral for plants: "I'm still religious, dear! I just don't believe in the mucky bits any more." Presumably, the crucifixion is one of "the mucky bits," given Brenton's delight in iconoclasm.

In *Our Country's Good* (1988), as in *Red Noses*, English dramatic literature supplies the inner play. Timberlake Wertenbaker's play is adapted from the novel *The Playmakers* by Thomas Keneally, which is in turn adapted from historical record. *Our Country's Good* is at once an implicit plea for humane treatment of prisoners and a celebration of the cathartic power of theatre. In *Our Country's Good*, Farquhar's *The Recruiting Officer* is performed by eighteenth-century English convicts newly arrived in Australia. Even at home in England, the condition of prisoners was deplorable, but far from home there was scant respect for even the letter of the law.

Captain Phillip, recalled from retirement to colonize Australia with a shipload of convicts, conceives of substituting theatre for hanging as an entertainment for his prisoners, and it is apparently he who chooses to revive *The Recruiting Officer* (first performance 1706 for a play set in 1697), perhaps because it involves military men. The director and actor of Captain Plume is a second lieutenant, but the other actors are prisoners, of whom few are literate. Five women prisoners are assigned the women's roles, and the cast is completed by a token Jew and a Malagach black. In spite of the scorn of the other officers, the rivalry of the women prisoners, the escape of a key actor, the

6 The burlesque contains its own sexism in a year that witnessed Mrs. Thatcher's overwhelming electoral victory.

rejection by the actors of the hangman in their midst, and the condemnation of four of the cast to chains, rehearsals persist. Never has the imperative of "the show must go on" overcome greater obstacles. Wertenbaker's play closes backstage, as *The Recruiting Officer* starts on the invisible forestage.

What Wertenbaker conveys during the course of *Our Country's Good*, what she imposes upon Keneally's diffuse novel, is the humanizing effect of theatre. In the Royal Court tradition of Wesker and Storey, who first dramatized work processes on stage, Wertenbaker dramatizes theatre as work: the copying of the script, the learning of the lines (whose elegance is at first barely comprehensible to the convicts), the entering into character, and the final weaving of the individual roles into the ensemble who perform *The Recruiting Officer*. These prisoners who "left [their] country for [their] country's good" also left their world for the good of the imagination.

In 1989, invigorated by a tour to Australia, where Wertenbaker's play is set, the Court actors alternated performances of *Our Country's Good* with *The Recruiting Officer*, so that the prisoner-actors of the play within the play actually performed the full roles in Farquhar's play. The spillover from the Wertenbaker play endowed that of Farquhar with rough energy, markedly different from (perhaps rebelling against?) the polish of William Gaskill's legendary production a quarter of a century earlier (with Colin Blakely, Sarah Miles, Laurence Olivier, Maggie Smith, and Robert Stephens). Wertenbaker's play ends on the opening speech of *The Recruiting Officer*, in which Sergeant Kite recruits by promising all things to all men. Farquhar's lying sergeant unwittingly speaks theatre truth for Wertenbaker's audiences.

When a play within a play consists of familiar material, a dramatic point can be conveyed economically. Of all modern playwrights, Stoppard is most partial to a device that enables him to champion the confused minor characters of fiction and history against the monolithic major personalities. A single classic – *The Beggar's Opera* – is grist to Ayckbourn's English suburban mill. For Bond, Arden, and, almost incidentally, Brenton, the inner play serves as the fulcrum to raise a social critique of the frame. In *The Sea* that frame is the privileged class of rural England before World War I. In *Pearl* it is the aristocratic subversion of the Puritan Revolution. In *Greenland* it is the unholy alliance of religion with conservatism. In *Our Country's Good* it is military rigidity. An old theatre technique can still cast light on new ways of viewing the world outside theatre.

Fictional plays within plays

Parody is more frequent than depth in fictional plays within plays, and a deft parodist is the inventor of the most intricate play within a play on the modern English stage. After Alan Bennett's triumph in the student revue *Beyond the Fringe*, he then looked for a larger frame for his pastiche. Extending the skits developed as an undergraduate, he fueled a "legitimate" play with a series of parodies of English cultural history.

Bennett's *Forty Years On* opened in the West End in 1968, a year in which student revolt was a potent social force, but Bennett preserved his light touch. Introducing the published play, Bennett outlines the complications of his structure: "It is a play within a play in which the time-scale of the first play gradually catches up with the time-scale of the second, one cog the years 1900–39, the other 1939–45, and both within the third wheel of the present day [1968]." That third wheel involves a student performance on the occasion of the retirement of a headmaster of the Albion school. His successor-to-be directs the second cog that lurches through World War II, while the first cog hiccups through English cultural history between 1900 and 1940, the "forty years on" of the title.

In the frame play an old-fashioned headmaster protests ineffectually against the untraditional antics of his liberal successor, as well as against the traditional mischief of the schoolboys. One of Bennett's inner plays satirizes an upper-middle-class couple and their nanny who spend World War II in the cellar at Claridge's, the aristocrat of London hotels, while their son fights valiantly but uncomprehendingly on several front lines. Against this stable ground Bennett speeds through four decades of British cultural history, caricaturing T. E. Lawrence, Virginia Woolf, and Wilde's (pre-*Travesties*) *Earnest*. After a barrage of Bennett witticisms, the middle-class family of the inner play leave their cellar, and the headmaster of the outer play leaves the stage. The new permissive headmaster leads the Albion school in a chorus of the first verse of the Doxology, "All People That On Earth Do Dwell."

As Bennett parodies the school play genre, Stoppard in that same year teases the murder mystery in his *The Real Inspector Hound* (1968), but the interplay is more subtle between frame and inner play. While an Inspector Hound hunts for a mad murderer in the fictional inner play (which resembles Agatha Christie's *Mousetrap*, the longest-running play in London), the two theatre critics of Stoppard's frame play are drawn, one by one, from their stall seats into the action on the stage. The murdered man proves to be still another theatre critic, who has already been murdered in the imagination of Moon, the second-stringer. As each critic discovers the identity of the corpse, he is shot by a character claiming to be "the real Inspector Hound" as well as the long lost husband of the titled heroine, and, more sinisterly, the third-string reviewer.

Shuffling identities, *The Real Inspector Hound* is a farce that pirouettes around a hackneyed thriller and the hackneyed responses of overworked reviewers: "Derivative, of course." Inventively, Stoppard blends the two strands of burlesque. Trespassing upon the traditional separation of characters from critics, Stoppard tosses the same sentences of dialogue into different mouths, so that the whole *Hound* thrives on *déjà entendu* in a new farcical configuration.

Other invented plays within the play maintain strict boundaries between stage and spectator. Political playwrights can disorient an audience by plunging at once into the inner play, and only later revealing it as a play within the framing play. The audience is thus compelled to reassess its own perspective. Howard Brenton, whose dramaturgy thrives on shock, entitles his whole play after its inner play in his *The Churchill Play* (1974) – the whole, as indicated in Chapter 2, emblematic of contemporary England.

To begin the action four members of the British armed forces stand guard over Churchill's bier. They are transfixed when Churchill abruptly emerges from his coffin.[7] At this point, when the original audience was shocked by the iconoclasm, Brenton halts the action, to shift us abruptly to the frame play for another shock. Set in the future (when first written), an English concentration camp is named after Churchill. Within this totalitarian context, a liberal medical officer has encouraged the camp's inmates to present a performance for the visit of a parliamentary committee. That visit is a hypocritical formality, since the members are empowered only to rubber-stamp the actions of the monolithic government. Nevertheless, "the Churchill play" goes on – for the fictional audience, and for us, the real audience in the theatre. Much later in the play Brenton again raises the inner curtain – a Union Jack – upon "the Churchill play." Although we are again confronted with four soldiers guarding Churchill's bier, the dialogue is more formal and aggressive. Our own witness is now mirrored in that of the parliamentary committee. (In the 1988 RSC

---

7 Brenton has revealed that emergence as the germ of the play: "I had the idea of [Churchill's] coming out of the catafalque in Westminster Hall while he was lying in state, coming out and addressing the young soldiers around him" (*Voices*, p. 95).

revival, we saw the reduced makeshift stage behind a row of parliamentary backs.) As the critic David Ian Rabey points out: "To react like the surrogate audience is to lay oneself open to the same charges that are levelled at the surrogate audience (snobbery, complacency, complicity in social repression, self-congratulatory class-consciousness), whereas to sympathize with the performers' aggressive efforts is to side with a subversive force" (Rabey, *British and Irish Political Drama*, p. 146).

Blatantly critical of Churchill ("God rot great men") and evocative of popular contempt for him, the inner play appals the committee, who are soon at the mercy of the actors armed to escape. One of the rebels goes berserk, however, and fires a sten gun through the outer wall of the concentration camp. This alerts external forces, and the rebels are soon surrounded. They have the choice between surrender or a suicidal shootout. While they debate, the electric power is cut off. In the dark the commanding officer's wife pleads: "Don't let the future . . ." But the rebels may have no future, since Brenton's play ends with searchlights blinding them while their names are called over loudspeakers.

In revision for the 1988 RSC production, Brenton added the line: "The Third World War." The giant searchlights were turned into the audience, and putatively speaking for us, the ex-journalist inmate moans: "I never noticed." With his habitual hostility toward bourgeois audiences, Brenton is accusing us, the audience, of never noticing the erosion of liberty, until Britain becomes a network of concentration camps.

The Churchill Play shrieks Brenton's denial of the national myth of the Second World War: that a great man united Britain against a common enemy. In 1965, a decade before Brenton wrote *The Churchill Play*, the war leader's funeral was reported in newspapers throughout the world, and some of those headlines were reprinted in the program of the 1988 revival by the RSC. Wood's *Dingo* preceded *The Churchill Play* in its indictment of Churchill, but that was confined to a single scene. Between the plays of Wood and Brenton, the historian Angus Calder published *The People's War*, which documents the selfishness of the leaders, especially as contrasted with the sacrifices of the nameless people. Brenton reflects and contributes to the revaluation of Churchill's military ethic. Interviewed in 1988, Brenton insisted that his play was, unfortunately, more relevant than ever in a climate of shrinking civil liberties. Relevant it might be, but its first act is also undramatically freighted with an overlong exposition of England as a vast concentration camp. Most of the vigor of Brenton's *The*

Churchill Play lies in the subverted patriotism of the inner play – a vigor he was unable to sustain through the remainder of what should have been one long act of rising tension.

World War II also lurks in the background of a more recent and inventive Brenton play, *H. I. D. (Hess Is Dead)* (1989). The free verse frame dissolves into a journalist's interview of Charity Luber, a perhaps insane inmate of an expensive clinic. Widow of a Jewish intelligence agent, Charity shows the journalist videotapes that cast doubt on the official version of the suicide of Hess in Spandau prison. Juxtaposed against historic "facts," and sometimes accompanied by Charity's mime, the video fragments hint at a monstrous Allied conspiracy to preserve the legends of allied solidarity and Nazi disintegration: "We have become specialists, technicians of acceptable truths." Finally, the walls of Spandau prison are pulverized, but they predict future generations of conspiracy in the mammoth lies daily seen on television.

By contrast, David Edgar's *O Fair Jerusalem* (1975) is almost pastoral in its view of World War II. Examined in the chapter on verse drama, Edgar's *Jerusalem* also deserves mention in the context of theatre framing unfamiliar material. Like Barnes in *Red Noses*, Edgar plunges us into 1348, the year the plague reached England. The first five scenes of Edgar's sprawling drama paint medieval society, from the runaway freeman William to a noblewoman illicitly in love with a knight. Edgar also sketches a professional soldier, various levels of the clergy, and itinerant actors. Only in the final scene of the first act do we learn that we have watched a modern rehearsal of a play set in the Middle Ages.

We are still in 1948 when the curtain rises on the opening scene of Act II. A doctor explains to the modern actors (and the modern audience) the symptoms and extent of the plague, whereupon Edgar returns us to 1348: the ravages of the Black Death, the adventures of the runaway William, the separation of the Knight and the Lady whom he impregnated, the emergence of a dangerous preacher: "God is in each stone, and every limb, as sure as in the Eucharist bread. All is divine." As examined in more detail in Chapter 3, the rhythmic variety of the medieval society in the inner play is contained somewhat shakily within the modern prose frame.

Act III opens on that frame, with an argument raging between an ex-bomber actor and the playwright/director who denounces World War II, through the plague as its symbol. Suddenly fainting, the playwright is rushed to the hospital with tubercular meningitis, contracted in Hamburg when he worked among refugee German children bombed out by the British. On this suspense in the frame play, the medieval play continues. Easter Saturday witnesses the end of the plague, but the Lady dies in childbirth, the itinerant player adopts her baby, and the professional soldier stores gunpowder for the next war. Only the commoner William is heartened by the end of the plague. The mad actor closes the long, dense inner play with "Mebbe it's waiting," with the indefinite pronoun "it" applicable to plague and war alike.

The Clerk mounts the pulpit and announces that the plague killed one-third of the population of Europe. Then, without a break, he speaks *in propria persona* as a modern clergyman, to announce the casualties of the two atomic bombs dropped in August, 1945. Not expecting the sermon, the contemporary actors are confused, and matters are hardly clarified by the sudden appearance of the playwright, cured of his meningitis by streptomycin. For the first time in history mankind has the means of "eradicating war, disease and poverty," so that Fair Jerusalem is no longer a utopian fantasy. Yet no modern professional theatre has been drawn to Edgar's rough interweaving of two historical periods through the technique of the play within the play, with the inner play inflated by further plays of the medieval actor Ham.[8]

Like Edgar's *O Fair Jerusalem*, Charles Wood's *Veterans* (1972) juxtaposes two historical periods: the present day and, minimally, the mid-nineteenth-century *The Charge of the Light Brigade*. That title refers not to Tennyson's poem but to a film which was actually scripted by Wood. However, the film action of the inner play remains offstage, in this parody of two old male film primadonnas, whereas a film within the play is obstreperously onstage in Wood's *Has "Washington" Legs* (1978). Conceiving a film about the American Revolution to be marketed during the Bicentennial Year 1976, an American producer hires a burly, foul-mouthed director, patterned on John Huston, and an outdated English dramatist. In a perfect non-meeting of minds, the American John Bean and the Englishman Sir Flute, on location in Ireland, go their separate ways while the cameras turn. Burlesque monologues of film clichés punctuate De Mille-type mass scenes. On foot, the director John Bean agitates for more action: "Hey, hey you guys gimme a piece of the shit here . . . Bayonets, I want bayonets . . . *He spins round and an* EXTRA *gives him a bayonet where he would least*

8 A later Edgar play, *Entertaining Strangers* (revised 1988), weaves an ancient Mummers' play sparingly into a nineteenth-century action. "The mummers' play itself is a compound of many," rarely intruding into the main play's narrative line.

want it." Still directing the film action, John Bean dies, and the camera keeps turning. Sir Flute, shot with an arrow, asks for his fee as the stage curtain comes down on the film and on Wood's spoof of the film industry. Caricatured to a man, the characters indulge their author's verbal facility. It is as though Wood, frustrated by his work in the more visual medium of film, opened the verbal floodgates for the stage.

In the 1980s left-wing playwrights of the 1970s have diverged. One of the most overtly political, David Edgar has been active in community theatre and small experimental houses, as well as in large subsidized theatres. Also ready to shift venues, Howard Brenton continues to focus most of his plays on the underprivileged, whereas his occasional collaborator David Hare confines the underprivileged to the relentless background of his middle-class characters. This is most explicit in *A Map of the World* (1982), another play opening on its fictional inner play. To a Bombay Unesco conference on poverty come a young English journalist, a black American woman journalist, a young American actress named Peggy, and – reluctantly – an Indian comic novelist who lives in Surrey, England. A long exposition presents the Englishman and the Indian competing for Peggy's favors, but the scene ends abruptly when she appears. In its first London performance the lights brightened, and the actors suddenly shifted to a melodramatic key. Only then do we learn that we have been viewing an inner play, which is a movie based on a novel, which is in turn based on "fact." The scene has been filmed for a visitor, who is the original of the actress Peggy. When she protests against the fictionality of the filmed scene, Hare's play jumps into flashback, perhaps in the mind of the "real" Peggy.

At the conference on poverty the Indian novelist is expected to antagonize Third World delegates. He is therefore asked to preface his speech with an implicit disclaimer: "Fiction, by its very nature, distorts and misrepresents reality . . ." Outraged by this maneuver, the novelist nevertheless consents to participate in a debate against the radical English journalist, with Peggy offering herself to the winner.

Act II of *A Map of the World* is reminiscent of Pirandello's *Six Characters*, as the film actors are preoccupied with themselves until the filming starts again – set in the bedroom where Peggy has spent the night with Mehta. Soon, however, the movie rises to a loftier plane as the Englishman pleads with the Indian to help alleviate poverty in the world, even if that involves lies and loss of face. Then, withdrawing from the debate in order to work among the poor of India, the Englishman departs. We are shifted back to the frame for the entrance of the "actual" Indian novelist, who summarizes the core of his novel which the film neglects: "The novelist is accused of dalliance and asked to put a value on what he has seen as a passing affair. The actress questions her easy promiscuity and is made to realize adulthood will involve choice. And the journalist assumes the confidence of his own beliefs . . . And is killed."

Having married Peggy in "real" life, the novelist is somewhat reassured by the enthusiasm of the actors – "All the warmth, all the kindness we can bring, we will bring." The cameras turn again for a short scene depicting the pride and misery of a Third World delegate. As the film crew start back toward London, the Indian novelist murmurs what he has learned from the dead Englishman: "The feeling, finally, that we may change things – this is at the centre of everything we are. Lose that . . . lose that, lose everything."

Within the slender frame – will a novelist accept the filming of his novel? – Hare has enfolded scenes of a fictional film within a play to dramatize his favorite theme, the ethic of private behavior in a world mapped by inequities. Before pop stars publicized famine in the Third World, Hare committed his concern to a drama centered on the old device of the play within the play. Explicit in its statement of ethics, *A Map of the World* achieves some dynamic tension between the film actors and the "real" characters they enact, both played by the same actors in actual performance. Upon the actors of Peggy and Mehta, Hare also imposes the burden of more mature reflection. Hare's Peggy objects to the tone and the factual errors of the film, but Mehta, aware that "Everything is wrong," resigns himself to the betrayal – presumably because he is charmed by the youth of the actors. The death of the English journalist may have converted the Indian novelist to work for social change, but Hare's play omits the effect of such virtue on a *comic* writer. Hare's Pirandellian play of theatre and reality is theatrically lively, but it too often fails to shade the filmed scenes from putative reality.

Within the genre of farce Michael Frayn need not grapple with such serious concerns. In his review Michael Billington makes large claims for Frayn's *Noises Off* (1982). "In one sense *Noises Off* panders to our sadistic delight in things that go wrong: in another, it is a very intelligent joke about the fragility of all forms of drama." Despite inflation of a slight play to "all forms of drama," Frayn's farce has sent box-office takings soaring for both amateurs and professionals.

Frayn focuses on stereotypical actors who first rehearse, and then perform, a farce in the English hinterland. The setting is a *Mousetrap*-type country house, with that necessity for farce, an "extensive range of entrances and exits." In Act I we view the stage from the audience perspective; in the frantic Act II the set has been turned 180 degrees, and we are behind the stage (of a different theatre); in Act III we are back at the front again (at still another theatre), savoring the knowledge of backstage error – especially in the wittily designed set of Michael Annals.

The inevitable country-house set is at least as vital as the several characters: a fading actress who plays the all-important housekeeper of the premises, her new young lover who plays a dashing philanderer, his current victim – in the inner play – who is having an affair with the director, a dull actor who plays the owner of the farcical mansion, a backstage gossip who plays his wife, a drunken old star who is being given "one last chance" as a burglar and also as a sheikh who wishes to buy the English country house, doubled by the dull actor who can barely remember the cues for a single part, much less two. A stage-manager and a prop-girl understudy all the parts of the happily confusing and aptly named inner play – *Nothing On*.

In the Act I rehearsal, the actors substitute their own words for those of the script, they battle with recalcitrant properties, and they are leaden-gestured at points where alacrity is essential. By Act II a month later, several cross-couplings have taken place in the frame play, and these are evidenced in the interstices of the inner farce that we hear as noises off, since we are backstage. Out front the show goes on, but we see the actors emerge dizzyingly from the various exits, to live their real life in mime. By Act III *Nothing On* has suffered further improvisation, and three burglars enter the final scene, instead of the one thief demanded by the script: "I thought I heard my voice." Undaunted, they recite in unison, until the two understudies slither off. Despite residual confusion, the outer farce meshes with the inner one in a hastily improvised wedding prediction for the director and the stage-manager he impregnated. Far from the noises off of the title, it is the adroitly timed incompetence onstage in an invented play entitled *Nothing On* that has delighted audiences conversant with the mechanics of farce.

When Frayn, perhaps misled by ponderous readings of *Noises Off*, seeks deeper metatheatre, he loses both humor and depth. His *Look Look* (1990) attempts to stage the audience, but a disaffected playwright comments on these stereotypical spectators, and Frayn feels compelled in the second act to thrust the spectators into onstage roles. Half-spectator and half-actor, no single role coheres, and the play staggers from auditorium to stage without ever attaining equilibrium.

Tom Stoppard, in contrast, can introduce erudite subjects into farce and still maintain a tightrope balance. The urbane dialogue of *The House of Cards*, the invented inner play that opens Tom Stoppard's *The Real Thing* (1982), sounds like its author's nimble prose. Although Stoppard's playwright has the same Christian name as his amateur actor, Henry Carr of *Travesties*, he is in command of his language and memory, if not of his feelings. Since Stoppard's protagonist Henry is a comic playwright (with Roger Rees originally juggling the epigrams), his wit is plausible. In the frame play as in the inner play, as in the English comic tradition stemming from the Restoration, aphorisms dance around adultery. The infidelity dramatized in the fictional *House of Cards* soon penetrates the frame play as well. The wife deceives her husband in *The House of Cards*, and the actress who plays the wife deceives her husband about her love affair with the playwright Henry. Before we know that, however, Stoppard creates one of his most inventive stage effects: since the fictional philanderess lies that she went to Switzerland, she brings her husband a glass-enclosed snow scene. As the cuckolded husband shakes it and sobs, the snow envelops the whole stage in a spectacular non-realistic lighting effect.

Although Stoppard shows us no more of *The House of Cards*, he teases us with another fictional play within the play, *The Real Thing*. After the once adulterous playwright Henry is married to his actress, he finds it difficult to write her into the drama she requests – about a young political activist who has composed a play even though he is a "lout with language." Eventually, Henry does manage to revise the activist's script, but we hear only a few maudlin lines of his text – "I'll wait for you and for everything to change." On their own ground husband and wife, playwright and actress, prove to be happily compatible in their dislike of the rude young radical whose play they have produced. For all Henry's sophisticated wit in adultery plays, however, he suffers at his actress-wife's casual affair with an actor who played not only the radical activist, but also the brother-lover in Ford's *'Tis Pity She's a Whore* and the servant-lover in Strindberg's *Miss Julie*. As Hersh Zeifman summarizes these fragmented theatrical forays: "The love scenes from Ford and Strindberg function, structurally, as deliberately theatrical, 'artificial' models against which we are meant to judge the 'real' love of Stoppard's central characters" (Zeifman, "Comedy of Ambush," p. 146).

Suffering at his wife's adultery, the playwright Henry nevertheless learns to appreciate the stability of his marriage. By the end of Stoppard's play, the theatre couple are preparing for bed when they receive a telephone call from the actor who played the husband in the invented *House of Cards*; he announces his forthcoming marriage. Stoppard's play closes on Henry listening to the radio – "I'm a Believer" – and assuring the telephoning lover: "Yes, I'm still here." Both "here" and "believing," Henry is finally a happy man. Despite the brittle dialogue in both the frame play and the opening fictional play, Stoppard dramatizes the love between the playwright Henry and the actress Annie as indeed "the real thing."

Some fifteen years separate the only two Stoppard titles that boast the word "real," and it is a perverse word for a canny dramatist who has factored theatre in the theatre into several non-realistic forms examined in this survey: his plays comment upon themselves, juggle popular arts and learned allusions, leapfrog through classics or bounce about novelties, and always slide gracefully among the slippages of language; even an adaptation like *Rough Crossing* embeds an invented musical comedy in the rather silly action of the main play. Stoppard has challenged Pirandello's theatre trilogy with his own tetralogy – *Rosencrantz and Guildenstern Are Dead*, *The Real Inspector Hound*, *Travesties*, and *The Real Thing*. No other playwright resorts so consistently to theatre in the theatre, dynamically inventive in the forms of his play. Yet Stoppard's essential center – the real thing – remains a well-intentioned apolitical bumbler endowed with amusing logorrhea.

In this post-Pirandello time, theatre about theatre has become a staple of farce; Nichols, Ayckbourn, Wood, and Frayn brightly marry these two old forms. In a serious context, Bond in *The Sea* ridicules his inner play to discredit its actors, who are oblivious of what he views as the real thing – man's rational control of his destiny. As an honorable old device, theatre in the theatre has served Osborne's nostalgia and Saunders' existentialism, but the social criticism of Edgar, Hare, and Brenton sometimes seems at odds with so baroque a technique. In extending theatre in the theatre to its several popular forms, contemporary playwrights sometimes subvert those forms. Highlighting the artifice of theatre, all these metatheatrical dramatists flaunt a style rather than vaunt the real, in the wake of the naturalists. But is there a residual real to be salvaged from style?

6

Splitting images of the mind

Thus play I in one person many people
And none contented.   (Richard II)

Britain's position in the world. Screw that. What about my position?
                    (Bill Maitland in John Osborne's *Inadmissible Evidence*)

Critics of contemporary realism read binary divisions into drama –
not only surface and depth, but individual and society. However,
these divisions are also exposed by non-realistic means. In this
chapter, I focus on non-realistic devices that explore the individual
private life, and in my final chapter I travel through plays set in the
past, with contemporary England at their guilty heart.

Surface realism lubricates the mechanical plot of the late nineteenth-century problem play. In that time of confused copyrights
English dramatists appropriated The Repentant Adulteress of the
French problem play, but even less in England than in France did she
actually figure as an important social problem. By the turn of the
twentieth century Shaw creatively misread Ibsen as the defender of
unwomanly women and the attacker of villainous idealists. In Shaw's
view, Ibsen cleared the path for his own dramas of wider social
problems – slum landlordism, aberrant nationalism, divided families,
double sexual standards. For the most part Shaw corseted these
problems in the conventional form of the well-made play, even
though he mocked that form as Sardoodledom.

With his favorite play *Back to Methusaleh* (1921), however, laboriously composed when he was in his sixties, Shaw discarded the
frame of realism to render his cosmic vision. Still thinking on a global
and extratemporal scale, Shaw also gave expression to the inner life in
St. Joan (1923), the favorite Shaw play of many critics. Shaw's Joan is
at times deeply divided, buffeted between worldly forces and hea-
venly voices that inspired her to defy those forces. As Shaw wrote in

his preface to the play: "There are people in the world whose imagination is so vivid that when they have an idea it comes to them as an audible voice, sometimes uttered by a visible figure."

Before the advent of realism some two millennia of European drama conveyed a character's inner turmoil not so much by projected voices as by dreams, ghosts, and especially soliloquies, but twentieth-century English playwrights were slow to depict torment through such non-realistic devices. The main exception is T. S. Eliot in the plays he completed before World War II. His Thomas à Becket is confronted by four personified temptations in *Murder in the Cathedral*; his Henry Monchesney is haunted by recriminatory Erinyes in *The Family Reunion*. Other modern Christian playwrights adopted this allegorical mode, but most secular dramatists observed the conventions of realism, as did Eliot himself in his plays of the second half-century, when he concealed his verse line and subtle symbols.

In contrast, a number of intense dramas on the postwar English stage, inspired perhaps by American tragedies, glided between a world of daily familiarity and one of dreams, ghosts, doubles, or distortions. At mid-century powerful American dramas are centered on characters who tremble on the edge of madness: Blanche DuBois in *A Streetcar Named Desire* (1947), Willy Loman in *Death of a Salesman* (1949), and Mary Tyrone in *Long Day's Journey into Night* (1941, but first performed 1956). We empathize with these characters whose fantasies could not be contained within realistic frames. Music accompanies Blanche's hallucinations; Willy Loman zigzags through time and place; Mary Tyrone becomes Ophelia.

Slower than Americans to puncture the surface of realism, English playwrights did so differently. By 1960 Arden was firmly on epic ground, whereas Osborne retreated from staging England into representations of mind and nerves. During the 1960s both the geographical and the social spectrum were broadened on the London stage. But by the 1970s and all the more in the 1980s, English theatre moved away from social problems and into the individual mind, especially the workings of the unconscious, which was probed by means of dreams, ghosts, doubles, and images of distortion.

Dreams

In the Greek tragedies that seeded the drama of secular Europe, dreams are narrated rather than dramatized. We may recall the nightmares of worried mothers, Atosca and Clytemnestra in Aeschylus' *The Persians* and *The Oresteia* respectively, but these intimations of another world vanish from the tragedies of Euripides, only to return with a literal vengeance in the bloody melodramas of Roman Seneca. Inspired by that Latin source, Shakespeare also blends dreams and ghosts to signal a guilty conscience or an impending catastrophe. Richard III sees no less than eleven ghosts of those he murdered; Hamlet's father's ghost (perhaps played by Shakespeare himself) is one of the most famous and difficult roles in world theatre, but Banquo's silent ghost is as tensely dramatic.

Whereas we *see* these Shakespearean ghosts, we rarely enter into his characters' dreams. An exception is Pericles, dreaming of the goddess Diana, whose injunction leads him to a happy reunion with his wife, thought dead. In other Shakespeare plays, however, we hear about unghosted dreams – narration as opposed to presentation. So, too, in realistic drama of the nineteenth century: Strindberg's Miss Julie and Jean tell one another of symbolic dreams, but not until thirteen years later, in *A Dream Play* of 1901, does the Swedish writer actually stage a dream. Yet his dreamer's consciousness is less theatrical than his innovative characters, which "split, double, and multiply; they evaporate, crystallize, scatter and converge" (Author's Note to *A Dream Play*).

Strindberg's heady legacy was treasured by both the Expressionists and the Surrealists, but English realists ignored it. Even the less realistic, more venturesome playwrights treat dreams gingerly, and one Royal Court director is quite hostile to them: "I don't fancy dream scenes and have no original idea of how to set about staging them" (Stafford-Clark, *Letters to George*, p. 183). Yet directors are confronted with such staging when dramatists convey mental disturbance through making dreams concrete on stage. Absent from the drama of the 1970s, dreams appear fitfully in English plays of the 1980s.

Michael Frayn's *Make and Break* (1980) is a case in point, but the dream clashes with the remainder of the basically realistic drama. As the title implies, Frayn's play is a satire on cut-throat business practices – on the part of a firm that sells partitioning systems. (That product inspired Michael Annals, under Michael Blakemore's direction, to design a display of moving doors which would have honored a farce.) Some dozen characters swell the cast – employees or clients of the firm – but two principals soon emerge. Garrard's entire life is dedicated to his business, but his old friend Olley can still summon humane impulses in this ruthless world.

To each of these opposing characters Frayn accords a nightmare. After seducing his secretary, Garrard dozes off. In his dream he sees *"people appear and disappear and reappear in different combinations of salesman and customer."* The dream tells us nothing about Garrard that was not obvious in his wakened state, but perhaps its anxieties prime us to think "heart attack" when the indefatigable businessman suffers from sudden pains. Instead of heart trouble, however, Garrard's pain is diagnosed as a slipped disk, which the hotel doctor swiftly puts right.

Garrard's old friend Olley, exhausted and still worried about him, dreams of Garrard in a coffin, and, improbably, he tries to comfort the ruthless profiteer by fragmentary Buddhist sayings, which were earlier spoken outside his hearing. Again the dream reveals nothing new about the character, but the coffin sets the stage for Olley's own death before the night is over. When his body is discovered in the morning, Olley's colleagues utter a few platitudes, whereupon Garrard conducts business as usual. Dreams prove intrusive in this realistic satire with a foregone conclusion.

Howard Brenton, who often revels in non-realistic devices, designates his first full-length play, *Revenge* (1969), as a nightmare, but since the action consists of a long cops-and-robbers chase, with the same actor playing cop and robber, I delay further comment until consideration of Doubling. Similarly, in Brenton's *Thirteenth Night* (1981) a leader of the Labor Party has a nightmare that is patterned on *Macbeth* (as discussed in Chapter 4). Rather than revelations of the unconscious, Brenton's staged dreams function as political warnings to the audience: in the earlier play countrywide corruption has eclipsed the individual entrepreneur, as the criminal Hepple realizes: "My dream of a criminal England, it's all come true with the 1980s." In the nightmare of *Thirteenth Night* power-struggles within a socialist party grow monstrously criminal, proving more deadly than the struggle against fascism.

Caryl Churchill never commits a whole play to dreams, but they occupy the strategic beginning and end of her *Top Girls* (1983), lifting it beyond realism. The play opens on the elaborate dream of the protagonist Marlene, and it closes in the whimpering fright of her unacknowledged daughter who has had a nightmare. Although Churchill's opening scene has been widely admired, it is not always recognized as a dream, which predicts the closing nightmare.

In celebration of Marlene's promotion to manager of the Top Girls employment agency, she invites to dinner (in the Prima Donna Restaurant!) five "top girls" of myth and history: a nineteenth-century Victorian traveler, a ninth-century female pope, a thirteenth-century Japanese courtesan, Chaucer's Patient Griselda, and Breugel's Dull Gret (the only lower class character, who also attracted Brecht).

Across centuries and continents Churchill's top girls reveal the sacrificial basis of their celebrity – particularly Patient Griselda, the last to arrive. Marlene's main function in this dream scene is to elicit the details of the celebrity of her guests, but she is often distracted by her attention to the items on the contemporary menu. The banquet ends chaotically, with Gret's populist speech drowning out Pope Joan's Latin, with the Japanese courtesan weeping and the hostess Marlene drinking the brandy of her Victorian guest who is oblivious to her surroundings. Marlene's dream of celebration fragments into a nightmare. "The visual lesson of the opening scene . . . is to recognize the cultural relativity of certain norms" (Marohl, "De-Realized Women," p. 383). Marlene's smart modern clothes – not described in Churchill's text – are revealed as another period costume. This all-woman party establishes no feminine community. Each woman is selfishly alone in Marlene's dream, a blatantly non-realistic opening of a play that is otherwise realistically set in contemporary England, where top girls smother their passion and compassion.

Top Girls differs, for example, from Christopher Hampton's *Tales from Hollywood*, where Horvath's adventures among Central European refugees in California are "explained" as a retrospective on his fictional life in the moment before his death. Churchill never explains the non-realistic opening scene of *Top Girls*, but like a dream, it predicts dramatic fact. The top girls of the opening scene have purchased their fame through sacrifice; so, we learn in the second act, Marlene has purchased her executive status through the sacrifice of her daughter and her class identity. To make that point, Churchill violates chronology, setting the play's final scene a year before the main action of the remainder of the play. In performance, however, or in hasty reading, this time-shift passes unnoticed, and *Top Girls* ends on the nightmare of Marlene's daughter, who whimpers: "Frightening." We are never told, much less shown, the contents of the girl's nightmare, but her reaction – "Frightening" – reflects retroactively on all Top Girls.

My bald summary neglects Churchill's inventive theatricality for the opening dream scene: resplendent costumes, more or less familiar legends, and free verbal associations enliven the stage, even while we absorb the forms of gender oppression in the several cultural contexts. Although the initial scene of *Top Girls* does not, like the parallel scene of Churchill's *Cloud 9*, function in the plot, it does heighten the thematic resonance, relieving Churchill's drama from problem play tedium. As a discerning critic perceives: "The first scene prepares the audience to perceive the play's subsequent scenes in the light of

7 Act I of *Top Girls* by Caryl Churchill, directed by Max Stafford-Clark at the Royal Court, 1982

culturally-conditioned ideology," but it does so theatrically and not doctrinally (Marohl, "De-Realized Women," p. 386).

I close this swift survey of the few dream plays on the contemporary stage with Trevor Griffiths' *Real Dreams* (1986, two years after an American production). Adapted from a story by Jeremy Pikser, Griffiths creates a soliloquizing character with that author's name, who has a vivid dream of revolutionary action in the reactionary United States. Griffiths converts the original ironic ending of Pikser's book to revolutionary promise, which is predicted by the dream. A quondam dropout enunciates the hope: "But these are dreams that will not go away. These are real dreams." Unlike its source, Griffiths' play closes on Tai Chi exercises of members of the collective; they recite a Ho Chi Minh prison poem. Finally, a dangerous and drunken Puerto Rican raises the Sandinista flag. Although Griffiths labels the collective dreams as real, the final naive optimism contradicts the thrust of the body of his basically realistic play. Both in Griffiths' political drama and Frayn's anti-business play, dreams seem too facile an escape-route from realism.

Ghosts

Like dreams, theatre ghosts are often predictive or retributive. Dramatic tension may be aroused by the selective visibility of a ghost, as when Hamlet but not Gertrude is privy to old Hamlet's words, or when, in a completely different tone, Coward's blithe spirit is apparent only to her quondam husband and not his new wife. Unlike dreams, which are more often narrated than staged, ghosts appear in the problematic flesh, as it were.

Ghosts are palpably present in the theatre of other times and other cultures. In Japanese theatre the Ghost Noh is an important genre, which has influenced both Yeats and Beckett, but ghosts also materialize in earlier Western drama. In one of the earliest Greek tragedies, *The Persians* by Aeschylus, the Ghost of Darius, the dead Persian king, pleads the cause of peace. A rare shade in Greek tragedy, ghosts run rife in the melodramas of Roman Seneca – Achilles, Tantalus, Thyestes, and a whole underworld in his *Oedipus* (adapted by Ted Hughes and directed by Peter Brook in 1968). In Seneca's wake vengeful ghosts people Elizabethan drama, causing staging problems for some contemporary directors of Shakespeare. However Romantic drama follows the Bard, it fails to include ghosts, and in post-Ibsen drama ghosts haunt the imagination rather than the stage. Guilt about the past drenches the symbolic realism of Ibsen's *Ghosts* and the embryonic expressionism of Strindberg's *Ghost Sonata*.

In early non-realistic dramas the ghostly figures are recognizably costumed, but occasionally a figure returns from the dead quite casually. *A Scent of Flowers* (1964) by James Saunders is predicated on the stage presence of Zoe after her suicide. Surrounded by family members who understand her only partially or not at all, she engages in selective flashbacks. Only her married lover is absent from the group of characters who variously acknowledge her presence. A success on the West End, the play is an obliquely conventional drama of adultery which is enlarged by a ghostly protagonist. Comparably, the soldiers who return from the dead in Charles Wood's *Dingo* cause the play to resonate beyond horrors of the war. Dingo clings to life in the face of living corpses – his comrade Tanky and the blonde officer – who are unchanged by death. These ghosts are as real to Dingo as the putative German enemy, and Wood blends them into the popular Comic's irrational repertory, as discussed in Chapter 5.

Although Edward Bond calls his theatre Rational, he occasionally introduces otherworldly figures into his plays. Bond gained notoriety through outrageous murders in his first two plays to be performed, the realistic *Pope's Wedding* and *Saved*. He then shifted to political farce in *Early Morning* (1967) with its mordantly unrealistic picture of Victorian society, but Bond blatantly asserted: "The events of this play are true." Those events involve conspiracies and counter-conspiracies against Queen Victoria and her only children, the royal Siamese twins, Arthur and George. Bond's Queen Victoria strangles the Prince Consort Albert with the Royal Garter, but he rises from the grave to urge Crown Prince Arthur to avenge him – even as the paternal Ghost in *Hamlet* – by killing his mother as well as his dependent brother. Unlike old Hamlet, however, Albert's Ghost is chained to his grave; he not only urges death but is locked into it. Ineffectually, the ghostly father tries to cut the dying George away from his brother, but Arthur realizes that he alone can perform that act of severance. Albert's ghost, like that of Hamlet, disappears at cockcrow in one reference to the titular "early morning." A mere episode in Prince Arthur's growth to maturity, Albert's vengeful ghost is as ambitious as the living man ever was – in *Early Morning*.

A far more significant ghost contributes to another royal maturation in Bond's *Lear* (1972). Although that drama was necessarily discussed in the chapter on Shakespeare derivatives, its density justifies consideration in this context too, especially since there are no ghosts in Shakespeare's *King Lear*. The character of the Gravedigger's

Boy seeded Bond's play; in the author's account, "That, incidentally, was the image from which the play grew – this image of the Gravedigger's Boy. In some senses he is much older than Lear and Lear recognizes this – he has been in his grave, and Lear, who is a very old man, has still to go towards it" (*Theatre Quarterly*, [January–March, 1972], p. 8). A refugee king, Bond's Lear is offered shelter by the Gravedigger's Boy, who is a naive man and not a boy. The designation Gravedigger's Boy recalls Lear's Fool, who is often addressed as "Boy," and also Hamlet's Clown-Gravedigger. Moreover, Boy is an apt designation for one so innocent; in the midst of civil war he can think only of private happiness, but not egotistically for himself.

At the home of the Gravedigger's Boy Lear sees his disfigured former courtier Warrington. Believing him to be a ghost, Lear cries out in fear of his own death. However, the imagined ghost presages not the death of Lear, but of Warrington himself and of the Gravedigger's Boy – bloodily. Public purpose is foreign to the Gravedigger's Boy, and his ghost materializes only when Lear wishes to escape from the civil war. Ghost-boy and ex-king comfort each other, and the Ghost is able to whistle other ghosts into presence. Although Lear's daughters Bodice and Fontanelle are still alive, their ghosts arrive to remind Lear of their tender family life in the past. When Lear cannot detain these secondary ghosts, he turns to the Ghost of the Gravedigger's Boy as to a son.

The civil war continues unabated, and the Ghost of the Gravedigger's Boy grows increasingly weak and emaciated. There can be no private life in times of crisis, but the Ghost, who represents private life, appears in three key scenes: when Lear admires the design of his dead daughter's body, when Lear is blinded by the Fourth Prisoner, and when Lear finally confronts the new ruler Cordelia, who was once married to the Gravedigger's Boy. In the first two scenes the Ghost appears because Lear's private pain is too great to admit a public dimension, but in the face-off between a totalitarian Cordelia and a newly democratic Lear, neither pays attention to the Ghost of the Gravedigger's Boy, who is gored offstage by pigs. He stumbles onstage to die in the arms of a cradling Lear: "I love you, I'll always remember you, but I can't help you. Die, for your own sake die!" Because Lear has chosen public action, the private life must die. The Gravedigger's Boy "has been in his grave," but he has learned nothing of social responsibility.

The Gravedigger's Boy is the companion and comfort of Bond's Lear, much like the Fool in Shakespeare's *King Lear*, but the latter helps educate the king to his responsibility: "O, I have taken too little care of this." Bond's Boy, in contrast, innocent of social responsibility himself, cannot teach it to his king. As the private young man's ghost ages and decays, the old man slowly achieves social activism.

Bond embeds the ghost in the very fabric of his Shakespeare off-shoot, *Lear*, but Brenton merely follows the Bard in the ghosts of his *Thirteenth Night*, his 1981 adaptation of *Macbeth*. He also summons them for his own original plays both earlier and later. As previously mentioned, *Revenge* (1969) introduces the ghost of young Albert, a Policeman gunned down by the criminal protagonist Hepple. In a parody of the Senecan revenge tradition, Albert's ghost urges revenge upon the arch-enemies, Hepple the criminal and MacLeish the policeman. But petty murders prove anachronistic in a world that has evolved beyond such retribution to the massive crime of corporate enterprise. Easy to parody, the superfluous ghost reenforces Brenton's abrasive point about ubiquitous corruption in contemporary England.

More haunting is the Ghost of Emily Davison in Brenton's *Epsom Downs* (1977), mentioned in the chapter on staging England. She is Brenton's main device for subverting a festive occasion, whose surface cuts across class and sex differences. The bright holiday is shadowed by the supernatural presence of the woman who committed suicide on Epsom Downs on Derby Day, 1913. The historic Emily Davison, a militant suffragette, threw herself in front of the king's horse, in flagrant protest against women's inequality. She was trampled to death, but her massive funeral cortege alerted the country to women's inequality, whose redress began with the passing of the first Women's Suffrage Bill in 1917. In this Brenton play Davison's ghost is a tragic conscience on a day of general joy.

Like Emily Davison, the ghost in Brenton's *Bloody Poetry* (1984) is a historical figure. The "bloody" of his title puns on literal blood and the common English denigration; in his explanation: "I called it *Bloody Poetry* because of the philistine, playground attitude to poetry and because of the cost – literally in blood" (*Plays and Players* [April 1988], p. 10). The poetry is that of Byron and Shelley; Brenton's view of the latter was influenced by the recent biography by Richard Holmes, *The Pursuit*. In the words of the character Mary Godwin: "They who are in love with life in that way, cause only pain to those around them" – indifferently in Byron's case, unintentionally in Shelley's.

The first of Brenton's two acts dramatizes the meeting in Italy of Byron and Shelley, a meeting engineered by their mistresses, Claire Clairemont and Mary Godwin. The four characters spend a summer of pleasure and poetic composition. Abruptly, the second act opens on the London suicide of Shelley's wife Harriet. After Shelley agrees to marry Mary, he flees from England in her company and that of Claire, but also of Harriet's Ghost: "Hasn't my life become a kind of haunting?" An embodiment of Shelley's conscience, Harriet's Ghost haunts him whenever Byron is absent from the stage, but in the play's final brief scene, when Shelley's body is furled in a sail, Harriet's Ghost remains at the back of the stage while Byron orders "A great big, bloody, beautiful fire!" Shelley has drowned in the sea, but onstage we see the residual emblems of a self split between hedonism and the responsibility symbolized by a ghost – in what Brenton himself calls a Utopian play (*New Theatre Quarterly* [August 1987], p. 199).

Bond and Brenton dramatize their ghosts for symbolic significance, but Louise Page, like James Saunders nearly two decades earlier, treats her returnee from the dead casually. In *Salonika* (1982) that city has been virtually destroyed during World War I. An English mother and her middle-aged daughter arrive to seek the grave of Ben, who died there in battle. They are followed to Greece by the mother's swain, Leonard, who is in his seventies, and on the beach they meet a young Englishman, Peter.

Dead Ben rises from the sand, appearing first to his wife Charlotte, who converses quite naturally with him. He next appears to his daughter Enid, whom he never knew. Ben reappears when Peter and Leonard talk about him. The three men speak briefly of two world wars, as though one of them were not a ghost. Peter reveals his pointless existence in the contemporary world. Ben confesses to Leonard that he didn't die in action but committed suicide by drowning: "I couldn't stand the strain." Briefly, dead Ben and living Leonard compete for Charlotte, but the rivalry fizzles out. Ben suggests that Enid offer Peter money to be her lover, and she does. In the midst of this wooing, however, Peter dies, and Ben advises her not to revive him. Together the ghost father and his middle-aged daughter wash the body of the dead young man. To Enid's comment on the waste, Ben replies: "There were thousands here. Pointless deaths." Charlotte, disillusioned with the living Leonard, abandons him. When the unghostly ghost Ben leaves, mother and daughter are alone again; the women endure, looking at the stars.

This quiet play of courteous conversation indicts both world wars, where young Englishmen were pointlessly slaughtered, but *Salonika* also captures the rootlessness of youth in the 1980s, selling their own blood, only to sleep on foreign beaches; without ties, ideals, or commitments. Salonika, through the agency of its place-bound ghost, is Page's metaphor for the alienation of successive generations of young men, who leave women dissatisfied but interdependent and mutually supportive.

Caryl Churchill intrudes a minor ghost – also a soldier – into *Cloud 9* (1979), but ghosts are central to her *Fen* (1984). Ghosting has a double edge in the earlier play, for ghosts are first invoked as part of the drunken orgy of the contemporary Act II, but the spirits do not manifest themselves. What does appear unbidden is the ghost of Lin's brother Bill, who was killed as a member of the British army in Northern Ireland and who is not listed in the Cast of Characters. There is a sudden contrast between the careless abandon – the cloud nine-ism – of gay Edward, his intermittently gay sister, her lover Lin, and the angry frustration of Bill: "I got so I fucking wanted to kill someone and I got fucking killed myself and I want a fuck." Perhaps a figment of Lin's drunken imagination, Bill is visible to us, and he is the only Act II residue of Churchill's Act I equation of sexism and colonialism.

More critical are the ghosts in Churchill's *Fen*, a less flamboyant but more searching play. *Fen* is composed of twenty-one brief scenes on the English fen (strikingly designed by Annie Smart, so that even interiors were pervaded by the field laboriously tilled by women). The slender plot focuses on Val, who is buffeted between her love for Frank, who has left his own wife and children, and her love of her two daughters, whom she leaves with their father. Ostracized in her own community, incapable of choosing between children and lover, Val informs Frank: "One of us better die I think." Violence is the only recourse in these brutalized lives on the fen. Before the middle of the play a field-owner is briefly confronted by a ghost in nineteenth-century clothes: "I been working in this field a hundred and fifty years." Brooding and rebellious, the nameless Ghost expresses the festering fen anger that is vented in random cruelties, and this helps us understand Frank's murder of Val – by her request. That murder triggers the wholly non-realistic ending of the play. Frank kills Val with a hatchet and hides her body in a wardrobe, then *"sits on the floor with his back against the wardrobe door. [Val] comes in through the door on the other side of the stage."* In effect she is a ghost.

Instead of dwelling on her personal grief, however, Val's ghost reviews the ubiquitous suffering on the fen – of dead and living alike. The voices of the fen women repeat phrases we have heard earlier, and two cruel stories run parallel: Val murdered by Frank and Angela tormented by her stepmother. Frank complains: "I've killed the only person I love." Val's ghost tries to comfort him: "It's what I wanted." But he accuses her: "You should have wanted something different."

All the voices of the fen women, subject to the cruelties born of their cruel condition, "should have wanted something different." The two ghosts, one a nineteenth-century figure symbolizing all the women and the other a victimized protagonist, etch the fen life indelibly against the relentless background of hoeing in the fog-drenched fields.

A ghost joins other unrealistic characters (e.g. an angel, a vampire, and a dog) in Churchill's only play to be set outside of Britain. *Mad Forest* (1990) is the result of a collaboration between Churchill and personnel of the Central School of Drama on a "Romania project." After a week in Romania in spring 1990, the English company returned to London and began rehearsals in May for a series of performances in June. Even as a new dictatorship claimed Romania, Churchill used documentary material, eyewitness accounts, and her own structuring imagination to dramatize the texture of experience in that unfortunate country. Against a many-layered background, Churchill etches two families, one accommodating to the Ceausescu regime, and the other divided in its attitude. An elementary school-teacher in the first family, parroting the required lessons, can talk intimately only to the ghost of her dead grandmother, who accuses her of being far more dead. Listed in the program as "Grandmother," this ghost is not so much the schoolteacher's conscience as a prod to feeling in a stultifying atmosphere.

Churchill, Bond, and Brenton have accustomed audiences to their deviations from realism, and there is no indication that ghosts occasioned them more difficulty than any other non-realistic convention. All three playwrights are deft with parody of a traditional device – Churchill the opening dream of *Top Girls*; Bond and Brenton the ghosts of *Early Morning* and *Revenge* respectively. More searchingly than in parody, however, the three radical playwrights situate ghosts in a social context; in a time of civil strife, Bond's Lear has to conquer his inclination to a private uncommitted life, represented by the Ghost of the Gravedigger's Boy. The ghosts of two historical women, Emily Davison and Harriet Shelley, sound dissonant notes in their respective plays: by the recollection of her suicide at Epsom Downs, Emily Davison pierces the surface of a mindless holiday, and by *her* suicide Harriet Shelley shadows great poetry with its "bloody" cost. Most subtly, Caryl Churchill's nameless ghosts prepare a rebellious union of the living and the dead on the fen. In the final scenic direction of *Fen* a woman who never sang finally sings. It might serve as a metaphor for these voices of the dead.

Doubles

In the contemporary stretch beyond realism, the schizoid pace of urban life favors several kinds of dramatic doubling. Dramatic doubles differ from performance doubles where a single actor plays more than one role, a strategy which is at least as old as Greek tragedy and which is prevalent today for economic reasons. In other instances, deliberate doubling brings sparkle to a performance, as when a single actor plays both twins of Shakespeare's *Comedy of Errors*, or when Caryl Churchill in *Cloud 9* leaves to the particular ensemble the doubling of roles in Acts I and II. I am concerned, however, with doubling that is written into the dramatic text, removing the play from surface realism. At its simplest, this device functions like an extension of the soliloquy: a character speaks certain words aloud, but the same actor also admits us into her or his theoretically unspoken thoughts. More intricate are the rare plays in which a character plays more than one part, with the script calling for two actors. Most complicated is the schizophrenic splitting of a single character, necessitating two actors.

Bodies by James Saunders is an example of the extended soliloquy. Commissioned by a Richmond fringe theatre in 1977, *Bodies* moved on to the Hampstead Theatre in 1978. In Act I the stage is split between two living-rooms, each containing a middle-aged married couple. And the dialogue is split between naturalistic conversations within each married couple and unnaturalistic monologues – of each of the four characters. A decade earlier, the bodies had cross-coupled, and after years apart the couples meet again. Saunders' first act deftly dovetails the intensity of memory with the placidity of the present, and that becomes the theme of the straightforwardly realistic second act. One couple has undergone psychotherapy and can dismiss the past: "When it happened, it meant what it meant. Now, it means nothing." In the other couple, however, the husband Mervyn cherishes human irrationality that was earlier expressed through bodies rather than words.

The play loses tension in Act II, when the predictable disillusions are set against the background of Mervyn's dying student – an invisible body *in extremis*. Brooding on Mervyn's valorization of a poet's work above his life, that student had suicidally run his motorcycle into a wall. While the middle-aged bodies preserve social decorum, a young body is dying on a life-support system. At the end of *Bodies* Mervyn's drunken praise of the irrational as the quintessentially human is punctuated by the telephone call that announces the death of the idealistic adolescent. The two sides of the four characters – an effective doubling into conscious and unconscious aspects – highlight Saunders' effort to escape a banal realistic tale of adultery.

Tom Stoppard, whose several non-realistic devices have been examined in other chapters, cleaves unusually closely to realism in *Night and Day* (1978). Like James Saunders in *Bodies* a year earlier, Stoppard splits a single character, Ruth Carson, into her spoken and unspoken thoughts. The title *Night and Day* apparently refers to two sides of the play's only woman. Stoppard prefaces the play with a rather elaborate note on his doubling device: "When Ruth's thoughts are audible she is simply called 'Ruth' in quotes, and treated as a separate character. Thus, Ruth can be interrupted by 'Ruth.' This rule is also loosely applied to the first scene of Act Two, where the situation is somewhat different." Quotes are of course invisible to a theatre audience, and in the original performance it was not always evident when Ruth was speaking or thinking. Stoppard is correct that the device is "loosely applied."

What is puzzling is why Stoppard should have resorted to this brief throwback to the technique of *Strange Interlude*. O'Neill, reading about schizophrenia, assigned stage asides to thoughts that dared not be spoken – on the 1928 New York stage. A half-century later, however, Ruth is a privileged member of a wealthy household, and she speaks her mind at will. Wife of a mining engineer and mother of his son, Ruth Carson has had a one-night London fling with the veteran journalist Dick Wagner, and back home in Africa she is attracted to the young journalist Jake Milne. As the critic Tim Brassell notes: "What Stoppard broadly sets up is an emotional alliance between Ruth and Wagner on the one hand and 'Ruth' and Milne on the other" (*Tom Stoppard*, p. 216). When Dick Wagner fortuitously arrives in Ruth's African home, her unconscious has nothing to say. Only after her conscious mind parries witty thrusts does Ruth's shadow self (1) find Wagner unattractive in the sober light of Africa, (2) feel guilt toward her husband, whom she placates with imaginary confessions, and (3) toward the end of Act I express her attraction to young Jake Milne.

In Act II, however, it is a very vocal Ruth who woos Jake whereas "Ruth" is reserved for political comments that she stifles in the presence of the dictator of the fictional African state. Once Ruth in quotes calls for help from Jesus Christ, and twice from her husband Geoffrey. After learning of Jake Milne's death, Ruth's conscious self offers her body to Dick Wagner, but by this time her unconscious self has vanished from Stoppard's play.

Although the device has been said to round out the character of "the most successful female in any of Stoppard's plays" (Brassell, *Tom Stoppard*, p. 222), it shifts confusingly from the personal Ruth in quotes of Act I to the political Ruth in quotes of Act II. Perhaps Stoppard intended the device to trace Ruth's growth from the personal to the political, but should it then dissolve in a cynical adultery? The doubling does permit Stoppard a striking stage effect in this play that eschews his notorious flamboyant theatricality. When Jake Milne leaves Ruth, without accepting her invitation to make love on the sofa, she undresses mentally, and, naked, *"she follows Milne into the dark."* A moment later the surface Ruth is fully clothed on the sofa, asking her husband for a cigarette. It is not a pyramid of yellow-clad jumpers, but it is a swift scenic twist in this otherwise realistic Stoppard play, with its melodramatic plot that is derived from Evelyn Waugh's *Scoop*.

More rewarding for actors are those dramas that impose dual roles. Audience pleasure rests upon the deftness with which the two characters are kept apart, since an actor cannot confront him- or herself on stage. Brenton's first full-length play, *Revenge* (1969), opposes the megalomaniacal criminal Adam Hepple against the piously self-righteous Assistant Commissioner Archibald Macleish, who are played by the same actor. After spending their lives in vengeful deeds, each against the other, their final encounter is engineered by the Ghost of a dead policeman. Their mutual murder proves to be a nightmare, in which Hepple acknowledges their common obsolescence in a world of corporate criminality: "The whole country on the fiddle, the gamble, the open snatch, the bit on the side." Brenton's spirited and sardonic view of modern Britain exploits both dreams and a ghost, but suspense and comedy arise from the sustained device of a criminal and a policeman embodied in the same actor.

Trevor Griffiths' first stage play, *Sam Sam* (1969), juxtaposes two brothers played by the same actor, and both improbably named Sam. Born into the working class, one brother revels in class-conscious squalor, whereas the other affiliates himself with the Labor Party in an effort to better workers' living conditions. Sam I rages at wife, mother, and the sordid minutiae of his surroundings, but he does so as a standup comic, playing directly to the audience. In contrast, Sam II is framed by a realistic proscenium, where we see him in his comfortable home, but when he and his wife engage in sexual intercourse, it is spiced with insults against his class. Richard Cave has pinpointed Griffiths' intention with respect to Sam II: "Act II is set consciously within a proscenium and the conventions of naturalism that compel surface calm and inner turmoil. It is seen as the mark of this Sam's failure in integrity that he is determined by the theatrical conventions in which he has chosen to play" (*New British Drama*, p. 216). However, it is not Sam II but Griffiths who chose the conventions of realism, a trap both social and aesthetic. An exploratory first effort that predicts *Comedians* in its dependence on music-hall, *Sam Sam* provides scope for agile acting of the two dissimilar brothers.

The wittiest example of two-character, one-actor doubling is Tom Stoppard's *Hapgood* (1988), in which the device becomes a pervasive theme. Hersh Zeifman aptly describes the first scene as "a Feydeau farce peopled by the characters of a John Le Carré novel on speed." The same critic conveys a sense of that scene's action:

spy chases counterspy chases counter-counterspy in and out of slamming cubicle doors and all around the Burberry bush (for the still center of this storm is the raincoat-clad Elizabeth Hapgood, codenamed "Mother," waiting patiently in the men's shower under a pink umbrella). Adding to the bewilderment are identical briefcases, identical towels, and – crucial to the plot but impossible to detect at this point – identical twins.

(Zeifman, "A Trick of the Light," p. 182)[1]

Counter-espionage has rarely raced so cleverly, and spy-novel mystery has rarely reached so hard for metaphysical mystery. Spoilsport, I reveal at once that the traitor is quite literally a double agent, that is to say that the Ridley (riddle-y) twins are spying for the Soviet Union, although Ernest (shades of *Importance of*) Ridley pretends to spy for Britain, as a member of Hapgood's network. In dim light, we even see these twins embrace, so their duality does not violate a surface realism that is full of technical apparatus and codewords.

What does subvert the spy-laden surface is the title character of Hapgood, who is also called other names that are not germane to my argument. Not only is she "Mother" in the secret service, she is mother of an eleven-year-old boy, father unknown. And, in a counter-espionage maneuver to which we are not privy, she suddenly appears as her twin sister, Celia Newton: "*She is as different from her other self as the flat is different from her office.*" More importantly, her language is different, lilting with slang and obscenities – a quite literal "new tone." As though that transformation were not startling enough, Ridley coerces Celia into a disguise as Hapgood. Like Ridley, we "don't know which one you are." And that is Stoppard's thematic point. As adumbrated in the play by Joseph Kerner, spy, physicist,

1 Zeifman, a trickster critic of the light, illuminates other subtleties of the play.

and father of Hapgood's son, light is either wave or particle, depending on the angle of vision. So too identity depends on the beholder; it is, in a phrase from the play, "a trick of the light" and an entertaining rain of doubles.

Contemporary English playwrights who split single characters into actor doubles lack Stoppard's ontological reach, but they may achieve more immediate impact. Peter Nichols is the prime doubler, in two plays that dramatize the strains of modern marriage. *Forget-me-not Lane* (1971), Nichols' own favorite among his plays, contains the nostalgia of the eponymous song. In some dozen flashback scenes (divided into two acts) Frank Bisley at forty looks back on his life. As the play opens, he listens to records of popular songs while he desultorily packs a suitcase. He addresses the audience directly: "And when you consider how large packing has loomed in my family. Both my families. The one I was issued with and the one I escaped to. And eventually from." Actually, packing looms far larger in the first family, since Frank's father is a traveling salesman, packing every Monday for a week on the road – to the relief of his wife and son.

Since forty-year-old Frank and his wife Ursula refer several times to his desertion of his wife and three children, we at first view the play as a retrospective explanation of the separation. The doubles appear when Frank-at-forty confronts himself at fourteen, the victim of his father's nagging and the witness of his parents' bickering: "What did my own boy make of it when at thirteen he watched Ursula and me growling and roaring at each other? Yes, that's one of the reasons I left her. Having seen my parents like cat-and-dog year after year, I wanted to save my son that spectacle." Or so he rationalizes.

Nichols dovetails the narrative comments of forty-year-old Frank into the flashback scenes that pit him against his younger self, played by a different actor: Frank's close friendship with Ivor, their entertainment of the troops during World War II, Frank's brush with a homosexual magician, his sexual fumbling with Ursula, his father's plea that Frank not join his mother if she leaves him, and finally Frank's induction into the British army to serve in a war that has touched his family only glancingly. More perfunctorily, a teenage Ursula appears on stage, but she confronts Frank rather than her mature self, who merely witnesses the proceedings. Nevertheless, the two Ursulas offer a token symmetrical doubling.

Early in Act II we see the last of young Frank. Doubling is over when the man Frank impregnates and marries Ursula. Frank's father retires, and his mother grumbles that the loquacious old man is underfoot all the time. To brighten his mother's drab days, Frank takes her to the theatre, and during their absence from home, his father dies. It is his father's death that decides Frank to abandon Ursula and their children: "We're all in the genetic trap . . . here we are with our father's hands . . . our mother's sneeze . . . their middle-aged indigestion . . ." The brave new words and the unpacked suit-case become the objects of Ursula's impatience. Frank was to pack for a trip with his wife, a second honeymoon; instead, he has indulged in the trip of nostalgia, which binds him to his family, subject to the "genetic trap."

It is easy to be patronizing about Nichols' soap-opera story, enli-vened by modern doubling in which an ironic narrator confronts a younger, innocent self. Gradually, however, a more significant kind of doubling emerges, as Frank slowly slips into the speech tics of his father. In spite of the device of doubling, Nichols himself recognizes his basic realism: "no matter how they try to break it down, my plays remain bound by naturalism, inasmuch as the people behave some-what as they did in life and the events are never far-fetched" (Intro-duction to *Forget-me-not Lane* in *Plays*, 15 November 1987). Yet, "try-ing to break it down," Nichols' devices do alleviate the tedium of the domestic play with its upbeat ending.

A decade later Nichols again anatomizes a modern marriage in *Passion Play* (1981), and he again confronts the members of the mar-ried couple with their other selves. It is the play for which Nichols received his most favorable reviews, and considerable praise was lavished on the device of doubling. Instead of chronology splitting the husband-and-wife protagonists, as in *Forget-me-not Lane*, they are bifurcated into conscious and unconscious selves. A couple, James and Eleanor, live and work at home, the former touching up modern paintings and the latter giving music lessons. Married for twenty-five years, with children long gone, they live, as Eleanor says, "a very quiet life." The first scene finds James yawning, even though attract-ive young Kate has come to dinner, but the next scene displays him very wide awake, when he meets her for a sensual lunch. At his home afterwards, James is joined by his alter ego Jim, *"dressed the same as James."* James offers lying excuses to his wife Eleanor, even while Jim salivates at the anticipation of intercourse with Kate.

Inevitably, a telltale letter (that hoary device) and an even more telltale "friend" inform Eleanor of her husband's liaison. Enter Nell *"dressed like Eleanor,"* a jealous termagant. Soon proper Eleanor sounds like her alter ego Nell: "How long have you been shagging Kate?" Whereas Nichols clearly differentiates defensive James from lascivious Jim, Eleanor and Nell gradually merge. On stage, however, the lookalikes (who were *not* dressed alike) lend piquancy to the sexual accusations and counter-accusations in what the *Listener* reviewer John Elsom has called a "ménage à cinq."

Act II opens on a Chorale from Bach's *St. Matthew Passion*, pointing to the pun in Nichols' title *Passion Play*. Eleanor translates the German words: "head full of blood and wounds, full of sorrow and scoffing" – phrases obliquely applicable to the heads of Eleanor and James, although they have agreed to forget his brief affair with Kate. Jim, however, objects to "liv[ing] the rest of my life like this," and he is delighted when Kate appears unexpectedly to show "the tail-end of [her] tan," to titillate the now staid couple with an account of her sexual adventures, and to announce: "I've fallen head-over-heels in love." This time it is Jim who is jealous, and Nell feels sorry for James.

The conflict shifts to Eleanor and a philandering Jim (rather than an ingenious James), but it is Nell whose nightmares drive her to a psychiatrist; and it is Nell who quotes the psychiatrist to Kate, whom she misguidedly befriends. Eleanor soon learns of the resumption of the James–Kate affair. Accusing James once again, Eleanor insists that he choose between her and Kate. He chooses Eleanor, but Nell and Jim, wearing seductive nightclothes, *"are in the same emotional mood as James and Eleanor."* Confusingly, it is James rather than Jim who longs for Kate's bold sexuality. On the stage, conscious and unconscious characters become increasingly difficult to separate, and it becomes increasingly difficult to distinguish actual from imagined scenes. Then suddenly all four characters are looking back on a scene in which Eleanor tried to commit suicide. Again suddenly, we are at a Christmas party in the home of James and Eleanor, with Nell and Jim present. The party goes into full swing, and *"Jim goes down in front of Kate. Nell leaves by the front door,"* in Nichols' third and final version of *Passion Play*. But who is Nell, when she leaves?

Nichols' scenic directions stipulate a visual equivalent for passion below the surface: *"The set resembles (and at times represents) a fashionable art gallery . . . and is on two levels."* On a two-leveled stage move two levels of character, but their dialogue does not consistently reflect the split. In the first act the tired representation of adultery is spiced by the device of the doubles, especially since Jim is quick with sexual innuendoes and Nell is wittily bitchy. By Act II, however, the characters are virtually indistinguishable from their doubles. It may be that the respective professions of James and Eleanor, with concomitant references to great works of art and music, are intended to reveal the triviality of the adulterous passion. And yet that passion is the hub of this drama.

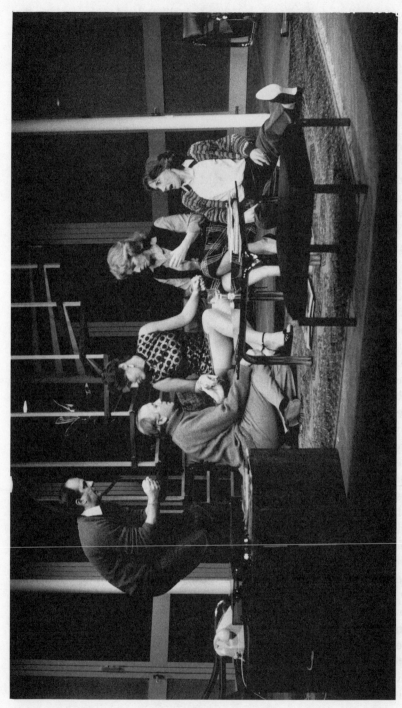

8 A full house, including doubles, in *Passion Play* by Peter Nichols, directed by Mike Ockrent at the RSC (Aldwych), 1981

Nichols, in a return to familiar material after some years of absence from the theatre, seeks to invest it with depth – the device of the doubles, the context of art and music, and, what was less apparent on stage, the growth of a character's understanding. In a note to his last revision of the play, Nichols insists that it does not matter whether Nell or Eleanor finally abandons the marriage: "the point being that where the wives have learned from and been changed by the events in the play, the husbands have not." Either ending seems implausible when, for most of the passion play, each member of a marriage has two faces – literally and figuratively.

In his autobiography *Feeling You're Behind*, Nichols betrays a certain bitterness at how little his work has attracted academic critics: "it lacks the crossword-puzzle element – those ambiguities, clues, arcane quotes and deliberately misleading allusions that are meat and drink to the scholarly mind" (p. 222). He supplies "the crossword-puzzle element" in *Passion Play*, but it animates a banal triangle, in which a middle-aged husband strays from his comfortable wife and life to an improbable siren who is younger than his daughter. Inventive devices and witty alter egos enliven *Passion Play*, as most reviews testify, but passion is elusive.

Moving into the late 1980s, we see the most extensive use of doubling in Alan Ayckbourn's *Woman in Mind* (1985), where a fantasy family is the idealized and distorted double of an actual family. The protagonist Susan is estranged from her son, ignored by her husband, and irritated by his sister who lives with them. She therefore fantasizes a daughter to replace her son, an adoring husband, and a younger brother, who are not only "tall, good-looking, athletic, easy-going and charming," but who surround her with affection.

When the first of the two acts opens, Susan is lying in her garden, having just fainted. A doctor, Bill, bends over her, and his words sound to her, and to us, like nonsense syllables, culminating in the play's subtitle "December Bee" – at once a phonic substitute for "Remember me" and a metaphor for a creature living out of season. When the doctor leaves, Susan's imaginary family envelop her in their concern. When her actual husband and his clumsy sister arrive, Susan faints again, unable to cope with both families. Later her husband keeps reiterating that their estranged son is coming to lunch, but Susan is absorbed in the wedding plans of her fantasy daughter. Gradually, the fantasy family voices hostility toward her actual family, and when Susan's actual son arrives to summon her to lunch, she faints for the third time.

Act II, *"a few seconds later,"* shows Susan in the same supine position with which the play began, but her son is bending over her, and there are no December Bees. He informs her that he has married a nurse, and that the newly-weds are going to work and live in Thailand. In effect, the son blames both his parents for their estrangement. When Susan's surly husband also blames her, the fantasy family reappear. Although Susan dismisses them, they again reappear when the doctor confesses erotic feelings for her. After a blackout, we again find Susan lying on the grass, but this time she is in a thunderstorm, and her husband accuses her of setting fire to his study. Battered by his blame, she summons her fantasy family: "Remember me?" They arrive dressed for a wedding, and Susan's mind is so unhinged that she sees her doctor and actual family members dressed for the event. Her son becomes her fantasy daughter's groom, and Susan is unable to prevent the marriage of the siblings. Her fantasy husband proposes a toast to "the most important person in all our lives," and as Susan expresses her appreciation, she lapses into nonsense syllables, ending in a reiterated "December Bee?" The question hovers over her in our final insight into a woman out of season in her suburban English family, in Ayckbourn's most daring deviation from realism.

A very different playwright, Sarah Daniels, resembles Ayckbourn not only in the exploration of doubling, but in a title that underlines the device – *Beside Herself* (1990). Evelyn's double, Eve, is quite literally beside her throughout the play, a rare deviation from realism on the part of Daniels, who usually dramatizes female bonding in short sharp scenes. It is true that Daniels' *Ripen our Darkness* (1981) contains a celestial scene that includes a female deity, and her *Byrthrite* (1986) contains a dumbshow within the play, but *Beside Herself* opens on a dream set in an infernal supermarket, then introduces the Evelyn–Eve couple in the second scene. As dynamically enacted by Marion Bailey, Eve was mercurial in her range of emotion from fear to aggression, on the border of hysteria.

Rather than focusing on a single protagonist, Daniels usually dramatizes a community of females within patriarchy – whether a family, a class, or a subversive cell. No male is sympathetic in her plays, and establishment figures are subject to her scorn – the psychiatrist, clergyman, and social worker of the "community group home," in which the play is largely set. Eve is everywhere ill at ease, urging escape or violence upon Evelyn, who, however, preserves the outward signs of social decorum. Only after the exposition of a child rape in another family does Daniels build up to the climactic scene in which Evelyn accuses her father of raping her when she was a child.

In the face of protests by the old man, Eve echoes Evelyn (rather than the opposite): "That's how it was." Cleansed by the accusation of child abuse, Evelyn and Eve take pleasure in wiping their hands, faces, and necks with a large white bath-towel. In spite of a tendency to pad her plays with case histories of women's subjugation, and in spite of lexical narrowness, Daniels attains a telling visual contrast between the outwardly placid Evelyn and her disturbed double Eve.

Distortions

Less blatant than dreams, ghosts, and visible or audible doubles, other stage images render the disintegration of the mind in modern English drama. Sometimes these deviations from realism disorient the audience at the same time that they reveal new depths of the mind. Examining the few plays that risk such disorientation, I disrupt chronology to conclude the chapter with the most striking example of distortion – Heathcote Williams' *AC/DC* (1970).

By the time John Osborne wrote *Inadmissible Evidence* (1964), he had already tried several escapes from the realistic anger that was synonymous with his name, but *Inadmissible Evidence* is his first and so far his only play to focus so relentlessly upon the unconscious of its protagonist. The tense drama might well carry the title that Arthur Miller finally discarded for his *Salesman*, *The Inside of His Head*, and the critic Ronald Bryden has described Osborne's protagonist as "a kind of Willy Loman in striped English serge" (quoted in Page, *Osborne on File*, p. 40).

The title *Inadmissible Evidence* situates us at a legal trial, but unlike Brecht's trial scenes, *Inadmissible Evidence* woos our sympathy rather than our judgment, and it does so by delving into the feelings of its protagonist in a way that would be inadmissible in a court-room. *Inadmissible Evidence* opens with the nightmare of its protagonist. Bill Maitland, a solicitor, dreams that, debilitated by a hangover, he is conducting his own defense against vague charges that add up to his life. Although Bill's offense is never explicitly stated, the word "change" cuts through his disjointed phrases, but we never learn what change whittles away at his sanity. The fragmentation and repetition of Bill's speech, like a slow-motion version of Beckett's Lucky, predict the fragmentation and repetition of his personal relationships, which will be dramatized in his waking life.

After a fade, the dream court-room dissolves into Maitland's office, which is the realistic setting for the remainder of the non-realistic two-act play. Osborne's scenic directions mark the transition from fantasy to fact: "*The actor has to indicate the painful struggle into con-*

sciousness, without, at the same time, making the physical metaphor too explicit . . . The dream, the prison of embryonic helplessness for the moment, recedes, but not altogether." "Not altogether," as we observe Bill's inability to communicate with his secretary, his clerks, his telephonist, and his client Mrs. Garnsey, whose invisible husband resembles Bill in that "everyone's drawing away from him."

At the opening of Act II, Bill, having spent the night in his office, struggles to escape from another nightmare, which we do not witness. He achieves a temporary rescue by that most banal of realistic props, the sound of the telephone, but Osborne converts it to an expressionist instrument by which Bill draws away from everyone. Again, Osborne's scenic directions are explicit: Bill's telephone conversations should *"progressively resemble the feeling of dream and unreality of Bill's giving 'evidence' at the beginning of Act 1 . . . sometimes it should trail off into a feeling of doubt as to whether there is anyone to speak to at all . . . The telephone is stalked, abused, taken for granted, feared. Most of all the fear of being cut off . . ."* In Act I Bill has more or less lucid telephone conversations with his wife Anna and his lover Liz, but by Act II it is not quite clear whether he converses with them or with his projections of them.

Osborne's small cast function to trace the disintegration of Bill's mind. Osborne, himself an actor, once played three roles in Nigel Dennis' *Cards of Identity*, and in *Inadmissible Evidence* the same actress plays Maitland's three women clients, whose ruptured marriages reflect obliquely on his own. As we in the audience see the same face on the three clients, we have glided into the mind of Bill, who cannot discern differences between them. But we are also aware of his escalating neurosis. In Act I his client Mrs. Garnsey describes her husband, whose emotional bankruptcy corresponds to that of Bill. By Act II Bill charges his client Mrs. Tonk with her husband's complaints, and Bill conducts a skewed defense against his client Mrs. Anderson. Against his three indistinguishable clients, then, Bill Maitland pits an aggrieved victim, himself.

Again we are in Bill's mind when the same actor plays the unattractive clerk Jones and the quick-witted homosexual client Maples – another merging of characters in Bill's professional life. Corrosively self-aware, the womanizer Bill Maitland recognizes his affiliation with Maples: "I should think Sir Watkin Glover Q.C. is sure to apply the full rigour of the law and send the both of *us* down" (my italics). After Bill's assimilation of his several professional relationships into one woman and one man, after everyone else draws away from him, it is something of a climax to behold his loving mistress onstage in the flesh. Bill and Liz exchange words of love, but they can do nothing for each other. Before a last telephone call to his unloved wife, Bill Maitland takes a pill. Suicide? Bill has swallowed pills at several points in the play, and Osborne's final scenic direction – *"He replaces the telephone and sits back waiting"* – is passive. Bill Maitland will wait until someone takes him away.

Unlike the angry young men who have been laid at Osborne's door, Bill Maitland is more anguished than angry, and he is nearly forty years *old*. Although he claims to love his daughter even more than his mistress, he flings his most vitriolic diatribe in the face of her youth. Bill's cynicism corrodes not only "good, brave causes" but even bad and surreptitious pleasures. Neither his personal nor his professional life affords Bill Maitland a sense of identity, and he is acutely aware of the acidity that dissolves his few human relationships. Osborne brewed that acid by seasoning his customary anguished monologues with the distortions of Maitland's mind, including nightmares and doubles.

In contrast to the progressive fragmentation of Maitland, the poet Verlaine experiences a single image of mental distortion in Christopher Hampton's *Total Eclipse* (1968, revised 1981). The playwright draws upon scholarship in French and English to trace the mutual interdependence of two poets during an intense two-year period punctuated by Verlaine's imprisonment and Rimbaud's withdrawal from poetry. The distortion is staged in Hampton's final scene, when Rimbaud is dead and Verlaine lives on in absinthe-induced nostalgia. The ageing poet eclipses his first sight of his wife into a vision of Rimbaud, and, more dramatically, he edits Rimbaud's cruelty from his memory.

During their tumultuous love affair, Rimbaud is brutally honest with Verlaine, refusing protestations of love. With both of them drinking absinthe, and the teenage Rimbaud perhaps taking stronger drugs, the latter commands: "Put your hands on the table. Palm upwards." (*Rimbaud looks at [the hands] for a moment, and then with short, brutal hacks, stabs at both of them.*)" Twenty years later Verlaine relives the scene. He receives the same command, and again complies, but this time "(*Rimbaud looks at [the hands] for a moment, and then bends forward and kisses them.*)" In a final speech Verlaine boasts that Rimbaud continues to live in him, but the sentimentalized image totally eclipses the fierce young genius.

Two decades later Simon Gray stages the distortions of the disintegrating mind of his eponymous protagonist in *Melon* (1987, revised 1989). Gray, a nimble-witted dramatist, tends to fit comfortably within the realistic picture-frame stage, where his friend Harold

Pinter often directs his drama to reveal an underlying menace. In the original version of *Melon*, however (not directed by Pinter, but by Christopher Morahan), Gray departs from that convention. Rather than the living-room set, four rooms are simultaneously visible: Melon's office at a publishing firm, the sitting-room of his home, the bedroom of that home, and a bleak psychiatric room. *"It would also be a good idea if playing space could be found between the rooms, so that Melon is seen crossing and arriving, rather than just entering the stage."* Physically, Gray's play departs only slightly from realism, but the dramatic departure is more drastic, for the play is set in Melon's memory. Melon is at once protagonist and narrator.

Like other narrators on the modern English stage – Bolt's Common Man in his *A Man for all Seasons* and Shaffer's Old Martin in his *The Royal Hunt of the Sun* – Melon tends to dispense his wisdom before he has earned it dramatically. Derived from Stuart Sutherland's confessional *Breakdown*, Melon lapses easily into the second person, with its implication that events do not constitute an exceptional case history but a human predicament that is widely applicable to you, the audience. Although Melon's obsession – sexual jealousy – constitutes the dominant passion of plays as different as *Othello* and Joyce's *Exiles*, it is scarcely the widespread existential phenomenon implied by the second grammatical person.

Socially and theatrically, Gray's *Melon* recalls Osborne's *Inadmissible Evidence*. Both solipsistic protagonists are professional men, husbands, fathers, philanderers in the thickets of contemporary London. Maitland and Melon both feel superior to their friends and/or subordinates, but both are subject to nightmares, and they are dependent upon pills to maintain their equilibrium. Both plays open in the protagonist's mind, with monologues that reveal their disturbed condition. However, Osborne's Bill Maitland utters speech fragments and repetitions, whereas Gray's Melon speaks in well-rounded generalizations, eschewing the first person, although he is apparently talking about himself.

Early in the first flashback Melon attacks a "harmless old bore" who quotes the medieval lyric: "oh summer is icumen in, louder sing, cuckoo," but Melon's rage is wildly disproportionate to the imagined jibe of "cuckoo." Soon sex becomes the leitmotif in the urbane conversation of Melon and his friends: a homosexual Jewish psychiatrist, a successful television interviewer, a would-be novelist and his colorless wife. But the drawing-room scene, so familiar on the realistic stage, veers disconcertingly when each character takes up a musical instrument and begins to play a different melody. Melon soon imposes his tune upon the others, and when discord is heard, the characters *"pack up their instruments and leave."* Only Melon's wife Kate continues to play. When the married couple are alone, Melon equates a false note with his wife's infidelity, to which his reaction is excitement: "And that's all there was to it. Not important to either of us at all." But Melon is lying; the importance of his unknown rival grows exponentially. Act I closes on Melon's adultery with a secretary, accomplished as the ritual he imagines between his wife and her unnamed lover.

Act II traces Melon's escalating mental lapses: he forgets the day of the week, imagines each of his friends as his rival, hears the word "cuckold" in magnificent chorus. As the Act I musical Tuesday was a conflation of several weeks, the Act II social evening is a painful phantasmagoria, through which Melon as narrator attacks the several psychiatrists who treated him. Obsessively, Melon questions his adolescent son about his wife's activities; he insults his friends and goads his wife. Eventually, however, Melon is cured of his obsession, and by the end of the play, all returns to normal. In the office *"Everything looks much the same."* At home we do not see the bedroom, but in the sitting-room Melon gives thanks for the joys of normalcy: "Safe and sane." All the characters take out their musical instruments, and finally, *"Gradually, led by Melon, they play in harmony, without passion or fire – humdrum in fact."*

The antithesis of the Osborne protagonist, whose neurosis is a form of rebellion against an unfeeling consumer society, Melon adjusts to that society, "without passion or fire." It is a sobering transition that may be clinically desirable, but is dramatically stifling. Theatre thrives on great eccentrics – characters *in extremis* – and even within the modest confines of Gray's own career his self-destructive Butley appealed to us by the sharp wit of his misery. Played by the same lubricious actor, Alan Bates, Melon (a name incongruously redolent of sweetness and roundness) is too monolithic to arouse dramatic tension. His constant retrospective interruptions become pretentious, and his final acceptance of sanity hovers at the edge of smugness. Since we are so exclusively in his mind, we find the space too small for his generalizations – four-room set notwithstanding.

Under the title *The Holy Terror* Gray revised *Melon* toward realism; the play's action is more obviously compounded of Melon's memories, which are evoked in his address to a specific Women's Institute audience; his mental illness is spelled out by his friends and family; he is not finally cured but prays that "neither the kingdom nor anything else, especially as powerful and glorious as a breakdown, will come in my, Mark Melon's lifetime." But he has already spent nine months in a clinic. Unfortunately for the drama, Gray expunged Melon's inventive musical distortions.

By the mid-1980s the anguished, astigmatic, monologue-centered drama had reached the West End, but in 1970 the most extreme example of this subgenre was relegated to the intrepid Theatre Upstairs of the Royal Court. When noticed at all, *AC/DC* was viewed as ravings of the psychedelic drug culture, as in this summary by the usually astute reviewer for the *Financial Times*, Michael Coveney: "*AC/DC* was exactly of its period, a junkie extravaganza which featured a character living off other people's 'voltage' and could not possibly have been written before the dawn of the Rolling Stones, communal sex, available drugs and schizophrenia about fame" (Edwards, *Celebration*, p. 51). In other words, the play reflects its time, but Coveney fails to recognize its intensity and depth for our time as well.

Triggered by M. Rokeah's *Three Christs of Ypsilanti* (1964), *AC/DC* by Heathcote Williams took some five years and a dozen versions to reach the stage. Before and after, Williams meandered in odd jobs and odd places, and he never did commit himself entirely to playwriting. *AC/DC* provides some insight as to why. Although the play received prizes in 1970, and although it was revived twice at the Court, it has never received the highly technical production it requires.

The title *AC/DC* points to electricity as a metaphor, but the play also draws upon the lexicons of physics, astronomy, astrology, mathematics, advertising, politics, anthropology, geology, chemistry, and biology, as well as obscenities and sexual puns on "come" and "eat." In Act I, entitled Alternating Current, electricity drives an Amusement Arcade, which is mindlessly inhabited by three Americans at 5 am. After a blackout we hear, but do not see, the three in a Photomaton booth, committing their copulations to illustration. The alternations would seem to involve trivial and deeper characters. Act II, set in the room of the protagonist Perowne, is entitled Direct Current, and electricity drives a bank of video-screens, but it has also functioned to photograph some two thousand personalities, whose pictures cover the three walls – an inventive mutant of the realistic picture-frame stage. The Direct Current confronts Maurice with Sadie and Perowne. In contrast to the two elaborate settings, a simple prop is seen in both acts – the pink shirt of the black American Sadie, which attracts Perowne.[2]

---

2 I consider Perowne to be the play's protagonist, even though Williams has said: "I didn't like anyone in the play except Maurice . . ." (*Gambit*, p. 144).

It is easier to describe the setting and prop than the plot of *AC/DC*, whose text is dense and layered. At its center is the oddly named Perowne (per own?), the last of five characters to appear on stage. Of the three Americans on which the play opens, two, trivial hedonists, are dismissed before the end of the first act: "You're agents from the abattoir, same as everybody else. You're just Mr and Mrs Jones." The third American, black Sadie (Say die?) has early announced: "I wanta go solo." In a symbiotic relationship are Perowne and Maurice, "an electrophiliac." The first act dramatizes the self-involved efforts of Sadie and more especially Maurice to help Perowne "go bald" or free himself from his "overloaded circuit." As Maurice narrates contemptuous anecdotes about his psychiatric treatment – detoxification, hypnosis, electric shock – he repeatedly tempts Perowne with "a clean break," but Sadie pours scorn on the whole electric spectrum by which we live.

Although Maurice's very first speech admits Perowne's power over him, the latter in Act II seems beholden to Maurice. Maniacally and yet methodically, Sadie tears photographs of "psychic parasites" from Perowne's wall. Increasingly, Sadie is aware of entering Perowne's "trip," and he often smiles assent to her attack on his "media rash." She is his bulwark against insidious television newsreaders, whom Perowne satirizes. Sadie supports Perowne morally through an epileptic fit. Vaguely bisexual, Sadie and Perowne have almost achieved a modus vivendi, when Maurice lays claim to his erstwhile lover, putting a bone into his jaw, then entering the television set with magnet and microphone. Nakedly, Sadie and Maurice vie for Perowne, screaming at each other in a counterpointed duet. Sadie stuffs photographs into her womb and masturbates at feverish length. Maurice in turn masturbates, and as they achieve a simultaneous climax, Perowne sobs. Liberated, Maurice confesses that he was not demagnetizing Perowne, but working for mysterious Saucer People.

Alone together, Perowne and Sadie drink like old friends. Then, in order to free the molecules of his brain, she *"presses the trephine onto his scalp."* The operation is painless, as Perowne keeps reiterating. He loses language while Sadie turns "every cell of his body into a brain cell." She shouts the play's last words at him, but he answers in nonverbal noises that are printed in hieroglyphics that vaguely resemble cells.

Williams specifies: "The text of *AC/DC* is convertible at all points to the frequencies of the actors and the director." Nick Wright, the first director, conducted the early read-throughs armed with the

9 *AC/DC* by Heathcote Williams, directed by Nicholas Wright at the
Theatre Upstairs of the Royal Court, 1970; the trepannation of Perowne (Ian
Hogg) by Sadie (Pat Hartley)

dictionaries that provide an entrance into the recondite worlds to which Williams alludes. Staged sparely in 1970, the drama was too easily classified as psychedelic stream-of-consciousness, instead of a dense and patterned arc of rebellion against the schizophrenia to which we are all condemned, unable to free our brain cells from the media in which we are immersed.[3] Finally, however, eschewing language, Perowne "goes off into that final speech in hieroglyphics [and] he's clear of all terrestrial vibrations and he's trying to convey what the Buddhists call 'Nadas' – the background noise of the universe, a kind of cosmic hum" (*Gambit* 17–18, p. 143).

What distinguishes *AC/DC* is the three-way interaction and the glorious arias that prefigure those of Sam Shepard at his best. As Katharine Worth has cogently written in her analysis of *AC/DC*, Williams shows "the mind in labour with itself" (*Revolutions*, p. 165). Maurice confesses his subservience to the Saucer People in a long monologue that ends:

We've SHAT on their Faustian universe. WE'VE SHAT ON IT, which is why None of the Super-Dwarves, and the Super Autistic-Schizo-Thalidomides that they're Spawning specially for us, in preparation . . . which is why . . . WHICH IS WHY NONE OF THEM FIT IN. They reward me sometimes by fetching me back into the original squitting sex noise that hasn't been in my bum since I was ten.

Sadie rhapsodizes: "When my fuckin revolution comes Everybody in the World's gonna be on television ALL THE TIME. THEN there's gonna be an 'Information explosion'. No more names. No more signature artists. No more selective newsreader psychosis. No more selective Beatle psychosis. There's gonna be TOTAL ACCESS . . . TOTAL ACCESS."

But access into this oxymoronic drama is arduous. Vividly original in its technical setting and vocabulary, *AC/DC* pleads implicitly for ecological equilibrium, as Williams would later plead explicitly in his books on whales, dolphins, and elephants. About *AC/DC* Williams himself has said: "The play isn't against technology, but against its abuse by monopolies," but he seems to me to be summarizing his own stance, rather than that of the play (*Gambit* 18–19, pp. 142 and 143). A later sentence in the same interview implies as much: "The human animal is totally convertible. Trepannation is a metaphor for this." Sadie's trepannation of Perowne, at once cruel and humane, is also intensely theatrical.

3 This is my reading of the play, but Williams claims that he has created five schizo-phrenic aspects of himself (*Gambit*, pp. 18–19).

The reader of *AC/DC* is guided by the different typefaces that distinguish the three central characters, and a chart magnifies the play's mystery. In performance, however, a director risks chaos unless a through-line is pursued. But few directors are bold enough to stage this remarkable work in a production worthy of its visual and verbal profundity, of its flights of fantasy, of its relentless theatricality. Within its dialogue appear no literal dreams, ghosts, or doubles, and yet their shades are ubiquitous in this trepannation of our media culture.

7

Fictional histories

I'm not a historian.   (Estragon in Samuel Beckett's *Waiting for Godot*)

Unlike Estragon, almost every English dramatist has been a historian
to the extent of setting a play in the past. From Zola on, realism in the
theatre focused on contemporary problems, and yet physical realism
on stage was influenced by the productions of the Duke of Saxe-
Meiningen, who costumed Shakespeare and Schiller in the dress of
their respective countries and periods. These ostensibly accurate productions appeared unrealistic by virtue of their distance from contemporary surfaces. "Costume drama" was a disparaging term for popular melodrama set in the past, but it was not so easy to dismiss
performances that looked authoritative of their period.

Critics like Jean-François Lyotard and Hayden White have subjected historical narratives (or, more accurately and clumsily, the
narrativization of history) to skeptical analysis, but earlier scholars
had already read in (or into?) works about the past a comment on the
present. It is hard to pinpoint the first example of re-viewing history
through a contemporary lens. The distinguished classical scholar Bernard Knox reads Sophocles' *Oedipus* plays as a criticism of contemporary Athens, and Queen Elizabeth saw danger to herself in Shakespeare's *Richard II*. Despite these examples, and others, the systematic
exploitation of history for modern instruction awaited the twentieth
century.

Brecht was the most self-conscious artificer in this aspect of theatre.
Although he valorized the word "realistic," he himself "estranged"
most of his dramas to other times and places, temporarily seducing
his audience into escape before bludgeoning them with contemporary parallels. Introduced to Anglophone readers by Eric Bentley,
Martin Esslin, and John Willett, Brecht's plays and theory had a
gradually widening influence. To this day the English theatre shows

the impact of the 1956 visit to London of his Berliner Ensemble (in the month of Brecht's death). Directly or indirectly inherited, the Ensemble insignia appear in denuded stages, harsh white lights, projected scene summaries, swirling banners, and direct address to the audience, mainly in Shakespeare productions. Scarcely less modest in their staging, many post-Ensemble English plays sprawl into scenes, rather than rise with the acts. A few plays sport narrators, trials, songs that are virtually spoken – all in Brecht's lineage.

Almost every modern English playwright has written a costume drama, and several of them estrange not only the garments but also the language of their characters. Scenically lavish, such plays reach the stage with decreasing frequency, and if they are staged, they are rarely revived. At a time when many novels have been adapted for the stage, these works of comparable scale were conceived as dramas, but the density of their language may relate them to that area dreaded in the theatre – literature. These dramas often stage apocalyptic events, far from the cool reason praised by Brecht.

The final device resisting realism on the stage is the fictionalization of history. At the simplest level, dramas set in the past *look* unrealistic, however authentic the surface. At a more sophisticated and theatrical level, such dramas can convey the texture of lived experience at another period. And with different degrees of complexity, the past may inform the present. I have tried to choose plays from the several levels, and in moving through them, I suppose that I impose my own narrative through a chronology. In so doing, I imitate modern chronological staging of Shakespeare's *Histories* – the order in which events happened, and not the order in which they were written. In 1963 John Barton collapsed four Shakespeare history plays into three, entitling them *The Wars of the Roses*. In 1964, under Peter Hall's overall direction, the sequence swelled to seven plays from *Richard II* to *Richard III*, following one another chronologically to dramatize some hundred years of British history. In 1989 the English Shakespeare Company under the direction of Michael Bogdanov and Michael Pennington presented those same seven plays with very different texts and approaches. Also in 1989 the Royal Shakespeare Company performed four Shakespeare *Histories* condensed to three as *The Plantagenets*.

Comparably, I propose to move chronologically through plays about Western history, non-realistic by reason of their visible pastness. Beginning with the matter of Greece and Rome, I advance through medieval, Renaissance, and Enlightenment times, to arrive at modernity. Unlike medieval drama that began with the Creation and ended on Judgment Day (which Bill Bryden staged in promenade fashion in a ringing version by Tony Harrison, *The Mysteries*, 1978), these modern quasi-historical plays are anchored to the earth and its all-too-sullied inhabitants. My selected sequence embraces a spectrum of approaches to theatre: the private and the public, the materialistic and the apocalyptic, fragments and wholes, all breaking the proscenium frame with its restricted probabilities.

The matter of Greece

Greek legend has been a mine of material for Western playwrights. In the twentieth century, with its paucity of students of classical Greek, playwrights nevertheless set special store by classical Greek culture. Cocteau, O'Neill, Giraudoux, Anouilh, Eliot dramatized Greek myth with an anachronistic fillip, but recent English dramatists have occasionally tried to probe to a meaning of myth, even while they hold the present firmly in mind. In that respect political dramatists are inspired by Brecht and his search for contemporary relevance, especially his adaptation of Sophocles' *Antigone*, which borrows lines of the Hölderlin translation, and sets the tragedy in the Third Reich. But whereas Brecht aimed for clarity both in staging and in the lessons of myth or history, English dramas can be complex and often perplexing. And none more so than recent dramas on the oldest Greek material, the Trojan War.

Edward Bond has borrowed Brecht's term of epic drama: "An epic play tells a story and says why it happened" (*Worlds*, p. 107). Like Brecht, Bond dramatizes national destiny through his individuals, and for neither playwright is that destiny inevitable. Human beings are born into certain historical situations, but they can choose their actions. The drama lies in the choice.

In Bond's *The Woman* (1978), set in a quasi-Homeric world, the playwright replaces Helen with a statue of the Goddess of Good Fortune. King Priam of Troy has stolen this trophy, and to recapture the symbolic statue the Greeks lay siege to Troy. Dead Priam's wife Hecuba is the woman of the title, who dominates both parts of the play, but the title also fits the invented character Ismene, wife of the Greek Commander-in-Chief Heros (and not the daughter of Oedipus). Part 1 of Bond's *The Woman* zigzags between the Trojan court and the Greek camp, as in *The Iliad*. Bond pits the military and mercantile Greeks against the religiously servile Trojans. The two "enemy" women, Hecuba and Ismene, connive toward peace in an armed world. They fail. Like modern politicians, Greeks and Trojans break their promises, and the Greek army loots Troy before burning the nation out of existence. As in Euripides' *Trojan Women*, the Greeks throw the Trojan child Astyanax to his death from the wall, despite the pleas of his grandmother Hecuba. Within the wall Bond's Ismene is immured for treason – the Greek judgment on her efforts to end the war.

Part II of *The Woman*, set twelve years later on a nameless island, finds Hecuba and Ismene living as mother and daughter, the one blind and the other half-witted after her incarceration. As Hecuba explains: "You're my eyes – and I make you eat, and wash, and rock you to sleep when you're afraid." The arrival of Heros and the Greeks cuts short the idyllic life of the two women among the island people. Heros seeks the statue which was lost in a storm. Vainly dredging the sea in his maniacal quest, Heros agrees to a race between himself and a runaway slave. At once superstitious and supercilious, Heros is outwitted by the rational Hecuba, and is stabbed to death by the former slave. After Hecuba is drowned in a storm, the lame ex-slave and the maimed Ismene will found a new civilization in harmony with the customs of the islanders. In this classical adaptation Bond blends the antiwar stance of his *Lear* and the cautious optimism of his *The Sea*.

Martin Esslin's review summarizes the intense theatricality of Bond's *Woman*: "it is the work of a real poet of the theatre: who thinks in entrances and exits, in ascents and descents of steps, in light rising to high intensity and fading, in the tension between groups of figures" (*Plays and Players* [August 1978], p. 27). It is also the work of a poet of startling images – the wall around Troy, the toy paper house of the child Astyanax, the bread and fish of the islanders, the cruel silver of the mines, the symbolic force of a waterspout. And a poet of telling scenes – the first meeting of regal Hecuba and hesitant Ismene, the blood-drunk, white-haired Nestor, the tender scene in which the lame slave tickles and teases the two women. Bond also reinforces the non-realism of a classical narrative with an early scene *"occurring in Heros's head"* and Hecuba's strategic late dream.

Having previously engaged in a long dialogue with Shakespeare, Bond in *The Woman* boldly challenges classical tragedy. Irving Wardle of *The Times* entitled his review "Classical Demolition Job," but Bond does not demolish the theme of Euripides' *Trojan Women*; he extrapolates the Greek poet's horror of the Trojan bloody War. As Jenny S. Spencer notes: "Bond's allusive technique allows him to recapture the texture and resonance of classical Greek theatre without needing to depend on precise parallels" ("Rewriting 'Classics,'" p. 563). Bond eschews a classical Chorus, but he emulates Shakespeare in sketching a population through a few remarks of the commoners: his Greeks are weary of the siege, and his Trojans return the statue; the islanders are dedicated to the rites that celebrate birth, death, and the changing seasons; the runaway slave paints a grim picture of the silver mines upon which Athenian prosperity depends. For the most part, this panorama of classes and nations is integrated into the story-line, demonstrating "why it happened" even while event and character engage our emotions.

Bond's first play to be directed by himself, *The Woman* was also the first modern play to be produced on the wide stage of the Olivier Theatre, and Bond, with his designer Hayden Griffiths, exploited its space with theatricalism. In Part I the stage was bared back to the metal fire-curtain, and in Part II the island was represented by a large canted disc. At the same time, Bond as both dramatist and director needed an outside critical eye. His scenes of tragic power were sometimes diluted by self-indulgent imagery or didactic monologues. Perhaps reluctant to render Heros simplistically villainous, Bond accords him too much attention – his skewed vision of the Trojan court, his insistence on political rhetoric, his Part II exposition of Athenian imperialism, and, finally, his mysterious acceptance of Hecuba's dream about a competitive race. If Heros is too subtle for his dramatic function, other characters can be too schematically good or evil. Thus, Bond caricatures the greed of priests – both Trojan and Greek – and he overstresses the simplicity of the islanders. On the whole, however, Bond's energy derives from his architectonics and verbal variety; if he occasionally lapses into didacticism, the boldness of his reach redeems him. In one of Bond's poems appended to the published version of *The Woman*, we read: "Energy occurs when an emotion is transformed into an idea." But Bond's theory contradicts his most searing practice, where the idea is transformed into emotion.

Like Edward Bond, his elder by a dozen years, Howard Barker rarely succumbs to realism, or what he calls "naturalism" in the following quotation: "Seeking meticulous reproduction of reality is a blind alley. In any case, as I like my plays to cover a wide range of social types, to describe a whole society, naturalism isn't an appropriate tool" (Kerensky, *New British Drama*, p. 242). Nor does Barker consider linear structure or psychological characterization appropriate tools. Michael Billington labeled him "a Marxist Christopher Fry," pointing thus to Barker's radicalism and his opulent dialogue, but dramaturgically Barker is anarchistic rather than Marxist. And although his prose brims energetically, he is lexically precise – unlike Fry. The actor Ian McDiarmid pays tribute to Barker's dialogue: "Every syllable, every punctuation point counts, so precise is its rhythmic composition, and sloppy elisions will obscure structure and meaning. It is no surprise that actors [like McDiarmid] who are used to performing classical texts are particularly attracted to his plays" (*Gambit* 41, p. 95). Such actors sing Barker's praises in interviews appended to David Ian Rabey's book about his drama. Detractors of Barker's work find it self-indulgent in its excess. Barker's so-called Theatre of Catastrophe has a quicksand quality, but even a momentarily stable footing can yield rewards.

Barker dramatizes the legend of Troy in his *Bite of the Night* (1988). Summarizing its plot is hard, but nevertheless easier than following it in the theatre. The program note for the Barbican Pit production reads: "In this epic play Doctor Savage, the last classics teacher at a defunct university, discarding his family in a wilful spasm of freedom and accompanied by Hogbin, a wayward student, revisits the eleven Troys of antiquity and encounters the source of Eros, Helen of Troy, as well as her creator, Homer." But Barker's three-act text rambles more waywardly than this single sentence suggests.

Not explicitly a play within the play, Dr. Savage's quest for Helen of Troy is nevertheless distanced by a Brechtian frame, the three free-verse Prologues spoken by Macluby, who is designated as a "soap-boiler" but who acts like a Narrator or Master of Ceremonies. Moreover, the several (not eleven) ancient Troys are neither historical nor mythic, but imaginary and even fantastic, e.g. Paper Troy (as celebrated in books), Mums' Troy (propagating infants), Laughing Troy (trivializing pain), Fragrant Troy (with compulsory scents). All Troys prove to be Infernos in which Helen is victimized, first of all by Homer: "If I had not made Helen, Helen would not have been disfigured." Barker's Helen knows that Homer is her creator, and she intuits that Dr. Savage will worship and destroy her.

Barker's drama is subtitled "An Education," and presumably the student is Dr. Savage, who journeys back to Troy, which is burned not by Greeks but by three soldiers with English names. Their leader Shade enlists Savage to write a constitution for the new Troy, freed of Helen's sin. Blamed on all sides, Helen suffers the amputation of her limbs, in what is cruelly called "The Pruning of Helen." Her voluble torso is wheeled around by a blind Homer. Since she is still considered dangerous, the soldiers arrange her execution by the ex-student Hogbin, who has been intermittently helpful to Helen.

Instead of killing her, however, Hogbin commits suicide. An imperturbable witness to these events, Savage cries out when he is given soap, for in it he smells the odor of Hogbin's body.

By Act III the forty-year-old Savage has reached the age of fifty, as though he were engaged in his own ten-year Trojan War. A totalitarian Fragrant Troy is to be celebrated in the public coupling of Savage and his wife Creusa (the name of the dead wife of Aeneas in *The Aeneid*). The son of Creusa and Savage is an adult soap salesman who addresses Helen with smooth clichés, and she senses that her end is near. When one of the soldiers strangles her, her mute husband breaks into speech, and the whole populace of Troy tries to touch her corpse for luck. In an armless, legless, indomitable Old Woman, Savage recognizes another Helen, and he systematically buries her alive, after which he throttles Helen's daughter Gay.

At the play's end Savage wanders through the rubble. Archaeologists who have figured briefly in the intervals of Barker's play point out the sights of the Trojan dig. Schliemann pontificates about the university: "The corridors of inordinate length where tortured thinkers thrashed each other in pursuit of a deity they called Truth." Barker's target is clearly a modern and not a Trojan university, but the sentence also applies to Barker's play, which ends, after Savage and a bespectacled Hogbin thrash about, on a high note of irony. Noticing Savage, the archaeologist Schliemann asks him: "Are you on the tour?"

The Bite of the Night is too dense to grasp on either one viewing or one reading, but its strands are provocative: the irreconcilability of private passion embodied in Helen and public responsibility claimed by the soldier Shade; the inadequacy of love as a way to public harmony, and yet the greater inadequacy of any substitute; the seduction of passion as opposed to reason; the triviality of comedy and laughter; the helpless witness of poets who flee from action; the innocence of children which all too quickly dissolves into the cruelty of adulthood; the tenuous bonds of family, fellowship, and friendship. Finally, a modern intellectual pointedly named Savage can be little more than a tourist, a spectator gaping at past civilizations, but a limbless and nameless Old Woman can resemble Helen, who will perhaps appear again in the most unexpected places, to ignite human imagination.

When Helen begs to be killed, she utters the phrase that gives Barker's play its title: "I wanted to be beaten out of life by some mad male all red about the neck and veins outstanding like the protesting prostitute in the bite of the night, discovered all brain and sheet and stocking." Elusive of meaning, this rich and confusing statement seems at once to celebrate and denigrate the violence of passion – masculine or governmental, ancient and modern.

In performance *The Bite of the Night* ran four and a half hours, and this always sours reviewers. The 200-seat RSC Pit was often half-empty, and even emptier after each intermission. Barker himself announced in the program: "the audience does not struggle for permanent coherence, which is associated with the narrative of naturalism, but experiences the play moment by moment, contradiction by contradiction." Some memorable moments: Hogbin in a coat of cloth-of-books, the ripping out of Helen's husband's tongue, Savage groveling at Homer's feet, the caging of Shade in a wicker basket, Helen's torso in a baby-carriage pushed by blind Homer, dictator Gay in a leather coat, Hogbin acting as limbless Helen's hands, Savage sniffing at a bar of soap.

For all its length and density, *The Bite in the Night* repays study. The text bristles with memorable images and quotable epigrams: "No ideology on the cheap"; "if love lies anywhere, it's on the other side of shame"; "Poets' Troy will be the worst yet"; "us and must, twin pillars of history"; "The Past never occurred"; "First Troy was burnt by foreigners. But last Troy the people burn themselves." Barker's stage holds a whole burning people, composed of striking and suffering individuals, each with her or his own rhetoric. On a mythic base, Barker's non-realistic play reaches through classical decorum to our own faulty archaeology.

Barker and Bond both ground their contemporary mythic plays on the Trojan War, whereas Caryl Churchill and David Lan in *A Mouthful of Birds* (1986) took Euripides' *Bacchae* as a springboard for their Joint Stock Company workshop on women and violence: "We began with *The Bacchae* and the idea of possession . . . *A Mouthful of Birds* tells the stories of seven possessed people . . . Our new play, which began with *The Bacchae*, is itself possessed by it" (Lan, p. 6). Churchill amplifies: "What really happened with *The Bacchae*, I suppose, was that it was one example of the kind of things that we were exploring, rather than it being that we were trying to find ways of doing *The Bacchae*" (*New Theatre Quarterly* [February, 1988], 9). *A Mouthful of Birds* is difficult to grasp because the seven modern stories come to us in fragments; none of them is linear, and none is realistically dramatized. Moreover, the presiding god Dionysos is split into two different actors – an arresting use of doubles – interacting not only with Pentheus and Agave, but with the modern characters. Crucial to any performance is the dancing skill of the actors who portray this androgynous god of drink and drama. Since the whole cast dances in two scenes, grace is essential.

The drama is the product of some twelve weeks of Joint Stock workshops, and a linear summary betrays the immediacy of this highly physical performance. On an "undefended day" each one of the seven modern characters is possessed by a spirit or a passion: (1) Lena, frustrated in her relationship with Roy, is possessed by a spirit that urges her to murder their baby, so as to be free of him; (2) Marcia, a black switchboard operator, is also a medium possessed by a Baron Sunday, but she is displaced by white Sybil who seizes her occult power; (3) Dan, a vicar possessed by Dionysos, acquires the ability to kill his victims in pleasurable deaths; (4) Paul, a married businessman dealing in wholesale meat, falls in love with a pig but loses her to an abattoir; (5) Yvonne, an acupuncturist, is also an alcoholic; (6) Derek and (7) Doreen are possessed by Pentheus and Agave respectively. The first act closes on a wild dance of the four possessed women, Lena, Marcia, Yvonne, and Doreen.

Costume and prop are central to Act ii, which opens on a long autobiographical monologue of the nineteenth-century French hermaphrodite Herculine Barbin. Unemployed Derek, now possessed by her, is dressed in her clothes, while repeating that same monologue, but this time intercut by comments of Herculine. The acupuncturist Yvonne has an alcoholic fantasy of women in golden shoes, but she overcomes that possession to grow absorbed in painting her room. Derek as Pentheus is dressed as a woman by the two Dionysoses in tandem. Doreen, a secretary who is possessed by the violent events she hears on the radio, reacts violently to her neighbors, who respond with reciprocal violence. Exacerbated beyond endurance, and possessed by Agave, Doreen tears Derek/Pentheus to pieces. After these events *"Pentheus is brought by Dionysos into a dance of the whole company in which moments of Extreme Happiness and of violence from earlier parts of the play are repeated."*

In Act iii the "undefended day" is over, and each character briefly reveals her or his new post-violence life. Lena sublimates her power drive by caring for helpless old people. Yvonne finds purpose in a career as a butcher. Dan leaves the spiritual world to plant a garden in the desert. Marcia escapes from extraterrestrial voices by living alone in a boat. Paul, having left his wife and demanding job, is an alcoholic vagrant who boasts of keeping himself receptive to a new experience: "It may not be love next time. You can't tell what it's going to be. You're lucky if once in your life. So I stay ready." Derek luxuriates in his female body: "Every day when I wake up, I'm comfortable." Six characters have embarked on new lives as a result of their respective possession. The exception is Doreen.

In an interview Caryl Churchill suggested: "It is not a linear piece and is best approached quite openly, more like dance, letting it wash over you." In performance, with Ian Spink's choreography, it was easy to succumb to the hypnotic visualization, if not quite to undergo possession. Memory, aided by the photographs in the published text, recalls Lena's involuntary infanticide, Dan's seriatim murders of happy victims, Derek's ritualized investment of female garments, Paul's comic dance with his pig, and the final quiescence after the Bacchic dance. The printed text, however, is less memorable. Sexes and races are blended, but their separate speeches are rarely distinctive. For the most part the characters speak in swift questions, exclamations, repetitions, without striking verbal imagery.

The exception is Doreen, the last character to speak and the only one for whom the long day of possession does not end: "I can find no rest. My head is filled with horrible images. I can't say I actually see them, it's more that I feel them. It seems that my mouth is full of birds which I crunch between my teeth. Their feathers, their blood and broken bones are choking me. I carry on my work as a secretary." Since these are the final words of the Churchill/Lan modernization of *The Bacchae*, they ring out resonantly for those who have enjoyed violence but who are at the same time horrified at its potential for destruction. For her, as for most of us, there is no choice but to "carry on my work."[1]

Like Bond and Barker, Churchill and Lan probed the matter of Greece for meaningful drama, and like them, the joint authors modify the ancient teachings. Euripides' tragedy is a warning against flouting the divine and the irrational, which may be synonymous. More determinedly optimistic, Churchill and Lan hint at the possibility of restructuring a life after possession by violence. Only Doreen abstains.

The matter of Britain

Whether or not King Arthur ever existed, he and his knights fed the imagination of Western Europe. The hero of *The History of the Kings of Britain* by the twelfth-century Bishop, Geoffrey of Monmouth, Arthur was depicted as warrior, scholar, and ruler. Hugh A. MacDougall in his *Racial Myth in English History* has analyzed the political use of this legend of Celtic Britain, but two playwrights preceded MacDougall in

---

[1] For a feminist reading of the play, see Diamond.

discrediting the heroic portrait of Arthur. *The Island of the Mighty* by John Arden and Margaretta D'Arcy was examined for its verse rhythms in Chapter 4, but its ambitious scope deserves further scrutiny.

While still a student at Cambridge, John Arden composed an Arthurian verse play. Once exposed to Brecht, whom he read in the 1950s, Arden reworked the Arthurian material to demonstrate that today's British imperialism in decline resembled its Roman precursor. Arden's play was rejected by the Royal Court as a "boring historical play written in phoney verse" (Gray, *John Arden*, p. 130). Further revised, the matter of Britain was by 1971 shaped into a theatre trilogy. As Malcolm Page notes: "The final version [of *The Island of the Mighty*], written in 1970–71, was influenced by D'Arcy's contributions, travel in India, conflict in Northern Ireland, and Indian folkplays" (*Arden on File*, p. 48).

The full title of the Ardens' trilogy is *The Island of the Mighty: A Play on a Traditional British Theme in Three Parts*. In the titles of those three parts, the Ardens indicate their sources: "Part One, 'Two Wild Young Noblemen,' Concerning Balin and Balan and how ignorant they were" (derived mainly from Malory); "Part Two, 'Oh, The Cruel Winter,' Concerning Arthur – how he refused to see the power of his army was finished" (derived mainly from Geoffrey of Monmouth); "Part Three, 'A Handful of Watercress,' Concerning Merlin – how he needed to be alone and then how he needed not to be alone" (derived mainly from the epic of Crazy Sweeney). The summaries are Brechtian in their brevity, and they do not convey the Ardens' pervasive concern with ubiquitous suffering during noblemen's wars.

The long saga opens with Merlin in ceremonial robes, singing to us, an audience of "Christian men." He informs us that wild men have invaded King Arthur's domain and conquered his armies. The play is thus a kind of flashback as to how this happened. The ruler confers in crisp prose with his allies. Twin brothers, Balin is recruited by Merlin for Arthur's army, but Balan demurs and later becomes king of the matriarchal Picts. Soon Balan and Balin, unknown to one another, engage in mortal combat: "Oh dear brother you never understood / One single thing you ever did."

Part I of the Ardens' trilogy closes on Arthur's direct address to the audience, calling upon them to support him in war, in a ringing rhetoric reminiscent of Churchill's World War II speeches: "Companions: you alone are responsible for the continued religion and civilization of Britain. This Island has been called by her poets 'The Island of the Mighty.' Do not betray that title." That phrase will be repeated in the long play, acquiring an increasingly ironic timbre as war breeds war.

Battles proliferate in Part II. Arthur needs Roman-trained Medraut to preserve his power, and yet he steals the young man's bride, Gwenhwyvar, whose divine origin is revealed by Arthur's sister–mistress Morgan, grown old and isolated. Father and son, Arthur and Medraut, kill one another, like the twin brothers of Part I. Although Merlin did not intend to survive Arthur, he lives on, cursed into madness by a rival poet Taliesin. Merlin believes he is a bird, perhaps to fly away from the civilization he helped destroy.

Part III explores the relationship of the poet to history. It opens on a song about Merlin by the popular poet Aneurin: "It has been said that the death he saw / And the blood he smelt and the cries he heard / Struck him so deep at his brain-root / What could he do but become a bird?" Later Aneurin the nature poet reflects: "Oh why and when did Merlin ever dream / That men of power and progress and authoritative domain / Would keep his pale blood warmer / Than a little green plant that grows in the running stream?"

With Arthur dead, another warrior Bedwyr seeks power, and he needs the poet Merlin to confer legitimacy on his enterprise. But poet and warrior soon realize that they are superfluous men in an egalitarian society. Bedwyr throws Arthur's sword away, and Merlin regains his reason through the good agency of Morgan. Sane and humble, Merlin pays for milk with a song to a Cowherd's wife. Just before being stabbed in error, Merlin breathes a final quatrain: "O the running of the deer / And the beating of my heart – / I am welcome at last for the man that I am / And neither for craft nor art!" Aneurin, the one poet to survive, closes the long play with a song about Lazarus rising from the dead – an emblem perhaps for commoners who will rise from their own deaths in the battles of power-hungry rulers.

The critic Javed Malick has published a persuasive Bakhtinian reading of the trilogy, but his account minimizes the diffuseness of the Ardens' dramatic canvas. The playwrights have peopled their trilogy with men of varied classes and motives, as well as with clear-sighted women who are nevertheless (or therefore?) victimized. The battle scenes recall Shakespeare, but the stubborn sense of a racial destiny is also relevant to modern Britain. The title – *The Island of the Mighty* – is, of course, ironic, and yet an eventual popular force whispers through the verses of the poet Aneurin and the tenderness of old Morgan and young Gwenddydd.

The Ardens and the Royal Shakespeare Company resemble two islands of the feeble in their conflict over the 1972 production of the epic play. Arden was present during six of the eight weeks of rehearsal, but D'Arcy arrived for the first run-through, whereupon both authors declared: "the meaning of the play had been crucially shifted out of balance, producing an imperialistic effect alien to our original intentions." Refused a meeting with the whole company, the Ardens picketed the Aldwych Theatre. In a climate of reciprocal aspersions (not clarified by the account Arden published in *To Present the Pretence*) reviews were negative, but Benedict Nightingale conveys the power of that maligned production:

The "untidiness" reflects an energetic, questioning, stimulating mind, grappling with perhaps too many ideas; and the length seems inevitable, given the subject, which is nothing less than the decline of Britain from Roman stability [and totalitarianism] into the disarray of the Dark Ages . . . only the old, unrepentant Arden would have dared stride in, with his songs, rhyming couplets, gnarled, knotty prose, and glorious imagination, to chronicle an entire civilization and refashion as elaborate a myth as exists.

(*New Statesman*, December 15, 1972)

A bad press also belittled the achievement of a very different Arthurian play – *The Romans in Britain*, by Howard Brenton (1980). After three young Celts gambol nude on the stage, two are killed and one is raped by a Roman soldier. The killings went unremarked in the reviews, but the simulated rape caused the indefatigably censorious Mrs. Whitehouse to demand public prosecution. Most reviewers condemned both Mrs. Whitehouse and Brenton's play (as I confess that I did myself), but a calm reading of *The Romans in Britain* now arouses my admiration for an innovative, decidedly non-realistic structure, of which Brenton was aware: "There is no lead character. There are no 'goodies' and 'baddies.' There is no obvious, or usual 'moral message.' The scenes of the past are haunted by the 1980s with another army, the British, blundering around in another foreign country, Ireland. And the play's dramatic shape is perverse, for it goes from 'dark' to 'light.'" (*Plays*, Vol. 2, p. viii).

Brenton's play divides in two: Part I is entitled "Caesar's Tooth," and Part II bears a symmetrical title, "Arthur's Grave." Part I is set on the Thames in 54 B.C., and, like Brecht in his projections, Brenton summarizes the action in terse phrases. However, he does not, like Brecht, discourage suspense by posting these summaries during performance. In my own summary, I follow Brenton's headings.

"On the run" refers to two Irish petty criminals; their plea for mercy is ignored by three Celtic brothers, who, in accordance with tribal law, kill one refugee and send their dogs after the other. "A family and its fields" portrays a Druid society where the Mother refuses the request of neighboring tribesmen that they join forces against the Romans. In private she confesses that her tribe is bound by treaty with fishermen who have concluded peace with the Romans.

"Two worlds touch" dramatizes the sudden arrival of the Romans among the Celts. First come three soldiers who kill two of the brothers and rape the third; the Romans act brutally not in the thick of battle, but in a pastoral calm, because the Celts are obstacles to a refreshing swim. The actions of these common Roman soldiers mirror those of Caesar, who marches at the head of his legionnaires, ruthlessly disciplining his own men and terrorizing his enemies. "Fugitives and refugees" include the raped brother who predicts the future of his tribe: "Change ourselves into animals. The cat. No, an animal not yet heard of. Deadly, watching, ready in the forest. Something not human." "Caesar's tooth," aching, is pulled by himself and thrown away; as Brenton notes: "That sums up what he thinks of Britain" (*Plays*, Vol. 2, p. vii). "The gods grow small" in their scorched earth policy, for the Romans were considered gods. "Two murders" are a striking finale to this act set in another era; the fleeing Irishman is murdered by the slave he abducted, but that slave is shot by the automatic guns of *modern* soldiers. Caesar is suddenly in command, in modern Northern Ireland: "That everyday life will begin again. That violence will be reduced to an acceptable level. That civilisation may not sink, its great battle lost."

Part II takes place in Britain in 515 A.D. and again in Ireland in 1980 A.D. Brenton continues to summarize the action in terse phrases, beginning with a noun that encompasses all the scenes of bloodshed – "A blunder." The particular error, however, is the 1980 arrest by British soldiers of one Captain Thomas Chichester, who has been assigned to kill the IRA man O'Rourke: "If King Arthur walked out of those trees, now – know what he'd look like to us? One more fucking mick." Blunder righted, Chichester remains on stage, and the abrupt shift to the year 515 may be his dream. "An old man [of an old time] and his fields" are inseparable, even in the face of an English invasion. "A soliloquy" and "A dead Saxon" reaffirm the old man's stubborn stand, but his daughters rebel and run away. In 1980 "A contact" is made by Chichester with the O'Rourke he is under orders to kill. As he waits for his prey, he stretches out to nap, and again 515 may be his dream. "The last Roman Lady" with her steward and two cooks, flees the invading barbarians. Plague-ridden, she is shunned by the cooks and murdered by her steward. In 1980 once again, Chichester confesses his mission to O'Rourke – and his guilt: "in my hand there's a Roman spear. A Saxon axe. A British Army machine-gun." Offstage "an execution" is heard, when O'Rourke orders Chichester shot.

The final return to 515 can no longer be the dream – or nightmare – of the modern English officer. The two ancient English sisters accept the company of the two cooks, one of whom declares himself a poet. In "The making of Arthur" he proves his calling by telling a brief story that ends in nostalgia, like Brecht's *Caucasian Chalk Circle*: "And when he was dead, the King who never was and the Government that never was – were mourned. And remembered. Bitterly. / And thought of as a golden age, lost and yet to come." When asked the name of this mythical king "who never was," the cook turns to his colleague, who responds: "Er – any old name. Arthur? Arthur?" Legend is compounded of chance and necessity.

Once past the tantalizing question of nudity, reviewers of *The Romans in Britain* reproached Brenton with substituting ideas for characters, but instead he has sustained drama without sustaining characters. At first the onrush of Celts, Druids, and Romans is confusing, but Brenton holds firm control of his material by the Act I curtain, with its astonishing metamorphosis of Romans into British. Again in Act II, the time zigzag is at first confusing, but the final parallels are clear, without degenerating into agitprop. Caesar, the Roman conqueror, and Chichester, who belongs to an old British army family, are two faces of the same coin; they both do their military and patriotic duty with rare efficiency. Living in 1980, however, Chichester comes to question his orders, as Caesar never does; in O'Rourke's description: "The assassin, humanized by his trade." What Brenton does, even while indulging in the shock tactics he loves, is to set the tribal community of 54 B.C. against its Roman invaders; the anachronistic community of 515 A.D. against Roman disintegration. The combined imperial heritage tears at the conscience of Chichester in the present. He is executed offstage, but Brenton hopes to shock us – theatrically – into opposing, or at least questioning, his mission.

Medieval matter

Medieval England, where four great cycles of drama were performed on Corpus Christi Day, is rarely the setting for modern plays, so that three dense and diffuse works are exceptional. In other contexts I have mentioned David Edgar's *O Fair Jerusalem* (1975), with its plays within the play, several verse forms, and the equation of the medieval plague with the modern atomic bomb. In contrast, two equally baro-que dramas embedded in the Middle Ages comment only obliquely on the twentieth century. Both these panoramic plays – Peter Barnes' *Red Noses* (written 1978) and David Rudkin's *Triumph of Death* (1981) – are set mainly in France, and both are excrutiatingly difficult to describe.

As noted in the chapter "Theatre Framing Theatre," the Red Noses of Barnes' title are red bulbous clown-noses that are ubiquitous on stage. Set, like David Edgar's *Jerusalem*, during the black plague of 1348, the two acts of Barnes' drama have a clean architectural line; the first act traces the rising fame of a company of clowns who combat the plague by evoking laughter. The second act traces the dissolution of that company called Floties after their leader Father Flote, played by athletic Antony Sher in the original production. As in several of these non-realistic, quasi-historical plays, the stage brims with representa-tives of several social classes, from Pope Clement VI to whores proud of their trade. Among the Floties are a nobleman, a warrior, and priests, as well as the lame, the mute, and the blind, with the mute character Sonnerie communicating through the bells that dangle from his limbs. *Red Noses* also brims with several kinds of theatricality. As Barnes wrote in a program note: "The aim is to create, by means of soliloquy, rhetoric, formalized ritual, slapstick, songs, and dances, a comic theatre of contrasting moods and opposites, where everything is simultaneously tragic and ridiculous."

At the beginning of Barnes' play the plague-ridden die while a doctor admits his "100% record of failure." Father Flote and the leader of the Flagellants disagree so heatedly that they exchange clumsy blows, arousing laughter in the onlookers. Suddenly Flote understands his role: "God wants peacocks not ravens, bright stars not sad comets, red noses not black death." (The play's original title was *Red Noses, Black Death*.) Father Flote proceeds to joke in the face of the Flagellants, the corpse-gatherers, and the bloodthirsty; he founds "a new order without orders." Punning, quoting, juggling, rhyming, and dancing, the Red Noses reach the papal court at Avignon to perform a play within the play – *Everyman*, whose subversion was described in Chapter 5.

By Act II the fame of the Red Noses has spread throughout France, and they award themselves a celebratory banquet, which proves to be a last supper. As two lame brothers announce the end of the plague, Sonnerie dies, its last victim. The aristocratic Flotie proves to be a Judas-figure, who stabs his friend and leaves the company. The pope and the bishop resume pre-plague politics, with its cruelties and contradictions. In the midst of a wedding of gold-merchants and former whores the corpse-gatherers are hanged. While the Flagellants are burned at the stake, the Floties present a Nativity play, as described in Chapter 5. When that play's Herod orders the massacre of newborn infants, Pope Clement complains: "It isn't funny," and Flote/Herod replies: "No, it isn't funny. In the days of pestilence we could be funny but now we're back to normal, life is too serious to be funny." Discarding his red nose, Flote condemns his way of life: "Our mirth was used to divert attention whilst the strong ones slunk back to their thrones and palaces where they stand now in their saggy breeches and paper crowns, absurd like me."

Some half-dozen loyal Floties imitate their leader in removing their red noses. With defiant quips, they join in a dance – and are shot by the order of the inclement pope Clement. *"Only Flote remains miraculously unharmed."* Telling a lugubrious joke, he stands on his head, thus disorienting his designated executioner. But the renegade aristocrat sends an arrow through Flote's head and then plays a funeral air. As in Elizabethan tragedy, the highest-ranking character announces the new order, but in Barnes' play Pope Clement announces a reign of darkness. Barnes, however, adds an epilogue for the spotlighting of the pile of false red noses. Familiar comic lines are repeated, and the play concludes with the Floties' chorus and their leader's ringing finale: "God, count us in."

In the only book on Barnes' work Bernard Dukore notes: "actors switch from intellectual discourse, to period argot, to poetry, to modern slang, to rhetoric, to musical comedy, to ritual, to dance, to opera, to slapstick" (*The Theatre of Peter Barnes*, p. 65). Under the lavish direction of Terry Hands in the Royal Shakespeare Company production, the clean arcs of each act were masked by acrobatics, musical accompaniment, and ornate lighting. A more scrupulous separation of dramatic from choral scenes – as in Shakespeare or Brecht – might have highlighted the complexities of clowning in a dark world. The heavy-handed jokes might be buoyed up by light physical images, rounded off by the red noses. Without overt reference to the twentieth century, Barnes nevertheless poses the question of the role of comedy, and, more resonantly, of art in a time of crisis. He does so obliquely, theatrically, and with prismatic good humor. He deserves a poorer, but crisper production.

Quite the reverse for David Rudkin's *Triumph of Death*, which has received only a Birmingham Studio production in 1981. From the opening rectal spasms of the gorgeously attired excremental Pope Papatrix to the final Pieta of Luther in the lap of a Mother Manus, "our modern incarnation of the alchemical Virgin of the Tarot," *The Triumph of Death* demands spectacular design and performing virtuosity. Without some knowledge of Rudkin's other works, it is virtually impossible to make sense of this play that telescopes the thirteenth, fourteenth, and fifteenth centuries, but Rudkin has been consistently hostile to rational sense. Brought up in a strict Evangelical tradition, he has retained its intransigence, if not its faith. His theatre portrays a world at once evil and inscrutable, with little hope of redemption.

The Triumph of Death, like *Red Noses*, is divided into two parts but Rudkin's narrative lacks Barnes' clean line. Both his acts zigzag between rational cruelty and what, for want of a better term, might be called natural love. In various guises and disguises, the former is represented by Papatrix, Mother Manus, two scholarly monks Peek and Pickavance, and a fanatical monk oddly named Artaud (who played the compassionate monk in the Joan of Arc film of Carl Dreyer, to whom Rudkin dedicates his drama). Colorful and unstable are the forces of love. The first avatar appears in the figure of adolescent and demonic Stephen of Cloyes, who, while closeted in a medieval jakes, is vouchsafed a vision of the Lord. Mother Manus bends that vision to launch the Children's Crusade, in which a whole generation perishes, with the exception of three maimed survivors.

The actors of these three roles then double in the roles of Iron Age siblings Jehan, Gil, and Brans, and it is not clear whether their afflictions are transferred to the new characters. It is clear that the family of a dying Mother Heniot live in primitive harmony with the natural seasons and with one another. Interwoven with their family scenes is a love relationship between Lord Enester and the young man Moralis whom he rescues from execution. Ethical confusion in the family follows Mother Heniot's death, and Lord Enester becomes their Lord "Satan, Cernunnos, Pan, call Him what you will." Shrinking from neither scatology nor carnality, the polymorphous lord straightens the crooked back of Jehan, but an army of golden automatons (led by an Artaud who speaks with words spelled in reverse) slaughters this natural family, except for Jehan who is pregnant by her two brothers.

Part II of *The Triumph of Death* is briefer and somewhat simpler. The trial of Joan-Jehan pits the earnestly orthodox power of the Church against the natural goodness of the terrified child/woman. Convinced of her Satanic ties, the judges condemn her to be burned after the birth of her daughter: *"In chaos and ugliness the child is born, umbilicus bloodily cut, slimed homunculus, hung up by the heels for LADY ENES-TER's traumatic slap. Theatre fills with child's screaming."* Jehan collapses with her arm pointing toward the judge Enester: "Jesu . . .!" The identification is never explained, but one of Jehan's husband/brothers reappears as a werewolf who, rocking his imaginary daughter, delivers a long lyric monologue on the barbarically human.

In the final scene bearing the title of the play *The Triumph of Death*, Luther appears as in the Cranach portrait; he claims Joan of Arc as his mother and Gilles de Rais (Bluebeard) as his father. Racked by constipation, he speaks in contradictions, at first claiming: "The Resurrection of the Body is in this life," but finally he acquiesces to the modern avatar of a grasping and orthodox Mother Manus. Her last words apparently explicate Rudkin's title, *The Triumph of Death*: "Heaven. Hell. All that antique delirium. We're humanists now. We've got it right." The unusual economy of phrase highlights the irony.

Relentlessly individualistic, Rudkin opposes the age of industrialization and its successor, the so-called age of communication. A linguist and musicologist, he subsumes Christianity into more atavistic faiths. Like many social realists, he peoples his drama with several social classes, but unlike the realists, he favors none of them. Rather, he dramatizes their interpenetration, implying that it is dangerous for all of them to distance themselves from primitive nature. Unlike modern ecologists, Rudkin is obsessed not with saving our earth, but with living at a primitive level. Anachronistic and apocalyptic, he dazzles by the brilliance of his stage images, the density of his language, and the shifting ground of his characters. Like Barnes, his dramatic intensity needs subvention and climactic direction. In the meantime, we can read him.

Renaissance matter

The Renaissance is of course the great age of English theatre. From Marlowe's mighty line to Brome's *Jovial Crew*, some six hundred English dramas testify, as recent revivals prove, to vivid theatrical imagination propelled by language in joyous self-discovery. Even aside from Shakespeare, the Renaissance has been the preferred period for costume drama performed between the Romantic age and the twentieth century, but in the second half of the twentieth century playwrights looked beneath costumes for structural contours. An anglicized Brecht inspired their examination. After the 1956 London visit of the Berliner Ensemble, journalists took the word "Brechtian" to mean epic, non-Aristotelian, dialectical, or simply any historical drama that criticized a ruler or a ruling class (*cf.* Hahnloser-Ingold, *Dar Englischer Theater, passim*).

Neither journalists nor playwrights bothered about Brecht's problematic gestus, which I understand as the convergence of the historical moment with the theatrical moment, to which all aspects of theatre contribute; the most celebrated example is Barberini's gradual hardening toward Galileo, as he dons the ceremonial papal garments. Linking the Brechtian gestus to Bond, David Hirst underlines its theatricality: "The concept of gestic acting and performances implies a combination of the implications of the words 'gesture' and 'gist' in English: a concentration of visual meaning" (*Edward Bond*, p. 136). At the same time, gestus should (as it rarely does in England) concentrate the historical meaning.

Two modern English plays were often linked to Brecht in the 1960s, and they have since found their way into school curricula and study guides. Like Brecht's *Galileo*, these two plays are set in the Renaissance, *A Man for All Seasons* in England and *Luther* on the continent.

A Man for All Seasons (1960) by Robert Bolt explores Renaissance history through some of its most powerful figures. In the wake of Shaw's St. Joan (and perhaps Brecht's St. Joan as well), Bolt's Sir Thomas More appeals to us as a historical figure victimized in his own time. Bolt, who read history at the university, in 1954 conceived a radio play about Sir Thomas More, but he adapted it for the stage only in 1960, after the Berliner Ensemble's London visit. Bolt has acknowledged his debt to Brecht:

The style I eventually used was a bastardized version of the one most recently associated with Bertolt Brecht. This is not the place to discuss the style at any length, but it does seem to me that the style practised by Brecht differs from the style taught by Brecht, or taught to us by his disciples. Perhaps they are more Royalist than the King. Or perhaps there was something daemonic in Brecht the artist which could not submit to Brecht the teacher. That would explain why in the *Chalk Circle*, which is to demonstrate that goodness is a terrible temptation, goodness triumphs very pleasantly. And why in *Mother Courage*, which is to demonstrate the unheroic nature of war, the climax is an act of heroism which Rider Haggard might have balked at. And why in *Galileo*, which is to demonstrate the social and objective value of scientific knowledge, Galileo, congratulated on saving his skin so as to augment that knowledge, is made to deny its value on the grounds that he defaulted at the moment when what the world needed was for one man to be true to himself. I am inclined to think that it is simply that Brecht was a very fine artist, and that life is complicated and ambivalent. At all events I agree with Eric Bentley that the proper effect of alienation is to enable the audience *reculer pour mieux sauter*, to deepen, not terminate, their involvement in the play.

(Preface to Heinemann edition of *A Man for All Seasons*, p. xvii)

None of Bolt's thumbnail summaries of Brecht's major plays shows an awareness of *how* Brecht theatricalized history for contemporary use. Although Bolt draws upon R. W. Chambers' biography of Sir Thomas More, the play is also a parallel to and a rebuttal of Brecht's *Galileo*, a man for certain scientific seasons (Harben, *Twentieth Century English History Plays*, pp. 161, 163). Bolt's More is "one man [who remained] true to himself," but Bolt's play skimps on the social repercussions of that truth. Moreover, Bolt's play specifically contradicts one of the most celebrated passages of Brecht's *Galileo*. The scientist's student condemns his fallen mentor: "Unhappy is the land that breeds no hero." And the old scientist retorts: "Unhappy is the land that needs a hero." Bolt's More is a hero despite his disclaimers, and he verbosely attitudinizes:

if we lived in a State where virtue was profitable, common sense would make us good, and greed would make us saintly. And we'd live like animals or angels in the happy land that *needs* no heroes. But since in fact we see that avarice, anger, envy, pride, sloth, lust and stupidity commonly profit far beyond humility, chastity, fortitude, justice and thought, and [we?] have to choose, to be human at all . . . why then perhaps we must stand fast a little – even at the risk of being heroes.

Bolt takes that risk for his hero.

Bolt's plot proceeds through the time-honored conflict of monolithic personalities: a steadfast hero (More) versus shifty villains (Protestant Cromwell and Catholic Chapuys, who finally "link arms"), with lesser characters faltering on the sidelines (More's wife, daughter, son-in-law, and friend). Although we know the outcome of the conflict, we are still caught up in the successive tribulations of More until his last heroic words before being beheaded: "[God] will not refuse one who is so blithe to go to him." Bolt does not quote the darker aspects of More's humor.

Passing mention of rebels in the north hints at a wider context for More's audience to his oath, and yet the focus of the action grows ever narrower as More is stripped of office, wealth, freedom, and finally life. At no point does Bolt invent a gestus, such as the belligerency that renders absurd the soldiering of Mother Courage's son Eilif. Determinedly non-realistic, Bolt calls images to his aid, opposing the superhuman imagery of water against the social imagery of land (Bolt's terms).

A Man for All Seasons, which was widely performed as a play for all tastes, adopted Brechtian estrangement techniques without understanding Brecht's commitment to social enlightenment through these techniques. As Bolt was well aware, his Common Man was his main alienation device, which he endowed with representative importance: "The Sixteenth Century is the Century of the Common Man. Like all the other centuries." However, unlike the Singer of the *Caucasian Chalk Circle*, Brecht's only play to use an epic narrator, Bolt's Common Man does not provide social background, or delve into the characters' minds. Even less does he enunciate the political meaning of an event; in short, he does not enlarge the story to an epic dimension.

Bolt has defended his Common Man:

the word 'common' was intended primarily to indicate 'that which is common to us all'. But he was taken instead as a portrayal of that mythical beast The Man In The Street . . . But once he was identified as common in that sense, my character was by one party accepted as a properly belittling account of that vulgar person, and by another party bitterly resented on his behalf. (Myself I had meant him to be attractive, and his philosophy impregnable.)   (*Preface*, p. xviii)

As played by Leo McKern, the Common Man is indeed attractive, but he grows increasingly more sinister with each change of costume. Wholly self-seeking, Bolt's Common Man is finally condemned by his heroic Sir Thomas More. As the Jailer of More in prison, the Common Man cuts short the family's farewell, pleading: "You understand my position, sir, there's nothing I can do; I'm a plain simple man and just want to keep out of trouble." More then bursts out: "Oh, Sweet Jesus! These plain, simple, men!" The blame is implicit in the pluralization. Although Bolt's More is a conventional costume hero, Paul Scofield's portrayal endowed him with humor and wiliness.

Luther (1961) by John Osborne sounds like the Protestant reply to Catholic More, and that reply leaned lightly on Brecht.[2] Osborne's narrator, a Knight with an occasional banner, appears only fitfully. Although Osborne relied on Erik Erikson's *Young Man Luther* (and possibly on Roland Bainton's *Here I Stand: the Life of Martin Luther*), he, like Bolt, was more faithful to personalities than to social forces. It is true that the Knight charges Luther with betraying the peasants in their rebellion against the nobles, but that remains a fact without an interpretation in Osborne's play, as one could not imagine it in a Brecht play. Although some critics viewed Osborne's drama as a neurosis magnified to destiny, the playwright does dramatize the corruption of the church and the hard materiality of daily life. Osborne's hero, far from being a man for all seasons, is a man against

2 Simon Trussler argues against Osborne's Brechtianism.

all reason in his tortured and tortuous rebellion. Finally, however, Osborne's Luther attains harmony in his private life and apparently abjures his public life, without a Brechtian gestus to link the two.

Another flawed hero comes to the fore in *The Royal Hunt of the Sun* (1964) by Peter Shaffer, in a play that rivals *A Man for All Seasons* in popularity, but, unlike Bolt, Shaffer acknowledges no debt to Brecht, in spite of the presence of a narrator. One of the first of Shaffer's several plays to dramatize the power of the irrational, *The Royal Hunt*, directed by John Dexter, benefited from a spectacular setting by Michael Annals. As Shaffer writes in a production note: "My hope was always to realize on stage a kind of 'total' theatre, involving not only words but rites, mimes, masks and magics." And further, "Avoid realism, and conjure effects (with the help of lighting of course) of jungles and mountains; and the immense over-organized ritual of Inca life from placing, gesture and acting choices." In no publication does Shaffer record his conceptual debt to Artaud's production plans for *The Conquest of Mexico*, but the similarities are too close to be coincidental.[3]

Artaud intended the first production of his Theatre of Cruelty to be *The Conquest of Mexico*, and he published his conceptual plan as part of his "Second Manifesto of the Theatre of Cruelty." Although Artaud and Brecht are polar opposites in some respects, the French prophet's opening sentences might have been written by the German Marxist: "[*The Conquest of Mexico*] will stage events rather than men. Men will appear in their proper place with their emotions and psychology interpreted as the emergence of certain powers in the light of the events and historical destiny in which they played their role."

Brecht tends to dramatize "events and historical destiny" as civil war between classes, but Artaud was prescient in his valorization of what has come to be called the Third World:

From a historical point of view, *The Conquest of Mexico* raises the question of colonisation. It revives Europe's deep-rooted self-conceit in a burning, inexorably bloody manner, allowing us to debunk its own concept of its supremacy. It contrasts Christianity with far older religions . . . It contrasts the tyrannical anarchy of the colonisers with the deep intellectual concord of those about to be colonised . . . From a social point of view, it demonstrates the peacefulness of a society which knew how to feed all its members and where the Revolution had taken place at its inception.

3 Robert Brustein mentions Shaffer's debt to Artaud in *The New Republic* (May 29, 1965). See also Peter L. Podol, "Contradictions and Dualities in Artaud and Artaudian Theater: *The Conquest of Mexico* and the Conquest of Peru," *Modern Drama* (December, 1983.)

Theatrically, Artaud is excited by these events and forces, harmonizing in a gigantic spectacle composed of "images, moves, dances, rituals, music, melodies cut short, and sudden turns of dialogue." Mexico was a mythic land for Artaud before he set foot on its soil. Although he hopes to stage events rather than men, the production plan does speak of "Montezuma's inner struggle, a king torn in two, history having been unable to enlighten us on his motives." Nor does Artaud enlighten us on the substance of Montezuma's inner struggle.

In *The Royal Hunt of the Sun* Shaffer transfers the setting from Mexico to Peru, but he accepts Artaud's view of history and his plans for its theatricalization. However, he transfers the inner struggle to his European protagonist Pizarro, who is torn between love for the Inca king Atahuallpa and the practicalities of his imperialist mission. Against this Artaudian background, Shaffer imposes a Brechtian narrator-figure, Old Martin, whose memory structures the play. More consistently than Bolt's Common Man, Martin guides our responses – by his idealism, fidelity, and final disillusion with Pizarro. And like Bolt's Common Man, Shaffer's Old Martin fails to draw enlightenment for our own time. Unlike Bolt and Osborne, who perused modern histories of their respective protagonists, Shaffer apparently relied on W. H. Prescott's *Conquest of Peru*, first published in 1847 (Harben, *Twentieth Century English History Plays*, p. 176 and *passim*).

At age seventeen Martin enlists as the page of the Conquistador Pizarro, and he looks back after half a century on "the royal hunt of the sun." Although Old Martin opens and virtually closes Shaffer's play, he intrudes only occasionally into the continuous action. In a few swift strokes Shaffer paints the Spanish poverty that enabled Pizarro to recruit a ragged army, the greed of the Spanish leaders, the opportunism of the Spanish clergymen, and the thirst for glory of Pizarro, a cynical self-made Renaissance man. In South America Pizarro undertakes what he senses is his last adventure. Although in his sixties, he leads his men in full armor across the Andes to claim the country for Spain, to convert the Indians to Christianity, and to amass booty for his troops – the colonization abhorred by Artaud. Since the Inca ruler Atahuallpa believes himself to be descended from the sun, the Royal Hunt of the Sun is the ignoble march into his kingdom.

In a daring exploit, the outnumbered Spaniards capture the Inca ruler, who barters for his freedom with the promise of a room full of gold. The stage glistens as Indians carry in the precious metal from all corners of the Inca kingdom. When the stage-room is full, the naive ruler expects to go free. But, pressured by representatives of Spain and the church, faced with the rebellion of his troops, Pizarro breaks his promise and allows the garrotting of the Inca king, who is calm in the belief that he will rise again with the morning sun. That is the second Hunt of the Sun, which proves to be an indifferent star when it rises on the corpse of the Inca ruler. A distraught Pizarro charges the dead Inca with cheating. In effect, Pizarro dies with Atahuallpa, for his spirit is deceived in its hope of immortality: "to speak truth, he sat down that morning and never really got up again." The royal hunt of the sun is at once the Spanish conquest of Peru, the Spanish greed for gold, and Pizarro's need for faith, temporarily localized in Atahuallpa.

The Royal Hunt of the Sun took several years and revisions. Shaffer has described his intention: "I'd always wanted to write a large epic play . . . What I learned from the production was that plays must centre on people; audiences mostly remembered the confrontations between Pizarro and Atahuallpa, although they don't meet at all in the first act and only have three scenes together in the second" (Quoted in Kerensky, *New British Drama*, p. 45). In the original production, passionate acting by Colin Blakely and Robert Stephens bolstered the impression of continuous confrontation and spiritual brotherhood. Shaffer's text deliberately ignores Artaud's intention of staging events rather than men. Although the phrase "large epic play" summons Brecht to mind, Shaffer retreats to that unbrechtian staple of Aristotelian drama, the conflict of heroic antagonists. In spite of its reach toward total theatre, *The Royal Hunt of the Sun* relies on the visual accoutrements of costume drama.

Shaffer does attempt to introduce a theological argument – the Spaniards' Christian God opposed to the Incas' sun god. Socially, Shaffer contrasts the unruly Spaniards with the disciplined Incas. Each is subservient to an iron-willed ruler, but the Inca subservience structures a whole society, whereas the Spaniards feed on greed. Finally, we admire Atahuallpa more than his "civilized" conqueror, for whom we feel most sympathy when he recognizes his defeat in his victory. Shaffer has offered us history as spectacle, as in nineteenth-century melodrama, but he also burdens that spectacle with a metaphysical message – divinity is what we believe.

In concept, staging, and dialogue *The Royal Hunt of the Sun* is diametrically opposed to David Storey's *Cromwell* (1973), a non-realistic play tenuously set in the English Renaissance. The jacket of the published play shows an etching of Oliver Cromwell, but the seventeenth-century Puritan does not appear in Storey's play; nor is his name mentioned. Far from a duel of opposing concepts embodied in their respective heroes, *Cromwell* stages opposing armies who cannot keep track of their leaders, much less their principles. Not only is there no resplendent burden of gold; even the uniforms are virtually indistinguishable. As Storey himself states his message: "The main point of *Cromwell* was that it has become immaterial which side you choose to be on. Political decisions make men destroy the values which they are ostensibly defending" (*Plays and Players* [September, 1973], p. 32).

Storey's plays usually adhere to surface realism, but *Cromwell* is like *Home* in its unlocalized setting, which dim light rendered mysterious in the original Royal Court production. Not literally a costume drama, *Cromwell* announces its period by the speech of the characters: one by one, they enter on scene – two Irish tramps, a Welshman, the English Proctor, and a chamberlain or Mr. Chamberlain who recruits the others for his unnamed army. Wandering through the woods, the men come upon a coffin on a cart, and one by one, the relatives of the dead man enter on scene – an old man, an idiot, a middle-aged woman Margaret, and her daughter Joan. The able-bodied men push the cart until they are stopped by rebel soldiers. When the coffin is opened, it is seen that the dead father of the family has been replaced by a soldier with his throat cut. His avengers interrogate each member of the group, torturing them offstage, but Proctor escapes.

In Act II the Irishmen and the Welshman are in one shabby uniform, and Proctor in another. He kills the Welshman and takes the Irishmen to prison: "You'll come with me . . . without ideals no man can live." But one of the Irishmen retorts: "And with ideals we end like this. (*Gestures round.*)" Before Proctor can find his army, Joan and the idiot offer bread and water to him and his prisoners, so that a weary Proctor is seduced by peace. Ignoring the rebel Cleet and his utopian vision of equality, Proctor and Joan agree to start a new life together, while the Irishmen wander on, refused ferryboat passage by a mysterious Boatman.

Time has elapsed before Act III, for Joan and Proctor have a child, and a farm where the Irishmen occasionally work. Again Cleet arrives with his egalitarian inducements, but Proctor replies: "No cause is greater than its means." The civil war grinds on, and soldiers burn the farmhouse containing the child. Proctor prays for a cause by which to live, but, broken in spirit, he receives no sign. At the last he and Joan are ferried by the Boatman into darkness. It is the same Boatman who earlier refused passage to the Irishmen; nor will he give them passage now, when Proctor offers to pay their way: "Each must find his ooown." What each finds is not revealed, for Storey's drama ends on Proctor's question: "Do you see the light?"

In his statement about the futility of war, Storey oversimplifies the effect of his play, which does not visit a plague equally on both warring houses: the rebel Cleet has more generous ideals than the government Chamberlain or the mercenary soldiers. Joan, who takes no sides, is indomitably ready to start again – after her parents are killed, after her child is killed. Above all, the Irishmen are jauntily dedicated to their own survival.

Except for offstage battle noises and onstage exhibitions of force, Storey gives few indications for the staging. In its original production at the Royal Court, stage darkness increased the ideological confusion, not only as to the identity of the troops but even as to the identity of the individual characters (played by such Court stalwarts as Joan Barrett, Brian Cox, and Albert Finney). Hard Brechtian lighting could make telling points in the staging: not only the "immaterial" nature of which side one chooses, but how individuals live through civil war. Or how they die.

The Royal Court production failed to articulate Storey's varied register of language, for which Shakespeare – no less – was the model. The Irishmen, first on stage, are a music-hall duet. Each at times utters the oath "To God . . ." and yet O'Halloran assures Joan: "There's nothing beyond death, you know." Linked to no faith, their oath is brief and blasphemous, much like an exclamation point. Sometimes their exchanges fall into split pentameters. So spirited is their self-preserving banter that it is hard to accept the Boatman's final judgment of these attractive Irish comics: "They hang like leeches to the things that others have . . . hands which always receive can offer nought." We have witnessed that the Irishmen put their hands to the cart with its burden, to the rope that imprisons them, to Proctor's farmland, but only reluctantly to weapons. Their voices are busier than their hands. At the very start of the play, they tease one another with insults, and they talk a fierce fight with a colleague, but they do not lift a fist. Bowing to anyone in power, they exaggerate their deference and thus subvert the power, like the Good Soldier Schweik.

In sharp opposition to their music-hall duets are the cadences of the overly symbolic Boatman, whose prose sometimes scans in rough pentameters: "the pattern of its light at dawn and dusk . . ." Cleet is less mysterious than the Boatman, but equally schematic, and his speech shifts between phrases of sympathy for the underprivileged and curt commands to his soldiers; he is the play's closest equivalent to the titular Cromwell. The speech of the other characters also falls into consistent patterns – the stiff declarations of Proctor, the warm phrases of Joan (both occasionally falling into pentameters), the staccato threats of soldiers of either side.

William Hutchings has written perceptively that in *Cromwell* the "concepts of madness and ideology are repeatedly conjoined . . . the presence of an ideology gives each person a semblance of madness in the estimation of those who do not share his views" (*Plays of David Storey*, pp. 38–9). Repetitions of the word "fool" underline the point, as well as the sporadic presence of the mute fool Mathew, who is sometimes a killer and finally a victim.

Although Storey himself has called attention to his blank verse cadences, I was not aware of them in the theatre, but in retrospect one can scan such prose as Joan's speech: "Let leaders lead: direct us as they will / – support the good, and fight against the ill . . . / what can't be taken is our joy in work / . . . our life, like theirs, is forfeit in the end / . . . But what you looked for was a kind of death / – the uniform . . . at first, and then a home – / inviolable extremes that like a hearse / can take you safely to a given end" (my scansion). The iambic rhythm is not "owned" by any single character, however, and were the drama played to emphasize that rhythm, one might recognize in it a counter-text to Shakespeare's depiction of history as the deeds of powerful men. In Brecht's opposition to the Great Man view of history, he sometimes used blank verse to satirize such figures, e.g. Mauler and Arturo Ui. Storey, in contrast to both Shakespeare and Brecht, presents his pentameters embedded in prose print.

The title *Cromwell* is ironic, for Cromwell is not only offstage but beyond reference. In Storey's play no one profits from the war, but, willy-nilly, little people live and die by the orders of heroic figures they never see – "A moving vapour," "the Big One."[4]

A Big One is very much in evidence in still another contemporary play with a Renaissance setting, Pam Gems' *Queen Christina*, (1975, revised 1982). Based on the life of the Swedish Queen, Gems' sprawling play "is not a documentary, thus characters have been concertinaed, and some events changed. All plays are metaphors, and the dilemma of the real CHRISTINA, reared and educated as a man for the Swedish throne, and then asked to marry and breed for the succession, is perhaps not irrelevant today." Gems rubs our noses in that relevance to a feminist perspective.

From her first appearance as a child who witnesses the stillbirth of her sibling, Christina is volatile. Full-grown and homely, she behaves

---

4 Howard Barker's *Victory: Choices in Reaction* (1983) introduces leading historical figures into the post-Civil War "reaction."

like a man, even to taking mistresses. At the same time, she is tempted by handsome men. The play itself does not dramatize what Gems calls her "dilemma," since Christina steadfastly refuses marriage for breeding. Instead, she fences philosophically with Descartes, and she contrives an end to the Thirty Years' War. Eluding both her Lutheran Chancellor and her French Catholic lover – both of whom wish to manipulate her as ruler – she renounces the crown and converts to the Catholicism described in the text as "A Warm Wind from The South."

Christina's first stop is France, where she finds the man-hating bluestockings distasteful, but they will bide their time: "We recruit them all as their breasts fall." In Rome, she is a valuable political pawn, in spite of her abdication. From Descartes she had learned of free will, but she accuses the Pope of stifling women's freedom through his insistence on chastity, with sex permissible only for procreation. Defiantly, she takes a Neapolitan lover, who pursues her for his own purposes. Tempted to deliver the kingdom of Naples from the Spanish yoke, Christina goes into battle, but she is defeated by the treason of her lover. She cuts his throat – and from that moment Gems' play begins to lose credibility.

This woman warrior is so horror-stricken by her bloody deed that she falls into a semi-coma, from which she recovers when an insouciant child slaps her. Cured, she is offered Poland by a handsome Cardinal, and although she refuses, she still tries to lure him to her bed. In a spontaneous moment, she saves the life of her servant's child (offstage), and she is soon preaching to the Cardinal equality of the classes and peace between nations:

Yet who are the poorest of all? Women, children . . . the old. Are they the fighters, the creators of war? You say you want me for the fight, and it's true, I was bred as a man, despising the weakness of women. I begin to question the favour . . . I begin to see that I have been a traitor to my sex . . . I begin to perceive that I am a woman. What that is, heaven knows . . . the philosophy is yet to be written, there is a world to be explored.

Like modern feminism, Christina has moved from competing with men to valorizing the feminine. Finally, she is resentful that she never had children – "Where's my daughter, where's my son, you've cheated me, all of you!" – as though the choice were not her own. With her whip she slashes at the Cardinal, while screaming that she will not fight. Then, abruptly, she drops the whip and embraces him. When he draws back, she becomes hysterical, but regains self-control and invites him on his next visit to see her library. When Christina leaves the stage, the servant and the Cardinal *"exchange a smile,"* the promise of an assignation.

Gems' Christina is a Renaissance women, in the popular meaning of the adjective – learned, imperious, iconoclastic, skeptical, and culturally alive. For all her belated feminism, however, she keeps abasing herself to handsome men. If the philosophy of womanhood "is yet to be written," with its intimations of the cultural definition of gender, Gems overemphasizes conventional sexual behavior with regard to desire and jealousy. And these emotions mix uneasily with Christina's phrases that coincide with those of contemporary feminist tracts. Until the last scenes, however, Gems' non-realistic chronicle play presents a vivid portrait of its protagonist moving within historical constraints.

English enlightenment

Gems' *Queen Christina* inaugurated her several woman-centered plays, usually set in the twentieth century. Although set in the eighteenth century, two historical dramas reflect on twentieth-century class and gender roles: *Restoration* by Edward Bond (1981) and *The Grace of Mary Traverse* by Timberlake Wertenbaker (1985). France rather than England dominates eighteenth-century Europe – intellectually with the publication of the Encyclopedia, and politically with the French Revolution. Yet Bond and Wertenbaker prefer to stage an England mired in aristocratic privilege and at the same time grinding toward industrialization. It is a daring subject, and both experienced production difficulties. *Restoration*, originally commissioned by the RSC, was returned to the author, who sent it to the Royal Court, straining that theatre's dwindling resources. (The RSC did produce a slightly revised version in 1988.) Wertenbaker, an unknown, was relegated to the upstairs studio of the Court.

Restoration seems an odd title for a play set in the eighteenth century in England, since it designates the seventeenth-century return of the monarchy after the Cromwellian Revolution. With his title, however, Bond suggests the witty flavor of that period, while also exposing its callous behavior. And "restoration" without the capital letter is an abstract noun, which points to the return of feudal fealty in the play. Bond may also intend his title to promise compensation by means of his play – the restoration of the good name of a servant who is hanged for his master's crime.

Bond draws the class lines through concrete stage details: the arranged marriage between business and peerage, the parallel commands of Lord Are to his footmen and Lady Are to her maid Rose, the cleaning of aristocrats' silver by servile Mrs. Hedges, the heavy trunks carried by the footmen Frank and Bob, the divergent ethics of Frank and Bob, which nevertheless lead them both to the gallows.

Unusually for Bond, he does not set his parable in the frame of a larger social canvas but contents himself with the representative status of his characters – stylish fop, ambitious merchant, accommodating clergyman, and overworked servants. As in Brecht's *Good Person of Setschuwan* or *Caucasian Chalk Circle*, morality is a luxury that the impoverished can not afford. Rather than insisting on his innocence, Lord Are's servant Bob depends upon the good will of his master, and is hanged. Yet his death is not a foregone conclusion, as we hope against hope that he will be pardoned for the homicide perpetrated by his master. Lest we miss the injustice of the social hierarchy, Bond points it out – as Brecht often does – in the songs of the underprivileged, and, as in Brecht, the working characters *sing* social truths to which they are blind in the dialogue of the play. More explicitly than in Brecht's fables, the black servant Rose, daughter of a slave, enunciates a final moral. Although my summary may sound like a socially realistic play transplanted to the eighteenth century, the songs, the aristocratic poses, and the discrete scenes slant the play toward Brecht's epic theatre.

Although Timberlake Wertenbaker is at least as scathing as Bond about aristocratic privilege, she offers no simple analysis or solution. Her title, *The Grace of Mary Traverse*, is ambiguous. Mary, an Everywoman name, traverses or crosses both class and sex boundaries in her quest for enlightenment or a grace by which to live. In a key scene of this female Rake's Progress Mary has been treated like a whore by her father, and she accuses him in puns that recall Restoration drama: "you make fatherhood an act of grace, an honour I must buy with my graces, which you withdraw as soon as I disgrace you."

The Grace of Mary Traverse progresses by cameo scenes rather than the cause-and-effect events of naturalism, a style antipathetic to Wertenbaker, as she notes in her preface: "My plays are an attempt to get away from the smallness of naturalism, from enclosed rooms to open spaces, and also to get ideas away from the restraints of closed spaces to something wider." Her protagonist Mary Traverse, schooled by her merchant father in a lady's graces, hungers for experience outside the closed space of her drawing-room. Abruptly, she is in Cheapside, escaping rape by Lord Gordon through the intervention of the country girl Sophie. Nevertheless, Mary's appetite for adventure is whetted, and she makes an informal Faustian contract with her servant Mrs. Temptwell who arranges her initiation into sexual pleasure, gambling, cock-fighting, and prostitution. But the greatest temptation proves to be the power to change the world. In a scene of few words the ingenuous Sophie falls in love with the radical Jack, whose egalitarian ethos inspires Mary.

The goal of the idealistic young women, Mary and Sophie, coalesces with that of the bubble-headed Lord Gordon, and the three characters become tools of the sinister Mr. Manners, who manipulates their separate purposes into anti-Catholic sentiment. What started as an urge to liberty terminates in the Gordon Riots, where many lives are lost: "More burning, more bones." Although Wertenbaker's Lord Gordon, like his historical prototype, goes unpunished for the riot, the worker Jack is hanged, and Sophie's optimistic spirit is broken.

The play's final scene, in a pastoral landscape outside of London, hints at enlightenment: Mrs. Temptwell returns to the land from which she was dispossessed by Mary's father, who learns in turn "Not to take orders. Not to give them. Not to want to give them." At the last it is Mary who encourages Sophie to seek human beauty, beyond nature: "One day we'll know how to love this world." Sophie is dubious, but she finally agrees with Mary that this world is "all we have." In contrast to *Restoration*, where the black servant Rose is the only clear-sighted character, all four of Wertenbaker's central characters learn through experience – at a cost: Mary's wealthy father renounces political ambition, and the servant Mrs. Temptwell renounces revenge. Mary Traverse renounces her quest for experience, but the generous country girl Sophie loses her child and her lover; the two young women still seek grace.

Timberlake Wertenbaker, bilingual in French and English, has translated plays by Marivaux, who was an habitué of salons where the questions of feminism were first raised. His elegance is congenial to her, and like Bond, she can turn a deft epigram, for example, "Talk of God leads to silence." She can contrast Lord Gordon's pernicious foppish speech with Jack's eloquent monosyllables. She can contrast three women and make them all credible. Mary Traverse herself is a mercurial protagonist, Faustian in her aspiration, picayune in her achievement, unremitting in her questions.

In a Note to the printed text of *The Grace of Mary Traverse* Wertenbaker claims: "Although this play is set in the eighteenth century, it is not a historical play." She is wrong. In spite of the analogy of the Gordon riots with events in Northern Ireland, the feel of the play is historical, from coffee-house to private club, from dispossessed

10 *The Grace of Mary Traverse* by Timberlake Wertenbaker, directed by
Danny Boyle at the Royal Court, 1985, with Janet McTeer as Mary

country people to new urban style, from marriageable debutante to women burned as witches, from hereditary privilege to the quest for enlightenment or grace. Wertenbaker claims that she "found the eighteenth century a valid metaphor," but she does not reveal for what, as she leaves questions unanswered. Any period of history may be a "valid metaphor" for our time, when we are perhaps more acutely conscious than ever before of unanswered questions, too often shrugged away as unanswerable.

This modern isle

In this trip through dramas of Western history which are by definition non-realistic, we arrive at the twentieth century. As the twenty-first century approaches, the twentieth recedes into history, and I select for comment a few non-realistic plays acutely marked by a consciousness of modern history.

Modern England may be dated from World War II, when Britain lost her empire. As Angus Calder revealed in his sobering study *The People's War*, the cooperation, self-sacrifice, and sheer tenaciousness of unsung heroes saved the island from invasion. Playwrights still unborn at that time have been drawn to World War II as modern matter. David Hare has set a television play as well as the first and last scenes of *Plenty* during World War II; Howard Brenton and Joe Orton have both chosen as a target Winston Churchill, the Prime Minister during World War II, and Stephen Lowe has washed the final events of that war over the daily lives of his characters.

Touched (1977) presents nine scenes in the lives of three Nottingham sisters during the hundred days between the German and the Japanese surrenders in 1945. On the page the play reads like a realistic dramatization of wartime privations – food, sex, and cigarettes – interspersed with war news heard on the radio. But atmospheric effect supersedes realistic detail: "*Lighting is crucial to the production. The set should be as simple as possible.*" In the wake of plays by Wesker and Storey, which showed people at work, the work of Lowe's women overrides their location: washing and ironing laundry at home, soldering phials in a factory, dismembering chickens in a hotel kitchen, and making sandwiches for a picnic to celebrate the end of World War II.

Lowe's skeletal plot centers on the emotional starvation of three sisters, Sandra, Joan, and Betty. Sandra and Joan are married to dimly remembered soldiers far from home, and Betty fondles love letters from a sailor she has seen only once. Joan's daughter Pauline is cherished by all three, but especially by Sandra, whose son was killed in an air-raid. Since his death, she has been untouched by feeling, until she shows signs of pregnancy. Subservient to their sexual code, Sandra's mother and sisters sentence her to an abortion, which she refuses. She is then ostracized by the women in her family. When a seventeen-year-old epileptic admits that he is the father of the unborn child, Sandra laughs derisively at him, then describes how she was "touched."

Along with other English women, she queued outside the Italian prisoner camp. When "her" prisoner emerged, Sandra led him into the woods, where she spread out her lace table-cloth with her rations and tea service: "I reached into his crumpled clothes, I touched him. Touched. I felt the shiver. The pulse. He is real." In gratitude for the joy of that "real"ness, Sandra prays. But the replacement child in her womb proves to be a hallucination, and she wonders whether the "real" touch was only her imagination. The epileptic adolescent re-assures her; he watched the coupling.

The last scene of *Touched* also takes place in the woods, on August 15, 1945. With the "bastard" gone, Sandra is included in her family's victory celebration. Her sister Joan dreams of taking her returned husband far from Nottingham. Her sister Betty displays the ring given her by a Polish pilot who has promised to take her to his country estate. After doubting the rosy future of her sisters, Sandra tells the child Pauline a mordant tale of a vengeful God: "And the best part of the joke for God is that we don't even see this . . . We don't see he's taken the life from us and replaced it with a dry warmth that –" Again Sandra spreads the lace tablecloth and sets it for a picnic. The loudspeaker intercuts the broadcast on which the play opened – British horror at the Nazi concentration camp – with General MacArthur's jubilation at the Japanese surrender. When we next see Sandra, she *"lies, face forward, on her cloth."* She is part of both announcements, at once a celebrant of victory and a helpless victim.

By choosing the hundred days between V-E and V-J Day, Lowe anchors us in the specific environment of the period, including radio news bulletins. Summaries of historic events are now a commonplace of theatre vocabulary, sometimes associated with Brechtian dramaturgy, although he did not originate the device. More subtly derived from Brecht is Lowe's sense of parable in the fate of these women, but Lowe spurns the distancing that Brecht viewed as an instrument to provoke audience meditation. Instead, Lowe provokes meditation by integrating history into the daily lives of the women: their failure to react to the description of the concentration camp; their suspicion that news of the end of the European war is withheld from them; their vagueness about the Pacific war; their anger against a privileged class, which leads to the landslide Labor victory; and the pitiful celebration of peace with its fantasy of a new and different life.

By choosing the small details of daily routine – laundry at home, unsanitary conditions at work, sensual deprivation everywhere – Lowe embeds the private in the public, and at the same time he plays private distress against public celebration. It is possible to view Sandra's false pregnancy as that of the new England; it is possible to read international cooperation in the sisters who are "touched" by an Italian prisoner and a Polish ally. The white laundered sheets may hint at a harmony that is never fulfilled. Although Lowe never pushes such interpretations in the manner of earlier playwrights of the 1970s, he shifts into a lyrical gear at moments of emotional intensity, departing from realism.

In plumbing the history of World War II, Lowe strips his plot to a very few incidents involving the central characters, but those incidents are carefully framed in historical context. Far more detailed in his attention to documents and his analysis of events, David Edgar has based some forty plays on contemporary history, even tabulating parallel paths for fictional and historical events. He has composed swift agitprop skits and adapted other people's books; he can spotlight a family or fill the stage with a whole populace. Capable of considerable variety, Edgar is proud of his consistent socialist realism. I have no quarrel with the socialism, but since I consider his *Maydays* (1983) non-realistic, I spend a moment on terminology.

Although Edgar derives his opposition of realism to naturalism from the Marxist critic John Berger, the distinction was already made by Stanislavski. Edgar summarizes Berger: "He argues that, unlike the bourgeois form of naturalism (which attempts to portray a surface view of human behavior as accurately as possible), realism is 'selective' and 'strives towards the typical.' The actions of people are presented within a 'total' context: the central character's actions are felt 'as part of the life of his [sic] class, society and universe'" (*Second Time as Farce*, p. 28). I maintain that all drama is selective, and that typicality is conferred by the director and the audience as much as the playwright. If, however, the characters represent more than themselves, i.e. their class or country – and such representation is written into the play in ways that I try to analyze – I label the play non-realistic.

Most of Edgar's main plays – *Saigon Rose, Wreckers, Mary Barnes, Teendreams, That Summer* – are realistic by both our definitions, and I admit that *Destiny* (1976) and *Maydays* (1983) are borderline cases. Although Edgar deliberately avoids "the degeneration of Brecht's techniques to the condition of theatrical cliché" (*Second Time as Farce*, p. 43), he is among those English dramatists who resemble Brecht in provoking the audience to think about and analyze social conditions. He does not, however, indulge in the "aggro" effects of Bond or Brenton; rather he charts the process by which men harden into their final political positions. Edgar, unlike Hare, is only minimally interested in the private lives of his characters, but at his best he theatricalizes their public roles.

Maydays (1983) was one of the first new plays to be produced at the Barbican, the 1100-seat London home of the Royal Shakespeare Company. The theatre's wide stage accommodated its epic sweep – the 1956 Russian invasion of Hungary, the anti-Viet War demonstrations in Berkeley, California, civil disobedience in the English countryside, a Siberian gulag for political dissidents, and a speaker's platform at a London right-wing meeting. Edgar changes scene as often as Brecht in *The Caucasian Chalk Circle*, and as in that play a few flats, props, and lights are sufficient unto the sense of locale. Unlike Brecht's parable, however, which is merely framed in contemporary history, Edgar's *Maydays* moves forward through public events, and poses today's dilemmas for the socially conscious intellectual, whatever his nationality.

In twenty-three scenes and four countries the action ranges over two decades. Such epic scope is at once a return to Shakespeare and a recent lesson from Brecht. Even in reading, one can sometimes be tangled in the several plot strands of *Maydays*, but Ron Daniels' direction highlighted the separate life-threads of (1) the middle-class radical Martin Glass, (2) the working-class turncoat Jeremy Crowther, and (3) the Russian dissident Pavel Lermontov – separate until the threads cross. The first scene offers us a brief view of Jeremy, a seventeen-year-old Communist on May 1, 1945, shortly before V-E day, and Act I drives forward to May 1, 1970, when American forces invade Cambodia. The betrayal of Western promise is announced as a major theme of *Maydays*.

The second scene, set during the 1956 Russian invasion of Hungary, introduces us to Lermontov, a Soviet Lieutenant who frees a young Hungarian rebel Paloczi. The third scene, set in 1962, shows us that Jeremy Crowther, the young firebrand of the first scene, has mellowed into a liberal teacher, who sympathizes with the rebellious instincts of the student Martin Glass, the protagonist. We follow Jeremy's step-by-step absorption by the political right; Lermontov's political education through forced labor; Martin's alternations between successively smaller left-wing splinter groups. Although the Hungarian Paloczi is limited to a before-and-after appearance, Edgar makes credible his conversion from left to right, in order to remain nationalistically Hungarian. As in Shakespeare and Brecht, even minor characters carry political weight: the secretary who denounces Lermontov because he called her an ignorant peasant; Martin's mother, a vicar's widow who lives in a Victorian fantasy; a red-diaper Trotskyite woman who works constructively in any collective where she happens to be; a party-line English Trotskyite who nimbly follows orders "objectively"; an American Jewish apologist for "the view that the West cannot be too fastidious about its choice of friends"; and an English right-wing politician who would rule out any dissent.

In the penultimate scene the main characters meet in London, but there is no meeting of minds: the ex-Communist, ex-liberal Jeremy is quite comfortable on the far right, as is Paloczi, the transplanted Hungarian. Lermontov, exchanged for a Soviet spy, rejects cooptation by the hard English right. Martin, disillusioned by both the many lefts and the rationalizing right, retreats into personal privacy. But there is a new generation dreaming of its own celebratory Maydays: the teenage daughter of the red-diaper woman joins anonymous activists on Greenham Common in the English countryside; the liberated cell-mate of Lermontov in the Soviet Union persuades a professor to carry a resonant message abroad. That newly freed Soviet citizen answers the professor's question as to how long the dissidents will last: "Who knows? 'May Days.'" He has proved prophetic.

Theatrically, the play opens on a red-bannered May Day in England, and Lermontov is taken to prison while Moscow's Red Square is literally in red for May Day. When Martin probes into the Trotskyite position, *"He makes the peace sign – Churchill's Victory-V,"* then *"He makes the clenched-fist sign."* It is a semaphore for the whole country's decline from peaceful hope to bellicose profits. Edgar is far more effective with such images, or with clipped verbal exchanges, than with such explicit didacticism as we hear on Greenham Common: "what we all are trying to do, in our many different ways, can only be accounted for by something in the nature of our species which resents, rejects and ultimately will resist a world that is demonstrably and in this case dramatically wrong and mad and unjust and unfair."

Despite such lapses, however, *Maydays* in its broad and cumulative sweep conveys the attrition of private life in the avalanche of politics. Edgar's characters tend to live politically. By judiciously selecting socially parallel members of opposing countries, by immersing them in key events of the last three decades, Edgar enlarges the epic to a panorama, while retaining the view of epic as a people's movement. But unlike agitprop, which posits an inevitable popular victory, Edgar's *Maydays* restrains itself to dissidence. The play's title and last word is a pun: May Days were compulsory festivals for Communist countries, but they carry the "may" of hesitant socialist possibility in democratic countries.

After World War II the memorable dates in modern British history are 1956 and 1968. World War II stripped Britain of its empire, but not until the Suez fiasco in 1956 was there widespread awareness of the loss of British prestige. 1968, the year of student revolt on the continent and in the United States, was a year of relative calm in England, and that very calm was a subject of concern for playwrights on the left. In other contexts I have alluded to the dramatic use of Suez by Osborne in *The Entertainer* and in *West of Suez*, and by Hare in *Plenty*, but David Mercer deliberately chooses 1956 as the springboard date for *After Haggerty* (1970), and although he does not mention Suez, the play seeks a global perspective.

A Marxist repelled by all actual governments, Mercer pits an ineffectual English Marxist against a virulent American radical in a non-realistic drama that essays several of the devices of my preceding chapters. The American Claire complains to the Englishman Bernard Link: *"God,* what a hunk of fly-blown little nothing England *is!"* And Bernard's loose, temporary household reflects that "little nothing" – old retired Mr. Link from Yorkshire, Chrissy the restless jack-of-all-decorator-trades, Roger his inept assistant who yearns to be an actor. Although Haggerty and his infant son Raskolnikov remain offstage, they separately and resonantly announce their presence.

Making free with time, place, and two decades of recent history, Mercer economically stages several conflicts; the absent Haggerty against the five main characters, a passive Englishman against his father, that same English intellectual against a British workman, that same English heterosexual against a gay man, and that same English spectator against the violence of world events. As deft as Pinter, Osborne, Gray, or Stoppard with the dialogue of the comedy of manners, Mercer subverts it through the absent Haggerty. As the writer explained: "[*After Haggerty*] was precisely about the fact that the Haggerties of this world are not standing about in drawing-rooms being agonised or mocking or rhetorical" (*Plays and Players* [November 1978, p. 10).

Through the wit and non-realistic devices threads a simple plot.

Claire, having lived with James Mawnan Haggerty in a London flat, has returned to her native United States to bear his child. The drama opens when, with baby shitting offstage, Claire descends upon the theatre critic Bernard Link, who has leased the London flat from Haggerty's agent. In the first act the domestic accommodations and flat renovation of Claire and Bernard are intercut with the latter's lectures in various Marxist countries, and it is through these glimpses that we view history: in 1956 in Budapest Link mentions Fry and Whiting; shortly afterwards in Moscow he designates *Look Back in Anger* as the pivotal point of modern English drama; in Havana he wafts off into theory, but in Prague, 1968, he cannot bear to mention theatre in the wake of the self-immolation of Jan Palach. Each of Bernard's trips is followed by his dialogue with his father, exposing their "conflicting views . . . On everything."

Act II opens on Bernard's submission to the plangent attack of the Living Theater actors, and he mutters venomously: "I'll bet they leave this country fully dressed. Passports firmly gripped in paws. Cakes of hash in their tooth-paste tubes. AND A LOT OF OUR MONEY!" (He was wrong on the last point.) Into the ill-matched household comes Bernard's working-class widower father – by 1970 a stereotype on the London stage, but Mercer subverts audience familiarity to expose the old man's racism, homophobia, provincialism, and vulnerability.

As Act I interrupts the narrative line with Bernard's lecture fragments and his feud with his father, Act II does so with Claire's obsession with Haggerty and her political flashbacks: the 1968 Democratic Convention in Haggerty's native Chicago, the New York anti-war demonstration where Claire was beaten by police while an underground Haggerty planned revolution, and her rich Long Island home to which she returned to bear Haggerty's child. Bernard and Claire, the Englishman and the American woman, are at once siblings under the skin and diametric opposites. Both have made a shambles of emotional ties – Claire, having left family and friends, is abandoned by Haggerty; Bernard, having dissolved two marriages, is at home nowhere. While the one taunts his father for cultural inferiority and travels through the world as a passive spectator, the other allies herself with a black rebel bearing an Irish name, and rears his child (Raskolnikov Haggerty) to claim a future. Both Claire and Bernard are cruel to old Mr. Link of the outworn attitudes, and both are left to face themselves when an empty coffin arrives bearing a devastating inscription: "James Mawnan Haggerty. Guerrilla. Killed during a skirmish between Government Forces and a rebel unit. Africa. Nineteen seventy." After Haggerty, Eurocentrism is as anachronistic as old Mr. Link. Mercer closes the drama on an enigmatic scenic direction: "*The coffin remains downstage of the curtain.*" Are all guerrilla movements doomed, while effete intellectuals wallow in private neuroses, however they may proclaim their allegiance to the left?

Although Mercer sets his play in that realistic staple, a middle-class English living-room, he contrives to connect it with Eastern Europe, Cuba, the United States, and Africa. Witty and swiftly paced, *After Haggerty* begins and ends on death. In the first scene the furniture is covered with sheets – a funeral custom in some countries; our final post-curtain sight is a funeral wreath on a coffin. Those two sober symbols enclose a variety of lively non-realistic devices: placards register the place, and time is spotlit through Bernard's lectures and Claire's memories. Haggerty's sporadic telegrams demand symbolic interpretation.

11 A mysterious coffin arrives in *After Haggerty* by David Mercer, directed by David Jones at the RSC, 1970

In terms of re-treats from realism, Mercer stages England in the context of American liberty (and libertinism) of the 1960s. At age seventeen Claire is aware: "I mix my vernaculars because I am an adolescent in a condition of revolt." By the time she meets Bernard, the revolt has fizzled, but the vernacular remains, especially toward Bernard: "You are the kind of Englishman I really hate. London is full of you." As a theatre critic, Bernard seems to specialize in contemporary drama, since there is no mention of the Shakespeare that was and is ubiquitous on London's stages. Bernard's calling endows *After Haggerty* with some muted metatheatre; the Living Theater actors mouth actual phrases from *Paradise Now*. More importantly, the implicit contrast of Bernard and Haggerty and, to a lesser extent, the triviality of Roger the would-be actor, belittle theatre in the context of history. At the same time, in a contemporary democracy such as England or the United States, privileged people can enjoy the luxury of neurosis. A heavy drinker, Bernard at first thinks that his father is a hallucination, but by that time we are aware that Bernard's life zigzags between his Marxist sympathies and his self-justifying filial antipathies. Between them, the lethal wit of Claire and the barbs of Bernard have "broken [the old man's] pride this day."

For an "aggro" playwright such as Brenton, no one is so blameworthy as the inactive liberal of humanist sentiments. To some extent, Mercer shares that blame, and yet he can find no other role for the Marxist intellectual who, unlike Haggerty, is incapable of suicidal guerrilla fighting. The theatre critic Bernard Link is not only passive but parasitic. In an early thrust at his name, Claire taunts: "Did the other kids at school call you Missing?" And that is finally his damnation: a spectator both in theatre and the theatre of history, Bernard Link is among the missing when it comes to forging links with nascent radical forces.

Belonging to no group, David Mercer was consistently welcomed in neither subsidized nor commercial theatre. Although his first love was the stage, he introduced non-realistic techniques to television – fracturing the narrative line, quoting from book and film, dissolving a surface into dream sequences, realizing the distortions of rebellious minds (Taylor, *Days of Vision*, p. 134). Clive Barker quotes Mercer as seeking "a synthesis between the problems of the individual in society and the problems of the society that produces the individual." On the stage, Mercer tends to confine himself within the realistic frame, in which private neurosis is aggravated by the political background. In *After Haggerty*, however, Mercer stretches his frame beyond realism. Like Lowe in *Touched*, he blends private experience into public events; like Edgar, he dissolves certain private lives into public passions. More incisively than either of them, Mercer etches tormented characters to whom he gives no quarter; Kenneth Tynan was not the model for Bernard Link, nor Patty Hearst for Claire. But Mercer predicts them in *After Haggerty*.

With a play about a theatre critic, this critic's journey through contemporary English non-realism ends. Given the quantity and quality of the dramas surveyed, there may be skepticism about my claim that realism remains the dominant mode on today's stage. My evidence is the recollection of tedium as the lights focus on yet another misnamed living-room, with its class-conscious furnishings. What I hope is not subject to skepticism is the dynamic way in which recent English dramatists mould old non-realistic patterns – metaphors for the country itself, adaptations of Shakespeare, a resurgence of verse, forms of metatheatre, fragmentations of the mind, and fictionalizations enfolded within historic events. I conclude with a quotation from Mercer's Bernard Link: "Most of the best playwrights don't give a damn about the notices. Quite rightly, I and my fellow criticism-grubbers are simply unreal to them."

Bibliography

Books about recent English drama

Anderson, Michael, *Anger and Detachment*, London: Pitman, 1976

Ansorge, Peter, *Disrupting the Spectacle*, London: Pitman, 1975

Barnes, Philip, *A Companion to Postwar British Theatre*, Buckingham: Croom Helm, 1986

Bigsby, C. W. E. (ed.), *Contemporary English Drama*, London: Edward Arnold, 1981

Bock, Hedwig and Wertheim, Albert (eds.), *Essays on Contemporary British Drama*, Munich: Max Hueber, 1981

Brown, John Russell and Harris, Bernard (eds.), *Contemporary Theatre*, London: Edward Arnold 1952
  Modern British Dramatists, Englewood Cliffs, N.J.: Prentice-Hall, 1984

Brown, John Russell, *Theatre Language*, London: Lane, 1972

Brown, John Russell, *A Short Guide to Modern British Drama*, London: Heinemann, 1982

Brown, Terry, *Playwrights Theatre*, London: Pitman, 1975

Bull, John, *New British Political Dramatists*, London: Macmillan, 1983

Cave, Richard Allen, *New British Drama in Performance on the London Stage*, Buckinghamshire: Colin Smythe, 1987

Chambers, Colin, *Other Spaces*, London: Methuen, 1980
  and Prior, Mike, *Playwrights' Progress*, Oxford: Amber Lane, 1987

Colby, Douglas, *As the Curtain Rises*, Cranbury, N.J.: Associated University Presses, 1978

Cook, Judith, *Directors' Theatre*, London: Harrap, 1974

Craig, Sandy (ed.), *Dreams and Deconstructions*, Derbyshire: Amber Lane, 1980

Doty, Gresdna A. and Harbin, Billy J., *Inside the Royal Court Theatre, 1956–1981*, Baton Rouge: Louisiana State University Press, 1990

Duncan, Ronald, *How to Make Enemies*, London: Rupert Hart-Davis, 1968

Dutton, Richard, *Modern Tragicomedy and the British Tradition*, Nottingham: Nottingham University Press, 1981

Edgar, David, *The Second Time as Farce*, London: Lawrence and Wishart, 1988

Edwards, Sydney, *Celebration: 25 Years of British Theatre*, London: W. H. Allen, 1980

Elsom, John, *Postwar British Theatre*, London: Routledge and Kegan Paul, 1976
  Postwar British Theatre Criticism, London: Routledge and Kegan Paul, 1981
Findlater, Richard, *At the Royal Court*, New York: Grove, 1981
  These Our Actors, London: Elm Tree, 1983
Garstenauder, Maria, *A Selective Study of English History Plays in the Period between 1960 and 1977*, Salzburg: 1985
Gaskill, William, *A Sense of Direction*, London: Faber, 1987
Goorney, Howard, *The Theatre Workshop Story*, London: Methuen, 1981
Harben, Niloufer, *Twentieth Century English History Plays*, London: Macmillan, 1988
Hayman, Ronald, *Theatre and Anti-Theatre*, London: Secker and Warburg, 1979
  British Theatre Since 1955, Oxford: Oxford University Press, 1979
  Playback, New York: Horizon, 1974
  Playback 2, London: Davis-Pointer, 1973
Hinchliffe, Arnold, *British Theatre 1950–70*, Oxford: Oxford University Press, 1974
Hobson, Harold, *Indirect Journey*, London: Weidenfeld and Nicolson, 1978
Hunt, Hugh, Richard, Kenneth and Taylor, John Russell, *The Revels History of Drama in English*, Vol. 7, London: Methuen, 1978
Itzin, Catherine, *Stages in the Revolution*, London: Methuen, 1980
Kennedy, Andrew, *Six Dramatists in Search of a Language*, Cambridge: Cambridge University Press, 1975
Kerensky, Oleg, *The New British Drama*, New York: Taplinger, 1977
Lambert, J. W., *Drama in Britain 1964–1973*, London: Longmans, 1974
Lloyd Evans, Gareth and Barbara, *Plays in Review 1956–1980*, London: Methuen, 1985
  The Language of Modern Drama, London: J. M. Dent, 1977
Marowitz, Charles, Milne, Tom and Owen, Hale, *New Theatre Voices of the 50s and 60s*, London: Methuen, 1965
  The Encore Reader, London: Methuen, 1965
Marowitz, Charles and Trussler, Simon (eds.), *New Theatre Voices of the Seventies*, London: Methuen, 1981
  Theatre at Work, New York: Hill and Wang, 1967
Masler, Tom (ed.), *Declaration*, London: MacGibbon and Kee, 1959
McGrath, John, *A Good Night Out*, London: Eyre Methuen, 1981
Nichols, Peter, *Feeling You're Behind*, London: Weidenfeld and Nicolson, 1984
Nightingale, Benedict, *An Introduction to Fifty Modern British Plays*, London: Pan Books, 1982
O'Connor, Garry, *Ralph Richardson: An Actor's Life*, London: Hodder and Stoughton, 1986
Olivier, Laurence, *Confessions of an Actor*, London: Weidenfeld and Nicolson, 1982
  On Acting, London: Weidenfeld and Nicolson, 1986
Rabey, David Ian, *British and Irish Political Drama in the Twentieth Century*, London: Macmillan, 1986
Ritchie, Rob (ed.), *The Joint Stock Book*, London: Methuen, 1987

Bibliography

Roberts, Peter, *Theatre in Britain*, London: Pitman, 1973

Roberts, Philip, *The Royal Court Theatre*, London: Routledge and Kegan Paul, 1986

Salem, Daniel, *La Révolution théâtrale actuelle en Angleterre*, Paris: Denoel, 1969

Salmon, Eric, *Is the Theatre Still Dying?* New York: Greenwood Press, 1985

Smith, Leslie, *Modern British Farce*, London: Macmillan, 1989

Stafford-Clark, Max, *Letters to George*, London: Nick Hern, 1989

Taylor, John Russell, *Anger and After*, Baltimore: Penguin, 1962

   The Second Wave, London: Methuen, 1971 (paperback edition, 1978)

Trewin, J. C., *Drama in Britain 1951–64*, London: Longmans, 1965

Tynan, Kenneth, *A View of the English Stage, 1944–1965*, London: Davis-Poynter, 1975

   Tynan on Theatre, London: Pelican, 1964

Wandor, Michelene, *Look Back in Gender*, London: Methuen, 1987

   Carry On, Understudies, London: Routledge, 1986

Wardle, Irving, *The Theatres of George Devine*, London: Jonathan Cape, 1978

Worth, Katharine, *Revolutions in Modern English Drama*, London: G. Bell, 1973

Other works cited in the text

Brown, Paul, "*The Tempest* and the Discourse of Colonialism," in Jonathan Dollimore and Alan Sinfield (eds.), *Political Shakespeare*, Manchester: Manchester University Press, 1985

Calder, Angus, *The People's War 1939–1945*, New York: Pantheon, 1969

Calderwood, James, *To Be Or Not To Be*, New York: Columbia University Press, 1983

Cohn, Ruby, *Modern Shakespeare Offshoots*, Princeton: Princeton University Press, 1976

Connor, Steven, *Postmodernist Culture*, Oxford: Blackwell, 1989

Cook, Judith (ed.), *Backstage*, London: Harrap, 1987

Duncan, Ronald, *Collected Plays*, London: Rupert Hart-Davis, 1971

Grene, Nicholas, *Shakespeare, Jonson, Molière, the Comic Contract*, Basingstoke: Macmillan, 1980

Hahnloser-Ingold, Margrit, *Das Englische Theater und Bert Brecht*, Bern: Francke, 1970

Homan, Sidney, *When the Theatre Turns to Itself*, Lewisburg: Bucknell University Press, 1981

Kane, Leslie, *The Language of Silence*, Cranbury, N.J.: Associated University Presses, 1984

Kennedy, Andrew, *Dramatic Dialogue*, Cambridge: Cambridge University Press, 1983

Kott, Jan, *Shakespeare Our Contemporary*, New York: Anchor, 1966

MacDougall, Hugh A., *Racial Myth in English History*, Hanover, N.H.: University Presses of New England, 1982

Nelson, Robert J., *Play Within A Play*, New Haven: Yale University Press, 1958

Righter, Anne, *Shakespeare and the Idea of the Play*, London: Chatto & Windus, 1962

Ryan, Kiernan, *Shakespeare*, Hemel Hemstead: Harvester, 1989
Schmeling, Manfred, *Métathéâtre et intertexte*, Paris: Lettres Modernes, 1982
Weales, Gerald, "The Madrigal in the Garden," *Tulane Drama Review* (December, 1958)
Wright, Elizabeth, *Postmodern Brecht*, London: Routledge, 1989

Works on individual playwrights

JOHN ARDEN

Arden, John, *To Present the Pretence*, London: Methuen, 1977
and D'Arcy, Margaretta, *Awkward Corners*, London: Methuen, 1988
Gray, Frances, *John Arden*, London: Macmillan, 1982
Hayman, Ronald, *John Arden*, London: Heinemann, 1969
Hunt, Albert, *Arden: A Study of his Plays*, London: Methuen, 1974
Malick, Javed, "The Polarized Universe of 'The Island of the Mighty': the Dramaturgy of Arden and D'Arcy," *New Theatre Quarterly* (February, 1986)
Page, Malcolm, *John Arden*, Boston: G. K. Hall/Twayne, 1984
Arden on File, London: Methuen, 1985

ALAN AYCKBOURN

Billington, Michael, *Alan Ayckbourn*, London: Macmillan, 1983
Page, Malcolm, *File on Ayckbourn*, London: Methuen, 1989
White, Sidney Howard, *Alan Ayckbourn*, Boston: Gale, 1984

HOWARD BARKER

Barker, Howard, *Arguments for a Theatre*, London: John Calder, 1989
Rabey, David Ian, *Howard Barker: Politics and Desire*, London: Macmillan, 1989
Gambit 41, London: John Calder, 1984

PETER BARNES

Dukore, Bernard, *The Theatre of Peter Barnes*, London: Heinemann, 1981

EDWARD BOND

Bulman, James, "Bond, Shakespeare and the Absurd," *Modern Drama* (March, 1986)
"*The Woman* and Greek Myth," *Modern Drama* (December, 1986)
Coult, Tony, *The Plays of Edward Bond*, London: Methuen, 1979
Hay, Malcolm and Roberts, Philip, *Edward Bond: A Companion to the Plays*, London: TQ Publications, 1978
Hay, Malcolm and Roberts, Philip, *Bond: A Study of His Plays*, London: Methuen, 1980
Hirst, David, *Edward Bond*, London: Macmillan, 1985
Iden, Peter, *Bond*, Hanover: Friedrich, 1973
Lappin, Lou, *The Art and Politics of Edward Bond*, New York: P. Lang, 1987

Bibliography

Roberts, Philip, *Bond on File*, London: Methuen, 1985
Scharine, Richard, *The Plays of Edward Bond*, Lewisburg: Bucknell University Press, 1976
Spencer, Jenny S., "Rewriting 'Classics': Edward Bond's *The Woman*," *Modern Drama* (December, 1989)
Trussler, Simon, *Edward Bond*, London: Longmans, 1976

HOWARD BRENTON

Tony Mitchell, *File on Brenton*, London: Methuen, 1987

CARYL CHURCHILL

Cousin, Geraldine, *Churchill the Playwright*, London: Methuen, 1989
Diamond, Elin, "Refusing the Romanticism of Identity," *Theatre Journal* (October, 1985)
Fitzimmons, Linda, *File on Churchill*, London: Methuen, 1989
Marohl, Joseph, "De-Realized Women: Performance and Identity in *Top Girls*," *Modern Drama* (September, 1987)
Quigley, Austin, "Stereotype and Prototype," in Enoch Brater (ed.), *Feminine Focus*, New York: Oxford University Press, 1989
Randall, Phyllis R., *Caryl Churchill: A Casebook*, New York: Garland, 1989

DAVID EDGAR

Swain, Elizabeth, *David Edgar, Playwright and Politician*, New York: P. Lang, 1986

TREVOR GRIFFITHS

Poole, Mike and Wyver, John, *Powerplays: Trevor Griffiths in Television*, London: British Film Institute, 1984

DAVID HARE

Dean, Joan, *David Hare*, Boston: Twayne, 1990
Oliva, Judy, *David Hare: Theatricalizing Politics*, Ann Arbor: University of Michigan Press, 1990
Page, Malcolm, *File on Hare*, London: Methuen, 1990

DAVID MERCER

Taylor, Don, *Days of Vision*, London: Methuen, 1990

JOE ORTON

Bigsby, C. W. E., *Joe Orton*, London: Methuen, 1982
Charney, Maurice, *Joe Orton*, London: Macmillan, 1984
Lahr, John, *Prick Up Your Ears*, London: Penguin, 1980

Bibliography

JOHN OSBORNE

Banham, Martin, *Osborne*, London: Oliver and Boyd, 1969
Carter, Alan, *John Osborne*, London: Oliver and Boyd, 1973
Egan, Robert, "*Anger* and the Actor: Another Look Back," *Modern Drama*
    . (September, 1989)
Goldstone, Herbert, *Coping with Vulnerability: the Achievement of John Osborne*,
    Washington: University Presses of America 1982
Hayman, Ronald, *John Osborne*, London: Heinemann, 1972
Hinchliffe, Arnold, *John Osborne*, Boston: Twayne, 1984
Northouse, Cameron, *John Osborne: A Reference Guide*, Boston: Gale, 1974
Page, Malcolm, *Osborne on File*, London: Methuen, 1988
Trussler, Simon, *The Plays of John Osborne*, London: Gollancz, 1969

PETER SHAFFER

Klein, Dennis A., *Peter Shaffer*, Boston: Hall/Twayne, 1979
Page, Malcolm, *Shaffer on File*, London: Methuen, 1987

TOM STOPPARD

Bigsby, C. W. E., *Tom Stoppard*, London: Longman, 1979
Billington, Michael, *Stoppard the Playwright*, London: Methuen, 1987
Bloom, Harold, (ed.), *Tom Stoppard*, New York: Chelsea House, 1986
Brassell, Tim, *Tom Stoppard: An Assessment*, New York: St. Martin's Press,
    1985
Bratt, David, *Tom Stoppard: A Reference Guide*, Boston: Gale, 1982
Cahn, Victor, *Beyond Absurdity: The Plays of Tom Stoppard*, Rutherford, N.J.:
    Fairleigh Dickinson Press, 1979
Corballis, Richard, *Stoppard: The Mystery and the Clockwork*, London: Methuen,
    1985
Dean, Joan Fitzpatrick, *Tom Stoppard's Comedy as a Moral Matrix*, Columbia,
    Mo.: University of Missouri Press, 1981
Gabbard, Lucina, *The Stoppard Plays*, Troy, N.Y.: Whitson, 1982
Hayman, Ronald, *Tom Stoppard*, London: Heinemann, 1977
Hunter, Jim, *Tom Stoppard's Plays*, London: Faber, 1982
Jenkins, Anthony, *The Theatre of Tom Stoppard*, Cambridge: Cambridge University Press, 1987.
Levenson, Jill, "'Hamlet' Andante/'Hamlet' Allegro: Tom Stoppard's Two
    Versions," *Shakespeare Survey* 36
Londré, Felicia, *Tom Stoppard*, New York: Ungar, 1981
Page, Malcolm, *Stoppard on File*, London: Methuen, 1986
Rusinko, Susan, *Tom Stoppard*, Boston: Twayne, 1986
Sales, Roger, *Tom Stoppard: Rosencrantz and Guildenstern Are Dead*, London:
    Penguin, 1988
Whitaker, Thomas, *Tom Stoppard*, London: Macmillan, 1983
Zeifman, Hersh, "A Trick of the Light," in Enoch Brater and Ruby Cohn
    (eds.), *Around the Absurd*, Ann Arbor: University of Michigan Press, 1990

"Comedy of Ambush: Tom Stoppard's *The Real Thing*," *Modern Drama*
(June, 1983)

DAVID STOREY

Ansorge, Peter, "The Theatre of Life," *Plays and Players* (September, 1973)
Hayman, Ronald, "Conversation with David Storey," *Drama* (Winter, 1970)
Hutchings, William, *The Plays of David Storey*, Carbondale: Southern Illinois
University Press, 1988

ARNOLD WESKER

Alter, Iska, "Barbaric Laws, Barbaric Bonds: Arnold Wesker's *The Merchant*,"
Modern Drama (December, 1988)
Hayman, Ronald, *Arnold Wesker*, New York: Ungar, 1973
Leeming, Glenda and Trussler, Simon, *The Plays of Arnold Wesker*, London:
Gollancz, 1971
Wesker the Playwright, London: Methuen, 1983
Wesker on File, London: Methuen, 1985

Index of plays and playwrights

Index of plays and playwrights

Index of plays and playwrights